RETHINKING MEDIA, RELIGION, AND CULTURE

RETHINKING MEDIA, RELIGION, AND CULTURE

STEWART M. HOOVER
KNUT LUNDBY

SAGE Publications
International Educational and Professional Publisher
Thousand Oaks   London   New Delhi

For information, address to:

 SAGE Publications, Inc.
2455 Teller Road
Thousand Oaks, California 91320
E-mail: order@sagepub.com

SAGE Publications Ltd.
6 Bonhill Street
London EC2A 4PU
United Kingdom

SAGE Publications India Pvt. Ltd.
M-32 Market
Greater Kailash I
New Delhi 110 048 India

Printed in the United States of America

Library of Congress Cataloging-in-Publication Data

Main entry under title:

Rethinking media, religion, and culture / editors, Stewart M. Hoover and
  Knut Lundby
      p.   cm.
      "This book grows out of a conference titled Media-religion-culture which was
  held at the University of Uppsala, Sweden, in May of 1993"—Acknowledgments.
      Includes bibliographical references and index.
      ISBN 0-7619-0170-1.—ISBN 0-7619-0171-X (pbk.)
      1. Mass media—Religious aspects.   2. Mass media and culture. 3. Religon and
  culture.   I. Hoover, Stewart M.   II. Lundby, Knut.
  P94.R48 1997
  302.23—dc21   96-45894

97 98 99 00 01 02 03 10 9 8 7 6 5 4 3 2 1

Acquiring Editor:	Margaret Seawell
Editorial Assistant:	Renée Piernot
Production Editor:	Astrid Virding
Production Assistant:	Denise Santoyo
Typesetter/Designer:	Marion Warren
Indexer:	L. Pilar Wyman
Cover Designer:	Candice Harman
Print Buyer:	Anna Chin

Contents

II

Media, Religion, and Culture:
Contemporary Society

III

Media, Religion, and Culture:
Changing Institutions

IV

Media, Religion, and Culture:
Individual Practice

Acknowledgments

This book grows out of a conference titled "Media-Religion-Culture" held at the University of Uppsala, Sweden, in May of 1993. At Uppsala were participants from France, Hungary, Italy, Norway, South Africa, Sweden, Great Britain, and the United States. This meeting led to the formation of the "Uppsala Group," an international network of academics founded both to encourage and to carry out research at the intersection of media studies, religious studies, and cultural studies.

None of the papers from Uppsala survives here in its original form. Contributions were added to the volume after the 1994 conferences of the International Association for Mass Communication Research (IAMCR) in Seoul, South Korea, and the International Communication Association (ICA) in Sydney, Australia, where additional seminars on this theme were held. Several contributions here also represent input from the international public conference on Media, Religion, and Culture held at the University of Colorado at Boulder, United States, in January 1996.

The foundation of all of these activities was a major research effort on Media-Religion-Culture hosted by the Department of Theology, University of Uppsala, chaired by Sigbert Axelson. Participating in this project were Hilde Arntsen and Knut Lundby from the University of Oslo, Kerstin Skog-Östlin from the University of Stockholm, and Ove Gustafsson, Alf

Linderman, Thorleif Pettersson, and the late Jan-Arvid Hellström from the University of Uppsala. Alf Linderman also organized the original Uppsala conference, which was directly based in this research project.

Another important environment for these joint research efforts is the University of Colorado at Boulder, where Stewart M. Hoover and Lynn Schofield Clark shared responsibility for the Boulder conference on Media, Religion, and Culture.

As editors of this book, we want to thank all of these colleagues and also recognize that there are others who have contributed to this effort. We would especially like to extend our appreciation to Robert A. White (who with Michael Traber edits the Communication and Human Values series) for his scholarly encouragement throughout the work on this volume. At Sage Publications we have had special support from Sophy Craze, Renée Piernot, and Margaret Seawell. Hilde Arntsen helped with formulation and translation of important sections of the book. Judy Jensen, Diane Willian, and Giulia Rossi also deserve recognition.

Finally, we would like to thank our families for their support during this project.

—*Stewart M. Hoover*
Knut Lundby

Part III

Analysis of Media, Religion, and Culture

Chapter 1

Introduction
Setting the Agenda

Stewart M. Hoover
Knut Lundby

This book intends to link theories of media, theories of religion, and theories of culture into a more coherent whole. By such a triangulation of theories, we want to readdress the simpler, two-sided relationships between *religion and media, media and culture,* and *culture and religion* that up to now have characterized both theory and research. The view here is that media, religion, and culture should be thought of as an interrelated web within society. This volume represents a first step in the direction of this more complex understanding of these phenomena.

An Interrelated Web in Formation

A process of rethinking media, religion, and culture promises to offer a richer analysis by moving beyond the tacit naturalisms of modernity toward the cultural dynamics that form contemporary society. It might be argued our intent to triangulate is too comprehensive a task, given the fact that these three fields have tended to be researched separately in a kind of scholarly isolation. However, the defects of this isolation become obvious when we review the current state of knowledge about these issues.

Although mainstream study of media has deemed questions of religion insignificant, the theoretical and methodological point of departure in this book can be found within media studies. We cross a few other bridges as well by drawing on literature in religion, cultural meaning, and ritual. These foundations can be found in various of the book's four sections.

The Birmingham school turned studies of mass communication into critical cultural studies; however, the field of cultural studies has not seriously addressed religion in relation to culture and media. This is ironic, in that in one of its founding texts, *The Uses of Literacy* (1957), Richard Hoggart provided a glimpse into the potential of such a theoretical triangulation when addressing the question of religion in working-class life. Stuart Hall and Tony Jefferson investigated the phenomenon of *Resistance Through Rituals* (1976) in youth subcultures in postwar Britain without addressing the possibility of cultural resistance through religion. This may demonstrate a curious lack of interest within media studies in topics related to religion. Graham Murdock provides a fuller challenge to this practice of exclusion of religious elements in his contribution to this volume.

The field of sociology, even as it has taken religion more seriously than has media studies, has tended to ignore or minimize the implications of the media in this connection. Robert Wuthnow has contributed to the development of the field of cultural sociology through studies of religion in modern culture (1988, 1992). However, the media are left in a "rather spare and truncated place" in his works (Hoover, 1995). As society becomes more and more dependent on mediation of sociocultural relationships through mass media and computerized communication technology (as touched upon here by Clifford Christians) this has to be taken into account in studies of religion and culture.

Sociologists of religion have focused on religion in relation to the modernization of society. They have tended to avoid the problematization of media as rendering any unique contribution to modernity or postmodernity. They have not arrived at any general theory of how media fundamentally change cultures—and religion—in spite of the fact that much such work (cf. Beyer, 1994) is highly suggestive. Jesús Martín-Barbero, in his study of mediation processes in popular culture and religion in Latin America (1993), as in his chapter in this volume, explores the analytic dilemmas introduced by this separation of media from studies of culture and society.

▨ Trends in Contemporary Religion

Transformations in the religious cultures of the Judeo-Christian parts of the world, where religious institutions have been said to be in decline for most of the second half of this century, provide the setting for this theoretical project. This decline has taken place at a time when the institutions of the media have emerged as the most important actors in the public sphere. The media now condition and determine access to that realm—a situation that impacts religious institutions as it does all others.

The decline of religious structures and institutions is related to another major trend in religion—a trend toward increased emphasis on individualism and individual autonomy. Even in traditionally "religious" Western industrial countries, such as the United States and Canada, the decline of institutions has been parallel to a rise in the authority and autonomy of individuals over their own practices of faith and belief (Hammond, 1993). As a result, a number of "parachurch" organizations have emerged (Wuthnow, 1988) and a wide range of other activities, affinities, services, and products have been charged with religious significance. This marketplace of religious symbols and values has become a major point of affinity and practice today and is itself largely a function of the cultural commodification practices of the media industries (Moore, 1994).

▨ The Cultural Dynamics of Modernity

The intersection of media and religion must be studied through the processes and patterns of culture, and we begin our project of rethinking with contrasting sketches of media and religion within the overall cultural context of modernity. Media, as embedded in broader social and cultural settings, can be said to be related to religion in a number of ways. First, the media are commonly thought to have potential as successful or unsuccessful purveyors of religious "messages." This conception is obviously most consistent with a *substantive* view of religion and a concern for its historical and doctrinal institutions. However, the media can also be seen to be providing the raw material for the intended or unintended construction of religious meanings among people in various contexts, as would be understood from a more *functional* perspective. Thus, the media open up to religion both in the symbolic production processes—that is, in the symbols provided in media texts—and in the consumption and interpretation processes.

Generally, the term *media* has referred to the technological media, such as radio, television, and the printing press. In contrast, we will here attempt to introduce a wider argument about the process of *mediation*, where the whole context of the cultural practice of communication is implied, although the focus is on the media sphere.

Studies of the interplay between culture and the mediation of religion can thus be carried out at a variety of levels. One framework might suggest *macro-level* analysis of society as a whole, *meso-level* analysis of institutions and their practices, and *micro-level* analysis of individual reception and negotiation of meaning. We do not intend to imply by such a framework that culture is nothing more than a context for exchange between media and religion, however. These spheres are interpenetrated by one another. Religion as a symbolic universe or universes of ultimate values and knowledge, and media as mediators in communication, constitute fundamental dimensions of culture in their own right.

But the theoretical project here does not emerge *de novo*. On the largest of the analytical levels, the societal level, authors here link classical sociological theories of culture, religion, and society to these contemporary issues. Graham Murdock and Jesús Martín-Barbero, for example, root their analyses in the work of Max Weber, but move forward to more contemporary theories of modernity. Gabriel Bar-Haim, Knut Lundby, Gregor Goethals, and Bobby Alexander, among others, look to Emile Durkheim and further to Victor Turner and others for theoretical understandings of ritual in society.

Rallies, Rituals, and Resistance

The dynamics of media, religion, and culture are not unidirectional. Both on a phenomenological and on a theoretical level, their interaction can take a variety of forms and directions. Of these, the three major ones can be described as *rallies, rituals,* and *resistances.*

It is possible to ground ourselves in various understandings or definitions of religion. Although we have linked religion rather directly to culture on the one hand, and to media on the other, questions of the actual definition of religion arise. The approach here is to apply a wide range of understandings of religion, leaving space for both the more narrow, substantive definitions, and for wider, more functional definitions that address the religiosity of seemingly nonreligious phenomena. The challenge of definition is well illustrated here by Lundby's critique of the definition proposed by Clark and Hoover. A rubric such as "rallies, rituals, and resistance" is a way of recognizing the range of things "religious" within our overall field of interest.

Rallies refers to those situations where religious activity is linked to history, doctrine, institution, or structured practice. The phenomena of interest here are those that relate to the practices of the formal religions. U.S.-style televangelism is an example of this category, as are the public relations practices of religious institutions throughout the industrialized West. In general, the emphasis here is on the instrumental relationship of religious practice to the media, wherever that religious practice is lodged in structured or institutional religious history or doctrine.

The notion of *rituals* exposes an entirely different and rich field of analysis, as implied by Carey (1989). Media consumption takes place in contexts that are culturally and socially defined, and communication cannot easily be disengaged from these contexts. But Carey's invocation of the term *ritual* can be read as primarily metaphoric. We would argue for a move beyond Carey toward a new metaphor that has another implication: Media consumption is rooted in human ontological imagination and practice, and media may therefore play a quasi-religious role in everyday life. The category of rituals must acknowledge this broader scope. We suggest that there is a substantive, ontological, and authentic dimension to meaning-making that accompanies media behavior. In so doing, we are not necessarily suggesting that the media *constitute* religion, as might be superficially implied by the category of rallies. In fact, we would posit that such debates over "essentialism" are beside the point. Rather, we suggest that there are aspects of modern social and cultural embedment in the media that necessarily imbue the media's powerful symbols, icons, values, and functions with religious significance.

A category of *resistance* can be both theoretically and empirically derived. The British cultural studies tradition acknowledges that media texts present their audiences with an inescapable opportunity for cultural construction. The very act implies audience negotiation of power in the reading of a media text. This is consistent with the implication of theory in cultural analysis in sociology (cf. Wuthnow, 1987; Wuthnow, Hunter, Bergesen, & Kurzweil, 1984), which suggests that the popular environment acts as a kind of context of social dramaturgy against which individual and community consciousness is formed and shaped.

We suggest that this phenomenon can be religiously and ritually significant on at least two levels. First, constructive processes that result in new conceptions of truth, value, meaning, notions of "the good," "the right," and so forth are intrinsically religious matters. They are rooted in those centers in the human individual and human social network that give rise to the deepest and most transcendent meanings. Second, processes of cultural construction in the media have been shown to be sites of social and cultural struggle in their own right. To put it simply, religious and ontological elements embedded in media texts have recurrently been seen to be the bone of contention between people and groups.

▨ Rethinking

Rethinking does, however, have to begin with more general reflections on media, religion, and culture as they are embedded in ongoing changes in society. Our task must thus be understood within modernity. Hence, the scholars included in this book introduce some theoretical approaches through which to look in more detail at the propagating rallies, the common rituals, and the conflicting resistance from various agents that together constitute mediated religion in modernity and against the backdrop of modernity's claims and demands.

The works presented here intend to address these developments in light of these approaches and to do so in a way that takes account of theory. It is presumptuous to suppose that any particular theoretical perspective can ultimately account for the phenomena of concern here, and this volume will not attempt to enforce any such unitary framework. Instead, the editors and authors of this volume attempt to raise the discourse to a new level by presenting material that either illuminates or challenges the received assumptions about issues of religion and media, media and culture, and contemporary religious and cultural matters.

▨ Limitations of Previous Approaches

It is not a simple task to account theoretically for the situation of media, religion, and culture and the interrelatedness thereof. Certain attempts, admittedly, have already been made to contemplate across the disciplines. Often, however, these have taken place along bipolar lines, linking pairs, but not the overall structure.

There are ample studies of *religion and culture*. Recent studies of modern religion (Bellah, Madsen, Sullivan, Swidler, & Tipton, 1985; Hammond, 1993; Roof, 1993; Wuthnow, 1992) and postmodern religion (Beyer, 1994; Warner, 1993) have extended the understanding of religious practice. On the other hand, few of these works account for the media's contribution to these developments, despite the inclusion of much anecdotal evidence of the significance of the media sphere.

Theoretical elaborations of *media and culture* have surfaced in recent years. Most significantly, the field of cultural studies (cf. Grossberg, Nelson, & Treichler, 1992; Turner, 1989) articulates understandings of culture that recognize the role of media in cultural formation. As has been suggested elsewhere (Hoover, 1995), such understandings could be significantly elaborated through a conscious approach to religion and religious sensibilities. However, this has often been lacking.

Finally, a number of studies have contemplated relations between *religion and the media*. Few of these have seriously addressed the problem of culture, however. Studies of religion and the media have historically tended to fall into two broad categories: First, there are administrative studies, which have assumed an instrumentalist media theory and which have looked at the prospects, practices, and prerogatives of formal religious institutions. Second, there are studies that contemplate relations between media and religion in terms of an antagonistic dualism, where the media are seen as a threat to "authentic" religion, either in a fundamental, categorical sense or more explicitly in terms of self-consciously "religious" media and their impact on conventional religious institutions and expressions (cf. Fore, 1987; Muggeridge, 1977/1986; Olasky, 1988).

The rather extensive body of texts in the area of televangelism (e.g., Bruce, 1991; Frankl, 1987; Hadden & Shupe, 1988; Hadden & Swann, 1981; Horsfield, 1984; Schultze, 1991) falls into this latter category in that it addresses, to a greater or lesser extent, the capacities of media-generated religious activities to threaten the prerogatives of "authentic" religion. These studies have failed to consider possibilities that transcend the notion that religion and media constitute separate or equivalent and competing social categories. They have also failed to problematize culture, and thus they have not allowed for the possibility of convergence of religion and media within contemporary culture. A small but growing number of works have begun to take this more comprehensive approach (Alexander, 1994; Hoover, 1988; Linderman, 1996; Peck, 1993).

A Cross-Disciplinary Venture

The contributions in this volume demonstrate the potential of this more complex approach to media, religion, and culture and illustrate both the necessity of its being cross-disciplinary and the value of its being cross-cultural in nature. They are lodged at the intersection of cultural studies, sociology of religion, media studies, ritual studies, and religious studies. We seek here to establish new theoretical terms of discussion and debate. As a result, this effort may also serve to refine issues in broader arenas of cultural, media, and sociological studies.

There are some substantial challenges to such crossing of academic borders. Sociologists of religion, for instance, view religion as a fundamental dimension of culture, but have no theory of mediation. It seems impossible to reach a complete understanding of the relationship between religion and culture today without incorporating a theory of media and communication. Even the classical studies of secularization might be seen to have an implicit theory of communication. For example, how was the exchange between the Protestant ethic and the spirit of capitalism possible without accounting for the communication of these ideas? Today, due to the significant role of the technical media in the exchanges in society, the mediation between religion and culture has to be made explicit.

This volume attempts to establish that religion is no longer to be regarded as the stepchild of media studies, and that the media are no longer to be seen as lingering at the periphery of religious studies. We argue that major contributions to our knowledge of contemporary life and culture are to be made by addressing the interrelationships between religion and the media. This volume will not constitute the final answer to such a complex topic. It is nevertheless our hope that it is but among the first of many approaches to these questions.

▓ Background and Organization of This Volume

A number of contributions in this volume were initially presented as part of a conference on "Media, Religion, and Culture" held in 1993 at the University of Uppsala, Sweden. The conference brought together scholars from Europe, North America, and Africa. Additional contributions were presented at subsequent conferences in Korea and Australia during 1994, and in Boulder, Colorado, in early 1996. Along the way, others were challenged to reflect on these elements as seen from their various geographic and scholarly standpoints.

The contributions to this book have been organized into four thematic sections. The first of these presents three efforts at normative or foundational statements of the project at hand. In a critical bibliographical essay, **Lynn Schofield Clark** and **Stewart Hoover** discuss the status of scholarship on this interrelated web of media, religion, and culture. They provide a detailed account of the position of this volume vis-à-vis other contributions to the field and go on to a consideration of the limitations of other literature that might well have been expected to have better accounted for these questions. **Robert White** follows with a review of the theoretical ground on which a project such as ours must rest. He provides a helpful framework for the kind of analytic work needed. **Clifford Christians** recognizes that a fundamental problematic of media culture is technology, and he probes works in philosophy and theory for insights into the meaning of technology.

In its empirical and phenomenological chapters, the book turns first to the *societal context*. **Graham Murdock** begins with a broad argument for the introduction of the question of religion into the ongoing discourse of cultural studies. As we have already noted, the religious has often been left out of these considerations; and Murdock contends that for a variety of historical, empirical, and theoretical reasons, this has been unfortunate.

Jesús Martín-Barbero follows with a reflection on the issue of mediation and the linkage between the mediated sphere and the individual and community spheres of communication. His is a rather direct indictment of the traditional "technologization" of media and culture studies. **Gregor Goethals** investigates the status of visual communication within contemporary religious consciousness. She posits that to understand the religiosity of the media age, we must critically analyze the contributions of nonlinear modes of communication to religious consciousness. **Gabriel Bar-Haim** presents a more focused argument through an analysis of the contemporary question of meaning and its ritual attributes. Bar-Haim draws heavily on foundational social theory, particularly that of Durkheim, in demonstrating the depth and richness of cultural analysis that is possible when Murdock's invocation of "the religious" is taken to heart. In the concluding chapter of this section, **Knut Lundby** examines religious and quasi-religious public ritual in contemporary culture within the theoretical framework of mediation. He presents a case study of the 1994 Winter Olympics in Norway to propose a grounded perspective.

The next section addresses *institutions*. **Peter Horsfield** turns to a historical examination of the role and status of conventional, institutional religion in the media age. He considers a number of ways that the prospects of contemporary religion are shaped by the existence of the media sphere. **Chris Arthur** turns from questions of religious institutional practice to questions of the study of religion, again raising the particularities of the media age as a key problematic. The next two chapters deal with the phenomenon of televangelism. **Bobby Alexander** presents an account of televangelism as ritual that moves beyond the norm by taking seriously the culture and history of the form, its practitioners, and audiences. **Keyan Tomaselli** and **Arnold Shepperson** conclude this section of the book, drawing on theories of communication change, political economy, and semiotics to present a theoretically thick description of the phenomenon.

The final section of the book deals with *individual practice.* **Janice Peck** investigates popular culture as a site of ritual and religious meaning, using theoretical frameworks drawn from existentialist philosophy and cultural theory. **Claire Badaracco** follows with an analysis of meaning negotiation and struggle in contemporary religious readings of popular culture. **Alf Linderman** explores issues of symbolism and meaning in religious television. His contribution goes beyond this particular case, however, to a presentation of a novel and compelling analytic framework in cultural and symbolic analysis. **Stewart Hoover** concludes this section with a historical-theoretical perspective on the construction of the religious public sphere. He brings together literature from religious studies, ritual studies, and media studies into an argument for an understanding of religion in the media age that goes beyond conventional categories.

The last chapter of the book presents some speculations about the potential for synthesis of the emerging discourse represented by the book. The field of scholarly analysis represented here is just at its beginning. There are rough edges to the various approaches that may clash and grate; however, at their core is a dynamic appreciation for the extent to which media, religion, and culture are converging both in the world of scholarship and in the world of actually existing lives and experience. It is our hope that this book will help set the terms by which we may come to a better understanding of these interactions in contemporary life so that we may move scholarship and practice forward.

References

Alexander, B. (1994). *Televangelism reconsidered.* Atlanta: Scholar's Press.

Bellah, R. N., Madsen, R., Sullivan, W. M., Swidler, A., & Tipton, S. N. (1985). *Habits of the heart: Individualism and commitment in American life.* Berkeley: University of California Press.

Beyer, P. (1994). *Religion and globalization.* London: Sage.

Bruce, S. (1991). *Pray TV: Televangelism in America.* London: Routledge & Kegan Paul.

Carey, J. (1989). *Communication as culture.* Boston: Unwin Hyman.

Fore, W. (1987). *Television and religion.* Minneapolis, MN: Augsburg.

Frankl, R. (1987). *Televangelism.* Carbondale: Southern Illinois University Press.

Grossberg, L., Nelson, C., & Treichler, P. (Eds.). (1992). *Cultural studies.* London: Routledge & Kegan Paul.

Hadden, J., & Shupe, A. (1988). *Televangelism: Power and politics on God's frontier.* New York: Henry Holt.

Hadden, J., & Swann, C. (1981). *Prime-time preachers: The rising power of televangelism.* Reading, MA: Addison-Wesley.

Hall, S., & Jefferson, T. (Eds.). (1976). *Resistance through rituals: Youth subcultures in post-war Britain.* London: HarperCollins.

Hammond, P. (1993). *Religion and personal autonomy.* Greenville: University of South Carolina Press.

Hoggart, R. (1957). *The uses of literacy: Aspects of working-class life with special reference to publications and entertainments.* London: Chatto & Windus.

Hoover, S. M. (1988). *Mass media religion.* London: Sage.

Hoover, S. M. (1995, Winter). Media and moral order in post-positivist media studies. *Journal of Communication,* 136-145.

Horsfield, P. (1984). *Religious television: The American experience.* New York: Longman.

Linderman, A. (1996). The reception of religious television: Social semiology applied to an empirical case study. In A. Linderman, *Acta Universitatis Upsaliensis, Psychologia et Sociologia Religionum 12.* Stockholm: Almquist & Wiksell International.

Martín-Barbero, J. (1993). *Communication, culture and hegemony: From the media to mediations.* London: Sage.

Moore, L. (1994). *Selling God.* New York: Oxford University Press.

Muggeridge, M. (1986). *Christ and the media.* London: Hodder and Stoughton. (Original work published 1977)

Olasky, M. (1988). *Prodigal press: The anti-Christian bias of the American news media.* Westchester, IL: Crossway.

Peck, J. (1993). *The gods of televangelism.* Cresskill, NJ: Hampton.

Roof, W. C. (1993). *A generation of seekers.* San Francisco: HarperCollins.

Schultze, Q. (1991). *Televangelism and American culture.* Grand Rapids, MI: Baker.

Turner, G. (1989). *British cultural studies: An introduction.* London: Unwin Hyman.

Warner, R. S. (1993). Work in progress toward a new paradigm for the sociological study of religion in the United States. *American Journal of Sociology, 98*(5), 1044-1093.

Wuthnow, R. (1987). *Meaning and moral order: Explorations in cultural analysis.* Berkeley, CA: University of California Press.

Wuthnow, R. (1988). *The restructuring of American religion.* Princeton, NJ: Princeton University Press.

Wuthnow, R. (1992). *Vocabularies of public life: Empirical essays in symbolic structure.* London: Routledge & Kegan Paul.

Wuthnow, R., Hunter, J., Bergesen, A., & Kurzweil, E. (1984). *Cultural analysis: The work of Peter L. Berger, Mary Douglas, Michel Foucault, and Jürgen Habermas.* London: Routledge & Kegan Paul.

Chapter 2

At the Intersection of
Media, Culture, and Religion
A Bibliographic Essay

Lynn Schofield Clark
Stewart M. Hoover

Practicing journalists and religious adherents gaze at each other across a wide cultural gap of misunderstanding. This divide may be attributed to the fact that these spheres occupy the same cultural turf; both are invested in communicating meaningful narratives and "truths" using the cultural capital of symbols, sounds, and subtle evocations of rational and emotional response in the audience. Although scholars of religion and of media have in the past participated in the wider cultural standoff between the two fields, recognition of an interrelation between the two has emerged, specifically in response to the turn away from institutional and toward cultural and individual (reception) studies in both fields.

This chapter will explore that turn as an interdisciplinary dialogue. Our hope is that a broad overview of literature will introduce areas in which similar questions are being raised across disciplinary lines, perhaps suggesting fruitful areas for new exploration. We acknowledge that we

15

draw largely on literature from the United States in this endeavor due to our backgrounds and to the significance of the North American case in media and religion.

We begin by offering a challenge to received definitions of religion, looking to anthropology for a cultural approach. This reframes the media scholar's tendency to marginalize religion and the religion scholar's tendency to focus on institutions rather than on practices, recognizing that both fields ask similar questions of meaning and being. We then address the existing thread of research that explicitly examines religion and media, which has played itself out in three primary directions: in televangelism, in dualistic critiques of "secular" media, and in research on news coverage of religion. Although each of these has contributed to knowledge, a review of relevant literature in cultural studies, ritual studies, and religious studies suggests lacunae for further consideration. We conclude with eight areas of research that emerge from this review.

▥ Religion for Media Scholars

We begin with the obvious question: Why should media scholars, as individuals concerned with the "concrete"—with power, politics, institutions, economics, urbanization, and, in short, all things "secular"—be interested in religion? This question itself reveals several assumptions about religion that we seek to challenge. Common scholarly misconceptions have reduced religion to its institutionalized and bureaucratized forms on the one hand, or to its privatized and idiosyncratic practices on the other. Both of these aspects of religion are marginalized in the larger public sphere. Part of the problem lies in a tacit acceptance of the theory of secularization, which suggests that as societies and cultures become more rational, the social significance of religion will decline. Berger (1969) provides the definitive description:

> By secularization we mean the process by which sectors of society and culture are removed from the domination of religious institutions and symbols. . . . [A]s there is a secularization of society and culture, so is there a secularization of consciousness. Put simply, this means that the modern west has produced an increasing number of individuals who look on the world and their own lives without the benefit of religious interpretation. (pp. 107-108)

Media practice—particularly in news—has equated its task with a rational product—information—and thus assumes an implicit role in this secular project. Commitment to journalistic objectivity furthers the idea that although religious sentiments may be acceptable in private life, they must be kept out of public work, especially out of journalism.

The theory of secularization is increasingly contested in religion scholarship (Warner, 1993). It assumes religion once had social ascendance and has now lost it, a position that idealizes the past and assumes a homogeneous and static approach to religion in society. It also does little to explain either the continuing existence of religion or the emergence of religion as a source of political and social power (Hadden & Shupe, 1988). Yet the idea that religion is declining in influence in a secularized culture holds salience throughout academic scholarship.

We assert instead that religion is integrated into everyday life, although not necessarily in the forms assumed by conventional scholarship. For purposes of cross-disciplinary discussion, we posit an anthropological definition of religion: religion as the site of the synthesis and symbolism of culturally meaningful belief systems. Although the Durkheimian discussion of the "sacred" and the "secular" is important and informs many fruitful interrogatives into religion and culture, we wish to shift the notion of religion away from those debates and the institutional assumptions that support them and to focus instead on the more general questions of ontology.

Religion, we propose, is not limited to what happens in a "sacred" realm, traditionally conceived, but is that part of culture that persuasively presents a plausible myth of the ordering of existence. In this sense, culture and religion are inseparable; and what is "sacred" may be understood, in Lundby's phrase, "as a variable, ranging from the substantial to the functional" (see Lundby, this volume). As it exists in the wholeness of human thought and practice, religion is thus an important consideration in theories of culture and society. Peck (1993) notes the connection between religion and issues of meaning at both individual and social levels:

> Religion is explicitly concerned with both ontological and experiential dimensions of existence—with being and meaning. Religion provides meaning for individual existence by grounding it in a larger, cosmic framework of significance. (p. 32)

We argue that the time is ripe for media scholars to begin to probe questions of religion in culture more directly. The ground has been laid for such inquiries by the recent trends in media studies that have foregrounded questions of meaning and being and have adopted methodologies that examine the everyday practices and discourses of individuals and groups. We will examine these trends after we have first examined the ways religion and media have been addressed in the past.

Studies of Religion and Media

We begin with the genre most frequently studied at the juncture of media and religion in American scholarship: *televangelism*. Televangelism derives its cultural meaning from situating religion in the "secular" realm of the media, thus inviting exploration of the role this phenomenon has played in transforming both religion and broadcasting. In *Televangelism and American Culture: The Business of Popular Religion*, for example, Quentin Schultze (1991) argues that the gospel is secularized, "turning Christ into another consumer product," while the consumerist and individualist values of the culture (as expressed in the "health and wealth gospel" of the televangelists) are sacralized (p. 123).

Televangelism's popularity as a site of study in the United States can be attributed to at least four factors. First, televangelism has been a progenitor of the rise of the Religious Right in American politics primarily through the efforts of Pat Robertson. Robertson, who established the first Christian television station in 1961 and launched the first religious satellite network (CBN) in 1977, ran unsuccessfully for president of the United States in 1988 and has enjoyed increasing influence since then (Hoover, 1988).

A second and related reason for interest in televangelism is its ability to visualize and thus give public voice to the valences of the Religious Right, including authoritarianism, nativism, xenophobia, homophobia, and, in its extreme, militarism and the desire for a theocracy. Televangelism is not only the place of origin of the Religious Right, but offers a form of its ongoing public discourse (Bruce, 1990; Hadden & Shupe, 1988).

Third, televangelism is implicated in the restructuring of the religious sphere. Although the hypothesis that the collapse of the mainline religions could be directly attributable to this new form of religion has been disputed (Hoover, 1990), televangelism serves as a reminder of the ascendancy of evangelicalism to a position of greater cultural prominence. Furthermore, televangelism serves as the quintessential example of evangelical theology's willingness to approach communication technologies and marketing techniques instrumentally in the dissemination of the gospel (Schultze, 1991).

A final aspect of televangelism's appeal as a subject of study rests with the excessively moralistic claims of televangelists coupled with their questionable practices, particularly in the realm of fund-raising. When financial and sexual scandals occurred in the late 1980s, they served to confirm suspicions that were articulated in studies of financial indiscretions—including misappropriation of funds, improper business practices, fund-raising tactics that manipulate elderly viewers (Abelman, 1990; Neuendorf, 1990), and the moral failings of its personalities (Bruce, 1990).

Televangelism has also been an important topic of study in other parts of the world, as scholars have probed the role of U.S. televangelism in countries and cultures outside the United States (Arntsen, 1993; Linderman, 1996; Lundby, 1996; Nyborg, 1995). Related studies highlight the concerns of public broadcasting policies that do or do not restrict the distribution of this material in countries outside the United States (Gunter & Viney, 1994; Wolfe, 1984).

Despite many suggestive findings, there are two problems presented to those who would look to this research for its application to a larger project of understanding media, religion, and culture. First, televangelism is self-consciously "religious," and as such, its television content is recognizably religious, employing forms such as worship services and preaching, or, in the case of magazine format programs, using religious language and music. This undergirds a too-facile assumption that religious programming is recognizable primarily within the framework of the traditional religions and their formal practices. Second, the televangelism audience comprises a rather small and confined segment of the population. Although televangelism's small subculture of viewers can provide theoretical elegance, the total population of individuals who claim a religious identity is far larger, beckoning a question not addressed in televangelism: What does "religious" programming mean to those not in the televangelism audience?

Several writings on televangelism also fall into a second category of writings about religion and media: *religious media criticism*. Malcolm Muggeridge (1977) and Virginia Stem Owens (1980) are prominent in this tradition, arguing that the Christian gospel is cheapened or at least cannot be communicated authentically through the mass media. Works in this tradition are consistent with a broader category of popular media criticism that includes the writings of Boorstin (1972), Ewen (1976), MacDonald (1962), Mander (1978), and Postman (1985), as elaborated by Jensen (1990). In fact, many religious writers draw heavily on these prior texts. Addressing the religious community's inadequate response to television, for example, Fore (1987) borrows the Huxleyan metaphor Postman introduced in *Amusing Ourselves to Death* (1985), lamenting television's influence on a culture in which "we are dominated not by force but by trivialization, by infantile gratification, by what Kierkegaard called 'twaddle'" (p. 32). The media, and television in particular, are believed to offer competing values that challenge the religious worldview (Melchert, 1994) and harbor biases and hostilities against religion (Olasky, 1988). The appropriate response is "innoculation" against media effects (Melchert, 1994; Thoman, 1993). This debate feeds into a wider argument against modernity as voices in religion lament the changes that have occurred since the Industrial Revolution as detrimental to values of community, locality, and interrelation (Jensen, 1990).

A minor thread in religious media criticism takes a radically different view. Rather than lamenting the media sphere, it focuses on the importance of entering it and offering religious values as a counterpoint to those proposed by the wider culture. These writings tend to assume an instrumental approach that views the media as "tools" that are "neutral" and thus may be employed for good, such as when they are utilized to spread the gospel (Armstrong, 1979) or to communicate narratives of faith (Benson, 1988; Boomershine, 1987). Other texts in this tradition emphasize the skills and knowledge needed to gain entrance to the media sphere (Parker, Iman, & Snyder, 1948; Poltrack, 1983; Shawchuck, Kotler, Wrenn, & Rath, 1992).

Interestingly (and consistent with the larger debates around "secular" media), both the critical and instrumental approaches assume a "strong media" perspective, emphasizing the power of communication messages to shape cultural values while overlooking the role of media reception practices of everyday life that might shape the meaning given to those messages (Baum, 1993; Fore, 1990). As Jensen (1990) writes:

> It is assumed that we, the audience, somehow absorb the goodness and subtlety of worthy culture, thus becoming uplifted and refined ourselves. Similarly, we absorb the corruption or triviality of symbolic expression, becoming corrupt or trivial ourselves. Thus cultural forms are given the power to make us over in their (assumed) image. (p. 28)

As White (1991) notes in his review of the televangelism literature, because these studies assume an (often unacknowledged) normative framework, they tend toward the unsatisfying and uncertain claims that characterize communication effects research in general. It is ironic that voices in the religious community embrace this view of media, given the commonplace sensitivity to the importance of cultural context in the interpretation of religious messages (Benson, 1988; Fore, 1990).

A third strand of research into religion and media has garnered the most attention recently: examination of *religion in the news*. The early 1990s proved to be a watershed in this area in the United States: Three major studies on religion and the news were completed (Dart & Allen, 1993; Hoover, Hanley, & Radelfinger, 1989; Hoover, Venturelli, & Wagner, 1995); a conference was sponsored by the prestigious Freedom Forum Media Studies Center in 1993; and several other periodicals and texts devoted attention to the issue (Carter, 1993; Mattingly, 1993; Stout & Buddenbaum, 1996). In addition, the fact that ABC television network hired the first-ever national television religion reporter in 1993 was seen as a symbolic recognition of the growing importance of religion (Govier, 1994).

Research has examined the content of coverage, the audiences for the coverage, and the institutions that generate the coverage. Working in the latter tradition, both the studies by Dart and Allen (1993) and Hoover and his associates (1995) dispute the oft-cited Rothman-Lichter hypothesis (Lichter, Rothman, & Lichter, 1986), which has been taken to contend that media "elites" are far less religious than the general public and may, as a result, be hostile toward religion. Dart and Allen (1993) attributed the lack of religion coverage to ignorance rather than hostility on the part of editors and reporters, noting that reporters tend to avoid religion because they assume that such coverage carries the potential of controversy.

Hoover and his colleagues (1995) added that any analysis of religion coverage must be lodged in a discussion of the limits of public discourse—including, but not limited to, the topic of religion in public discourse. Media coverage operates within these limits and is guided by public perceptions of both religion and news.

Accounts of religion and the news, like those of televangelism but in contrast to those in religious media criticism, have emerged from scholars of media rather than scholars of religion. Such studies have included content and rhetorical analyses of religion coverage in the news (Buddenbaum, 1986, 1990; Hart, Turner, & Knupp, 1981; Hynds, 1987). Although several of these have documented general improvement in the amount of religion coverage, there is evidence that religion news is still approached with biases favoring local over national and international stories (Hoover et al., 1989). Each of these works contributes to an understanding of the interesting American situation in which, despite the high level of religiosity and the democratic protections of its public expression, religion is a problematic topic in news output.

Although this research raises interesting questions, it fails to address others. Religion is here viewed as a particular type of news, categorized within the prerogatives of journalism and competing with other categories such as sports, politics, or entertainment. Because few people are interested in the news of religion—the argument goes—it becomes a specialized, and (much like televangelism) a marginalized area of interest.

We argue that it is essential to understand the relationship of religion and media within the larger cultural and media sphere. Tools for the task of problematizing the site of reception as an intersection between the spheres of religion and media are offered by the field of cultural studies. Thus, we probe cultural studies as a means to understand religion as breaking out of its institutionalized and marginalized status.

Cultural Media Studies

Although cultural theorists in Britain take a Marxist critique of class structure as a starting point, they question the degree to which the superstructure of culture is determined by the base of economic relations, arguing that culture must be seen as conditionally autonomous. Gramsci's nuanced description of the process by which consent to the dominant ideology is won, a process he terms "hegemony," has thus shaped the central questions of the British cultural studies tradition, offering three questions as starting points: How do institutions of power in liberal capitalistic societies succeed in winning the consent of subordinated groups to the dominant ideology? Why and how is it that media institutions, free of constraint, articulate content within frameworks of the dominant ideology? And how are cultural practices of appropriation and symbolic creativity used subversively to counteract dominant ideologies? (White, 1994).

Gramsci's indictment of the role of the institutional church in the process of hegemony—noting that it preserves "the ideological unity of the entire social bloc which that ideology serves to cement and unify" (Gramsci, 1971, p. 328)—echoes Marx's and has contributed to a blind spot toward religion on the part of cultural studies. Religion has too facilely been dismissed as a hegemonic force whose only role is to frame competing definitions of reality and, in so doing, suppress ideas and conflicts.

There are other reasons contributing to the theoretical truncation of religion in cultural studies. The culturalists in mass media have tended to see their work, which foregrounds everyday experience and its intersection with popular culture, as in direct contrast to "high culture" analyses of art and religion. Mukerji and Schudson (1991) point out that the high art/low art distinction was underscored by the "mass culture" debates of the Frankfurt school in the 1950s, yet originated in the late 19th century, when the upper classes sought cultural distinctions between themselves and their tastes and those of the classes beneath them. Popular culture was rescued from the arguments over taste and aesthetics beginning in the 1960s with the antielitist intellectual movements and the accompanying British emphasis on social change in the working class. Religion and art, Mukerji and Schudson imply, were left to the elitists as subjects of study, offering a social and political explanation for the obscuring of religion.

We might also look at the founding texts, Raymond Williams, Richard Hoggart, and E. P. Thompson. Williams (1961) argues that values or "meanings" cannot be analyzed without reference to a particular social context, nor can they be viewed as derivative or determined by that context. Media messages thus are viewed, not as causes of culture, but as rich cultural texts that provide insight into the values and meanings of the "structure of feeling," or social and historical organization, of an era. Unfortunately for our purposes, Williams does not explicitly address questions of religion, and in this way truncates his description of where those shared cultural meanings and values might originate, be challenged, and be reconstituted.

Like Williams, Hoggart (1957) does not pay explicit attention to religion in *The Uses of Literacy*. His contribution, as well as Thompson's, lies in the presentation of the working class from the "inside," looking at individuals in this group not as passively exploited, but as creative in their development of traditions that incorporate but are not subsumed by various aspects of mass culture and modernization. (For a further exploration of Hoggart's approach to religion, see Murdock in this volume.)

Thompson (1963) explicitly recognizes a role for religion in class formation and conflict. He describes Methodism and Utilitarianism as the dominant ideologies of the Industrial Revolution, assisting in the transition from rural to urban life as semisubsistence peasant industries were destroyed and replaced with the capitalist economy of the urban industrial centers. The Methodist and Utilitarian ideologies, Thompson argues, provided support for discipline and repression in schools, factories, and even leisure activities, while also promoting a moral life among upper class evangelicals which was to serve as an example to the poor. Thompson does not wholly idealize what was lost in the transition, noting the growth in self-respect among working persons and the discontinuation of such practices as wife-selling, animal sexuality, orgiastic drunkenness, and games of mortal combat. The ideologies supporting these changes, he argued, contributed to the collective, disciplined, and sober efforts on the part of the working class to fight for their civil rights.

Stuart Hall, a prominent scholar in the British cultural studies tradition, coedited a volume with a promising title for our current project: *Resistance Through Rituals: Youth Subcultures in Post-War Britain* (Hall & Jefferson, 1976). Making an argument in the introductory chapter against the American tendency to speak of "youth culture" as a homogeneous group transcending class and history, Hall and his coauthors note the importance of the dialectic between youth and the youth market and the ways in which group identity is reinforced through practices and commodity forms. Unfortunately, the "ritual" of the book's title is defined broadly as the patterned practices of the everyday that reinforce the boundaries of social identity. Overlooked are the religious origins of the term and religion's potential multiple roles in youth culture.

Hebdige (1976) provides the most interesting discussion of the intersection of religion and youth culture, tracing the roots of reggae music to the experience of slavery, its role in language formation among black Jamaicans, and the redefinition of Christianity to serve different cultural needs resulting in the development of the Rastafarian religious system. Each of these elements combined with American soul music, Pentecostal "calling" traditions, and African rhythms, to create reggae, which Hebdige calls a "Rasta hymnal," a music of resistance. The adoption of this music in the South London black youth culture, he argues, provided an avenue for resistance and the development of cultural autonomy. Hebdige's analysis serves as an excellent model of the benefits to be gained from the understanding of religion's role in the development of popular cultural forms.

Although other texts of the Birmingham school have also failed to address religion (e.g., Hall, Hobson, Lowe, & Willis, 1980; Hobson, 1982; Morley, 1980; Willis, 1977, 1990), as a body of work, they are helpful in our project for their theory and methodology. In his essay "Encoding/Decoding," Hall (1980) concurs with the idea that there is a relationship between social situations and the way television programs are "read," yet he argues that television programs are "open texts" that involve a process of negotiation between viewers and texts. Viewers may be in conflict with the dominant ideology inscribed in the text. Morley (1980) confirms Hall's findings in his audience reception analysis, marking a turning point toward greater attention to the socially contextualized practices of media use. Lull (1990), with his observation of the interaction of American families around the television set, and Hobson (1982), with her accounts of housewives who were alienated by media yet also found resources for identity reinforcement within media, were particularly influential in this turn. Through these and other reception studies, which primarily employ ethnographic approaches, allowing categories of interpretation to emerge from the social and cultural context, a more sophisticated understanding of the use of media in individual and group contexts has developed.

Scholars in British cultural studies have also been influenced by structuralism and interpretivist traditions arising from cultural anthropology, a field in which religion is traditionally a more central concern. Because humans are symbol-producing creatures, or "animal symbolicum," as Cassirer (1944) argued, communication and cognition are only possible within the limited systems of symbols embedded in culture. This is the point at which the British and American culturalist traditions intersect, although the American school is less influenced by Marxist and more by anthropological and liberal pragmatist traditions. Particularly important in the American school is the work of anthropologist Clifford Geertz (1973), who emphasizes the process of meaning-production in culture and argues that culture does not reflect the social order but exists in the representation of a society to itself, allowing for reflexivity on social order. Carey (1988) provides a germinal reading of Geertz, as well as Chicago school sociologists Dewey, Park, and Mead, in his arguments for a cultural approach to communication studies.

Carey offers a bridge to understandings of media and religion in his introduction of a ritual metaphor for communication, which he argues can helpfully replace the transportation metaphor that has undergirded positivist and instrumentalist approaches to communication research:

> A ritual view of communication is directed not toward the extension of messages in space but toward the maintenance of society in time; not the act of imparting information but the representation of shared beliefs. (p.18)

Carey thus brings us to another body of scholarship that intersects with questions of media and religion: that of ritual studies.

▦ Ritual Studies

Although religion per se has had to be satisfied with a "spare and truncated space" (Hoover, 1995) in media studies, insights from the field of ritual studies have been appropriated for media analyses. Whereas some communication theorists have built on Carey's Durkheimian notion that ritual primarily serves to maintain social systems and reinforce norms, others, such as Ettema (1990) and Dayan and Katz (1992) have extended Carey's metaphor through exploration of the work of Victor Turner.

Turner (1974) develops Geertz's concept of cultural reflexivity through his analyses of social dramas and rituals. Each ritual, he argues, consists of three stages: the initial phase, which divides participants from their everyday life; the liminal phase, which suspends all previous under-standings of the social order, allowing for both reflexivity and considera-tion of change; and the final phase of reintegration, in which participants are afforded a new status in social life. He argues that film and other media forms grant individuals a liminal moment in which they are removed from their daily lives and are open to the possibility of change, thus affording ritual a creative rather than conservative function in society (Turner, 1986).

Bell (1992) offers a critique of such essentialist approaches to ritual studies. Understandings of ritual have evolved out of a dichotomy that separates thought from action and sees ritual as the action in which the beliefs of a people are encoded, according to Bell. She addresses this false dichotomy through the use of the term *ritualization* to refer to the way in which certain social activities are distinguished from others:

> [R]itualization is a matter of setting some activities off from others, for creating and privileging a qualitative distinction between the "sacred" and the "profane," and for ascribing such distinctions to realities thought to transcend the powers of human actors. (p. 74)

Wuthnow (1987) makes a similar argument, noting that all actions that are expressive or communicative are, to some degree, rituals; and thus ritual is a part of all social activity. The cultural anthropologist Mary Douglas (1973) also asserts the communicative nature of ritual that high-lights social and cultural boundaries. Both Wuthnow and Douglas pro-vide important bridges between religious and cultural studies because each wants to separate the exploration of ritual from its formalist roots and examine these activities in everyday life.

Grimes (1976) also explores ritual in everyday life, examining ritual in a public, not exclusively religious, context. He describes the ways in which the performances of the annual Fiesta de Santa Fe not only serve to express the community's self-identity, but become the means by which the community may reflect on its advances as well as its shortcomings. He explores the city's symbols both in their historical development and in their relation to one another currently, noting that symbols are at once part of a timeless system and yet constantly reworked in a temporal process. Ritual thus points to a dynamism in religion, in social processes, and in their attendant symbol systems.

These trends in ritual scholarship highlight the public and procedural aspects of religious behavior, contradicting the idea that religion is limited to the private sphere. This is particularly relevant as scholars in the fields of sociology of religion and religious studies move away from institutions and structures and toward studies of religion in private life. Studies in religion are not irrelevant to our project, however, in that they contribute important insights not only into the realities of religion in everyday life, but also in the methodologies by which questions of meaning and being in everyday life (the setting where audiences interact with media) may be addressed.

▓ Religious Studies

It is common wisdom that institutional religion has been in decline in Europe and North America—a trend that seems on its surface to support the overall secularization hypothesis. It is significant to our purpose here that the majority of Americans still identify themselves as religious or spiritual (Roof, 1993). Clearly, what is meant by the terms *religious* and *spiritual* has changed. The authority over religious experience and expression is increasingly in the hands of the individual; and thus some scholars in religion have turned toward a model of "rational choice" to explore the ways in which individuals create their belief systems from symbols and other resources that constitute the "supply" in the religious "marketplace" (Finke & Iannaccone, 1993; Iannaccone, 1991), constructing a kind of "religion a la Carte," as Bibby (1987) has called it.

Warner (1993) relates this process to identity construction: "What the new religious voluntarism amounts to is a centrifugal process, sorting elemental qualities on the basis of which identities are constructed" (p. 1078). Marty (1993) notes that while this new voluntarism has individual actors creating a self-legitimated bricolage of various traditions, these practices of appropriation do not at the same time undermine the importance of religion itself:

> While one is free to violate inherited cultural bonds and instinctive social boundaries, there is a continuing use of religion to define who one is, to what one belongs, and whom one can trust. (p. 17)

The extent to which symbolic resources of the mass media are drawn into these processes is an essential question for our inquiries here.

Another area of religion research that connects with current work in mass media is the examination of the increasingly blurred boundaries between religion and psychology (e.g., Spilka, Hood, & Gorsuch, 1985). The therapeutic aspects of religion and an increased emphasis on healing are found in quasi-religious organizations such as 12-step programs (Marty, 1993), and such language increasingly makes its way into the public sphere, as Albanese (1993) notes:

> With what many would regard as unpromising beginnings in individualistic mystical themes, their metaphor of healing as reconciliation had led them to a concern for healing relationships with others. From there, in a move that fit their mentality as nature religionists, they had turned to a cosmological concern for healing the earth and reconciling the human community with it. . . . Perhaps, to the chagrin of some and the delight of others, new spirituality people were talking to the body politic and moving comfortably into its central square as the old religious and philosophical establishment was leaving. (p. 143)

There is thus a connection between religion scholarship and media scholarship as both examine the role of therapeutic discourse in television. Mimi White (1992) notes that the languages of psychology and therapy significantly frame the television viewing experience: "The idea that television functions as a therapeutic apparatus, and should be explored in those terms, is an integral part of the everyday discourses and practices of regular television viewers" (p. 27).

Historical and pragmatic connections between religion and therapeutic discourse are explored in Peck's (1993) work, as she draws connections between the centrality of therapeutic discourse in television talk shows and the influence of individualism in both American Protestantism and democratic liberal thought. Future research might examine the ways in which therapeutic discourse is "read" as religious among audiences, while also exploring how therapeutic discourse is employed to describe the religious aspects of mass media interaction.

Linked with this turn to the therapeutic is a rediscovery of the experiential and affective in religion, problematizing the extent to which questions of meaning and being have been limited to the cognitive sphere under the enlightenment regime. As Albanese (1993) writes: "The insistence on the joys of physicality and sexuality, the rewards of massage and bodywork, the importance of touch and contact in relationship all tell of a past in which such themes were denied or underplayed" (p. 140).

Roof and Taylor (1995) describe the "Rave in the Nave," a popular religious expression that embodies the experiential and affective in religious worship for the twenty-something generation. The pleasure of sensation is an important aspect of the ritual, which Roof and Taylor argue affords the "transport" to the mystical (using William James' term) that might be likened to Turner's "liminal moment." Engaging the emotions and senses is imbued with religious meaning, Roof and Taylor argue, thus offering a bridge to a development of religious understandings in the "pleasures of the text" described by mass media scholars such as John Fiske (1987).

Albanese (1993) and others argue that religious themes emerge in public discourse. Approaching a similar question from the stance of religion in popular culture, Jindra (1994) has examined the sacralization of cultural and therapeutic concepts in *Star Trek* fandom. He argues that the *Star Trek* cycle is a location for nonconventional religion and illustrates how fandom shares such religious practices as the formation and maintenance of a "canon," a "theology" that extols the virtues of technology and humanity's ability to solve problems, a group identity, pilgrimages to exhibitions and conferences, and a stigma of difference. This research reflects an important movement toward the examination of the interplay between mass media and religion in everyday experience.

Why these themes of therapy or the "religion" of *Star Trek* have gained salience in the public sphere is an open question. Research might examine the evolution of these symbols and discourses, as well as those being replaced, in the public expression of religion.

An important contribution of contemporary sociology of religion is methodological. In the move toward the examination of religion in everyday life, a number of scholars have adopted qualitative, in-depth techniques, developing insights into how researchers might approach the elusive questions of meaning and being (Roof, 1993; Stacey, 1990).

▓ Conclusion

We have suggested several studies that might be indicative of research at the intersection of religion, culture, and the media. Out of this review emerge at least six additional areas that seem worthy of further exploration.

The first two of these would refine and extend current research: studies of *religion and the news* that focus on producers, texts, and audiences (Dart & Allen, 1993; Hoover, 1995; Stout & Buddenbaum, 1996) and studies of *televangelism* (Bruce, 1990; Peck, 1993). Recent work in each of these areas has continued to extend the field of knowledge and to produce new and interesting ideas (see chapters in this volume by Linderman, Tomaselli and Shepperson, and Alexander, for example).

The third area of potential research, reflected in Hebdige's (1976) work on reggae and Jindra's (1994) analysis of *Star Trek* fandom, would examine the *interplay between religious thought and popular culture*. Whereas the former suggests the study of historical religious roots of particular genres and texts, the latter examines the ways in which religion emerges in everyday life in unexpected forms mediated by popular culture. As Mukerji and Schudson (1991) note, there is little research on the interconnection between popular culture and religion, although this is a field of growing interest (e.g., Clark, 1996; Pardun & McKee, 1994). Such research requires an understanding of both popular culture and popular religion (see chapters in this volume by Goethals and Hoover).

A fourth area of research is suggested by Albanese's (1993) work on *new modes of spirituality*, and would examine how religious symbols are contested and constrained in the public sphere to create a public discourse of religion. Some work is already being done in this area (Hoover & Clark, 1995; Redal, 1995), although much remains in the analysis of the construction of public identity and the complex relations between religious institutions and the media (see chapters in this volume by Lundby, Bar-Haim, and Badaracco).

A fifth area is suggested by Mimi White's (1992) and Peck's (1993) work on *mediated therapeutic discourse*. As the field of religion explores the relationship between the psychological and the religious in both the private and public spheres, how popular culture discourse emerges as "religious"—in both public texts and audience perceptions—remains to be explored (see Peck's chapter in this volume).

A sixth area, and perhaps the least explored, is the minor but simultaneous call for examination of *the affective* that is occurring in both religion (cf. Roof & Taylor, 1995) and media (cf. Fiske, 1987) scholarship.

Underlying several of these areas are three themes that are particularly relevant for the project with which we began. The first of these is the shift from *modernity to postmodernity*, which has foregrounded the roles of commodification, transnationality, and globalization, and in general the flattening of time and space occurring simultaneously in both media and religious practices (see chapters in this volume by Murdock, White, and Christians).

The second, which grows out of the conditions of the first, is *identity negotiation*, both individual and collective. Bellah and his colleagues (1985) have noted that the search for meaning, often associated with religion, has become for many a search for the self and its expression in American individualism, thus foregrounding the relationship between religion and identity formation. Studies in religion and personal autonomy have emphasized that individuals create their own identities, but within the storytelling and ritual traditions of the culture in which they find themselves. Media present possible identifications to "try on" in a safe way, enabling audience members to consider who they are and are not (see chapters in this volume by Martín-Barbero, Badaracco, and Peck). Furthermore, through the collapse of the public sphere into the *mediated public sphere*, the media are also the primary public forum for the debate over cultural identities (see chapters in this volume by Bar-Haim and Hoover).

The third theme, which grows out of the previous two, is the postmodern question of the creative *reworking of the text at the site of the audience*. We need much more information about the role of religion in this process. How are people using existing media texts and converting them to stories of religious inspiration, for example? Do those stories have connections to deep myths of the Abrahamic faiths, or do they resonate with other traditions (perhaps civil religion, or other religious traditions)? How do these readings work themselves back into the production of media? (See chapters by White, Tomaselli and Shepperson, and Alexander.)

We have argued for a broader conception of religion that provides space for questions of meaning, identity, and ontology to emerge in cultural studies. This is necessary for studies of both religion and media as the two increasingly intersect in the practices of everyday life. Religion undergirds the production and reading of media discourse; while the images, narratives, and symbols of the media become resources in the ongoing construction of individual and collective religious identity. The fact of media's religious significance should not be cause for alarm, nor should it be overlooked. Clearly, we need more information on the ways in which this religious significance is played out in people's everyday lives.

References

Abelman, R. (1990). The selling of salvation in the electronic church. In R. Abelman & S. M. Hoover (Eds.), *Religious television: Controversies and conclusions* (pp. 173-183). Norwood, NJ: Ablex.

Albanese, C. (1993, May). Fisher kings and public places: The old new age in the 1990s. *Annals of the American Academy, 527,* 131-143.

Armstrong, B. (1979). *The electric church.* Nashville/New York: Thomas Nelson.

Arntsen, H. (1993). *The battle of the mind: International media elements of the new religious political right in Zimbabwe.* Unpublished thesis, Department of Media and Communication, University of Oslo, Norway.

Baum, G. (1993). The church and the mass media. In J. Coleman & M. Tomka (Eds.), *Mass media* (pp. 63-69). Maryknoll, NY: Orbis.

Bell, C. (1992). *Ritual theory, ritual practice.* New York: Oxford University Press.

Bellah, R., Madsen, R., Sullivan, W. M., Swidler, A., & Tipton, S. N. (1985). *Habits of the heart: Individualism and commitment in American life.* Berkeley: University of California Press.

Benson, D. (1988). *The visible church.* Nashville, TN: Abingdon.

Berger, P. (1969). *The sacred canopy: Elements of a sociological theory of religion.* Garden City, NY: Anchor.

Bibby, R. (1987). *Fragmented gods.* Toronto: Irwin.

Boomershine, T. (1987). Religious education and media change: A historical sketch. *Religious Education, 82*(2), 269-278.

Boorstin, D. (1972). *The image: A guide to pseudo-events in America.* New York: Atheneum.

Bruce, S. (1990). *Pray TV: Televangelism in America.* London: Routledge & Kegan Paul.

Buddenbaum, J. (1986). Analysis of religion news coverage in three major newspapers. *Journalism Quarterly, 63,* 600-606.

Buddenbaum, J. (1990). Religion news coverage in commercial network newscasts. In R. Abelman & S. Hoover (Eds.), *Religious television: Controversies and conclusions.* Norwood, NJ: Ablex.

Carey, J. (1988). *Communication as culture.* Boston: Unwin Hyman.

Carter, S. L. (1993). *The culture of disbelief: How American law and politics trivialize religious devotion.* New York: Basic Books.

Cassirer, E. (1944). *An essay on man: An introduction to a philsophy of human culture.* New Haven, CT: Yale University Press.

Clark, L. S. (1996, January). *Media, meaning, and the lifecourse: Religious imagery in the music video "One of Us" and its interpretation by Gen Xers.* Paper presented at the Media, Religion, and Culture Conference, Boulder, CO.

Dart, J., & Allen, J. (1993). *Bridging the gap: Religion and the news media.* Published report of the Freedom Forum First Amendment Center, Vanderbilt University, Nashville, TN.

Dayan, D., & Katz, E. (1992). *Media events: The live broadcasting of history.* Cambridge, MA: Harvard University Press.

Douglas, M. (1973). *Natural symbols.* New York: Random House.

Ettema, J. (1990). Press rites and race relations: A study of mass-mediated ritual. *Critical Studies in Mass Communication, 7*(4), 309-331.

Ewen, S. (1976). *Captains of consciousness: Advertising and the social roots of the consumer culture.* New York: McGraw-Hill.

Finke, R., & Iannaccone, L. (1993, May). Supply-side explanations for religious change. *Annals of the American Academy, 527,* 27-39.

Fiske, J. (1987). *Television culture.* London: Routledge & Kegan Paul.

Fore, W. (1987). *Television and religion: The shaping of faith, values, and culture.* Minneapolis, MN: Augsburg.

Fore, W. (1990). *Mythmakers: Gospel, culture, and the media.* New York: Friendship Press.

Geertz, C. (1973). *The interpretation of cultures.* New York: Basic Books.

Govier, G. (1994, May). Religion reporter at ABC. *The Communicator* (Radio-Television News Directors Association) pp. 23-24.

Gramsci, A. (1971). *Selections from the prison notebooks.* (Q. Hoare & G. N. Smith, Trans.). New York: International Publishers.

Grimes, R. (1976). *Symbol and conquest: Public ritual and drama in Santa Fe.* Albuquerque: University of New Mexico Press.

Gunter, B., & Viney, R. (1994). *Seeing is believing: Religion and television in the 1990s.* London: John Libbey.

Hadden, J., & Shupe, A. (1988). *Televangelism: Power and politics on God's frontier.* New York: Henry Holt.

Hall, S. (1980). Encoding/decoding. In S. Hall, D. Hobson, A. Lowe, & P. Willis (Eds.), *Culture, media, language.* London: Hutchison.

Hall, S., & Jefferson, T. (Eds.). (1976). *Resistance through rituals: Youth subcultures in post-war Britain.* London: Center for Contemporary Cultural Studies.

Hart, R., Turner, K., & Knupp, R. (1981). A rhetorical profile of religious news: *Time,* 1947-1976. *Journal of Communication, 31,* 3.

Hebdige, D. (1976). Reggae, rastas and rudies. In S. Hall & T. Jefferson (Eds.), *Resistance through rituals: Youth subcultures in post-war Britain.* London: Center for Contemporary Cultural Studies.

Hobson, D. (1982). *"Crossroads": The drama of a soap opera.* London: Methuen.

Hoggart, R. (1957). *The uses of literacy.* London: Chatto and Windus.

Hoover, S. M. (1988). *Mass media religion: The social sources of the electronic church.* Newbury Park, CA: Sage.

Hoover, S. M. (1990). Ten myths about religious broadcasting. In R. Abelman & S. Hoover (Eds.), *Religious television: Controversies and conclusions* (pp. 23-39). Norwood, NJ: Ablex.

Hoover, S. M. (1995, Winter). Media and moral order in post-positivist media studies. *Journal of Communication,* 136-145.

Hoover, S. M., & Clark, L. (1995, October). *Negotiating the boundaries between religion and the media: A case study of the re-imagining controversy.* Paper presented at the annual meeting of the Society for the Scientific Study of Religion, St. Louis, MO.

Hoover, S. M., Hanley, B., & Radelfinger, M. (1989). *RNS-Lilly study of religion reporting and readership in the daily press.* Unpublished manuscript, Temple University, Philadelphia, PA.

Hoover, S. M., Venturelli, S., & Wagner, S. (1995). *Religion in public discourse: The role of the media.* Unpublished manuscript, Center for Mass Media Research, University of Colorado, Boulder.

Hynds, E. (1987). Large daily newspapers have improved coverage of religion. *Journalism Quarterly, 64*, 444-448.

Iannaccone, L. (1991). The consequences of religious market structure. *Rationality and Society, 3*, 156-177.

Jensen, J. (1990). *Redeeming modernity: Contradictions in media criticism.* Newbury Park, CA: Sage.

Jindra, M. (1994). Star Trek fandom as a religious phenomenon. *Sociology of Religion, 55*(1), 27-51.

Lichter, R., Rothman, S., & Lichter, L. (1986). *The media elite.* New York: Adler & Adler.

Linderman, A. (1996). The reception of religious television: Social semieology applied to an empirical case study. *Acta Universitatis Upsaliensis, Psychologia et Sociologia Religionum* 12. Stockholm: Almquist & Wiksell International.

Lull, J. (1990). *Inside family viewing: Ethnographic research on television's audiences.* London and New York: Routledge.

Lundby, K. (1996, January). *Media, religion and culture in community communication: Case studies in Zimbabwe and Norway.* Paper presented at the Conference on Media, Religion and Culture, University of Colorado, Boulder, CO.

MacDonald, D. (1962). *Against the American grain.* New York: Random House.

Mander, J. (1978). *Four arguments for the elimination of television.* New York: William Morrow.

Marty, M. (1993, May). Where the energies go. *Annals of the American Academy, 527*, 11-26.

Mattingly, T. (1993, July/August). Religion in the news: Are we short-changing readers and ourselves with biases that filter news? *Quill*, 12-13.

Melchert, C. (1994). TV: A competing religion. *PRISM: A Theological Forum for the UCC*, pp. 88-96.

Morley, D. (1980). *The "Nationwide" audience: Structure and decoding.* London: British Film Institute.

Muggeridge, M. (1977). *Christ and the media.* Grand Rapids, MI: Eerdmans.

Mukerji, C., & Schudson, M. (1991). Introduction: Rethinking popular culture. In *Rethinking popular culture: Contemporary perspectives in cultural studies.* Berkeley: University of California Press.

Neuendorf, K. (1990). The public trust versus the almighty dollar. In R. Abelman & S. M. Hoover (Eds.), *Religious television: Controversies and conclusions* (pp. 71-84). Norwood, NJ: Ablex.

Nyborg, G. (1995). *Conquest, dominance or spiritual reformation? Bolivian Quechua families watching U.S. televangelism.* Unpublished doctoral dissertation, University of Bergen, Norway.

Olasky, M. (1988). *The prodigal press: The anti-Christian bias of the American news media.* Westchester, IL: Crossway.

Owens, V. S. (1980). *The total image: Or selling Jesus in the modern age.* Grand Rapids, MI: Eerdmans.

Pardun, C., & McKee, K. (1994, August). *Strange bedfellows: Symbols of religion and sexuality on MTV.* Paper presented to the Mass Communication and Society Division, Association for Education in Journalism and Mass Communication, Atlanta, GA.

Parker, E., Iman, E., & Snyder, R. (1948). *Religious radio: What to do and how.* New York: Harper and Brothers.

Peck, J. (1993). *The gods of televangelism: The crisis of meaning and the appeal of religious television.* Cresskill, NJ: Hampton.

Poltrack, D. (1983). *Television marketing: Network, local, and cable.* New York: McGraw-Hill.

Postman, N. (1985). *Amusing ourselves to death: Public discourse in the age of show business.* New York: Viking.

Redal, W. (1995, May). *Waging the culture war: Media strategies of the Christian right.* Paper presented at the International Communication Association, Albuquerque, NM.

Roof, W. (1993). *A generation of seekers: The spiritual journeys of the baby boom generation.* San Francisco: Harper.

Roof, W., & Taylor, S. M. (1995). The force of emotion: James' reorientation of religion and the contemporary rediscovery of the body. In D. Capps & J. Jacobs (Eds.), *The struggle for life: A companion volume to William James' The Varieties of Religious Experience* (Monograph No. 7). West Lafayette, IN: Society for the Scientific Study of Religion.

Schultze, Q. (1991). *Televangelism and American culture: The business of popular religion.* Grand Rapids, MI: Baker.

Shawchuck, N., Kotler, P., Wrenn, B., & Rath, G. (1992). *Marketing for congregations: Choosing to serve people more effectively.* Nashville, TN: Abingdon.

Spilka, B., Hood, R., & Gorsuch, R. (1985). *The psychology of religion.* Englewood Cliffs, NJ: Prentice Hall.

Stacey, J. (1990). *Brave new families: Stories of domestic upheaval in late twentieth century America.* New York: Basic Books.

Stout, D., & Buddenbaum, J. M. (Eds.). (1996). *Religion and mass media: Audiences and adaptations.* Thousand Oaks, CA: Sage.

Thoman, E. (1993). Media, technology, and culture: Re-imagining the American dream. *Bulletin of Science, Technology, and Society, 13*(1), 20-27.

Thompson, E. (1963). *The making of the English working class.* New York: Vintage.

Turner, V. (1974). *Dramas, fields and metaphors: Symbolic action in human society.* Ithaca, NY: Cornell University Press.

Turner, V. (1986). *The anthropology of performance.* New York: Performing Arts Journal Publications.

Warner, R. (1993). Work in progress toward a new paradigm for the sociological study of religion in the United States. *American Journal of Sociology, 98*(5), 1044-1093.

White, M. (1992). *Tele-advising: Therapeutic discourse in American television.* Chapel Hill, NC: University of North Carolina Press.

White, R. (1991). Televangelism and the religious uses of television. *Communication Research Trends, 11*(1) 2-33.

White, R. (1994). Audience "interpretation" of media: Emerging perspectives. *Communication Research Trends, 14*(3), 3-40.

Williams, R. (1961). *The long revolution.* London: Chatto & Windus.

Willis, P. (1977). *Learning to labor: How working class kids get working class jobs.* Farnborough, UK: Saxon House.

Willis, P. (1990). *Common culture: Symbolic work at play in the everyday cultures of the young.* Boulder, CO: Westview Press.

Wolfe, K. (1984). *The churches and the British Broadcasting Corporation 1922-1956: The politics of broadcast religion.* London: SCM Press.

Wuthnow, R. (1987). *Meaning and moral order: Explorations in cultural analysis.* Berkeley: University of California Press.

Chapter 3

Religion and Media
in the Construction of Cultures

Robert A. White

The current questions about the politics and cultural influence of the religious broadcasters of fundamentalist leanings in various religious traditions raise many of the classical issues regarding media and religion in public discourse. Is religion part of the public cultural patrimony, or is it a matter of personal opinion that is best consigned to the private sphere? Does the decline of some of the institutional churches confirm predictions of inevitable secularization, or do the new religious movements signal a resurgence of the sacred in the public sphere? These quandaries about the public role of religion, especially in broadcasting, reflect the erosion of old certainties in the sociology of religion and echo the call for a paradigm change in theories of religion, culture, and media.

Policies regarding religion in public discourse have followed closely our social theories of religion and culture. This is another example of the "double hermeneutic" noted by Giddens (1984), in which there is a constant moving back and forth from the first level of interpretation of meaning in everyday lay language to a second level of interpretation developed by the metalanguage of the social sciences (p. 374). The Enlightenment political-economic project removed theological discourse as a basis of public consensus but continued to see religion as somehow important for the development of modern industrial societies. Social theories of religion followed suit. The Durkheimian tradition of social theory considered religious sentiment to be a foundation for the social integration of modernizing societies. Weber interpreted religion as the motivation for the personal and social mobilization needed for industrial progress. Ernst Troeltsch viewed religion as a positive ethical foundation for a new social order, but the Marxist tradition considered religion to be an obstacle that must be replaced with a secularizing "religion" of socialist progress. In one way or another, all of these theories of religion reduced public religious discourse to a function of industrial progress in the new nation-state (Beckford & Luckmann, 1989, pp. 1-2).

As the public sphere began to be identified with the state, the discourses of the press and other forms of mediated communication were also considered a volatile threat to orderly public consensus and, like religion, were either consigned to the sphere of private opinion or were allowed into the public sphere as a form of circulating the information necessary for industrial progress. Later, broadcasting was defined as having a public function needing public regulation, but only reluctantly, under the guise of technological orderliness. Not surprisingly, religious studies and media studies developed with little theoretical interrelationship, especially as regards their common role in the public sphere.

When broadcasting began in the 1920s, these conceptions of the role of religion and media in national development provided a framework for including a kind of nondenominational religion in the programming. The presence of religion in the new medium legitimated the entry of media into the privacy of homes, where "religious" religion was consigned, and made broadcasting a supporter of the kind of civil religion that Bellah (1967) has described. Mainline religious leaders joined hands with broadcasters and political leaders to ensure that their message was recast into the nondenominational language of public progress, instrumental rationality, and nation building; competing sectarian groups were excluded from broadcasting (Horsfield, 1984, pp. 3-8).

The postmodernist movements of the 1960s and 1970s have profoundly unhinged the Victorian solution to the interrelation of religion and media in public discourse. The new ethos questions a worldview

based exclusively on instrumental rationality and claims that each subculture based on ethnicity, race, language, gender, personal interests,
region, or cult has its own epistemology and its own logic. Every subculture should be provided with the means to project its identity into the
public forum. The new definition of *democratization* as privatization has
suddenly seemed plausible; and this has led to policies of deregulation of
the public sphere and a kind of consensus formation founded on single-
issue, polling-based politics. The ensuing "culture wars" are raising fears,
but there seems be no theory of the new public sphere to explain what to
do (Hunter, 1991; Wuthnow, 1989).

Religious studies are increasingly aware of the breakdown of 19th-
century conceptions of religion and society and are attempting to create
a new theoretical formulation that is broad enough to explain not just the
new religious movements, but religious phenomena across time and
space. Religion is not just a factor of social integration, but points beyond
the present organization of society and is just as likely to be socially
disruptive, culturally ecstatic, and politically revolutionary (Beckford,
1989, pp. 170-171). Sociologies of religion are moving beyond a simple,
linear model of religion and society that presumes a steady march of
secularization (Warner, 1993, p. 1048). There is a theoretical and methodological capacity to see the manifestation of religious phenomena in myriad sociopolitical contexts and in all social formations. Religious aspirations and motivations are no longer seen as located largely within specific
institutions and ecclesial organizations. The sense of the sacred and
religious sentiments may be part of the revitalization of churches, cults,
and movements; but even here, they are seen more as general, autonomous symbols of "ultimate meaning, infinite power, supreme indignation
and sublime passion" (Beckford, 1989, p. 171).

Media studies are likewise moving away from a paradigm that
reduced media to the function of transporting and circulating the information needed for rapid industrial progress (Rowland, 1983). The focus is
shifting to the many actors who are creating cultural meaning in the forum
of the media and in the struggle of audiences to define their identities in
interaction with the media (Morley, 1992).

The present chapter examines the emerging trends of religious studies and media studies to construct a theory of religion and media in the
public sphere in a postmodernist context of radical cultural pluralism. On
the one hand, there is an affirmation of the need and the right to project

diverse value identities in the public sphere, continually contesting the validity of a single hegemonic national culture, language, and religion. On the other hand, the new context demands a process of global peace and negotiated cultural consensus in which all persons and subcultures can immediately recognize something of their identities.

A central question of this chapter is how to allow discursive autonomy to the sacred, with its implications of unity, ultimateness, and transcendence, in a public sphere that is increasingly pluralist, secular, hegemonic, and pragmatic.

A central argument of this chapter is that the modernist oppositions of sacred versus secular, poetic imagination versus instrumental rationality, subjective versus objective, person versus society, and pluralism versus personal conviction are better expressed in terms of what Giddens (1984) has characterized as *dualities* that are enabling conditions for each other. The sacred and the secular are two autonomous but interdependent discourses within a multiplicity of categories of meaning that interpret different modes of existence (Jensen, 1995, p. 31). The autonomous "symbolic realism" of the sacred, to use Bellah's term (1970, pp. 3-19; Wuthnow, 1992, p. 53), affirms an equal autonomy of the secular. The imaginative, exploratory, prefiguring discourses of what Klaus Bruhn Jensen (1995) has referred to as "time-out culture" are not simply subordinate to and measured by the "time-in culture" of pragmatic agency (pp. 56-58). Rather, these two cultures are mutually interpellating and complementing each other. Instead of the modernist solution of making the secular and instrumental efficiency the norm of public discourse, this theory sees these as a continual mutual affirmation in which the sacred evokes the secular and the secular evokes the sacred.

The Religious and Mass Media as Discourses of Reflexive Prefiguring of Culture

Religious studies and media studies have freed themselves from the reductionist functions of social integration and modernization largely by aligning themselves with the cultural sciences; and they have found common ground as discourses that monitor, evaluate, and orient the integrated development of cultures (Geertz, 1973; Wuthnow, 1992, pp. 37-58). Both religious studies and studies of public communicative discourse start with the awareness that humans *create* the conceptions of their past and future history. Both religion and media stand at the edges of the construction of the islands of commonsense meaning. On the one hand, both religion and media explore possible alternative meanings of history outside of these islands; and on the other hand, they continually validate and maintain the internal coherence of the world of constructed meanings. Both theologians and rhetoricians are constantly monitoring public discourse to ensure that the rules of sense and nonsense, the rational and the irrational, are working—or if not, finding ways of adapting these rules to new situations.

Religious and media studies are an instance of what Giddens (1984) refers to as "reflexivity" in social theory. Just as it was not possible to explain and predict religious or media behavior as deterministically related to the functional prerequisites of social systems, so also Giddens seeks to avoid both the imperialism of subjectivity and the imperialism of social structure by defining social practices as a process of reflexive "positioning" and "negotiating" between one's personal existence and social rules as one goes about the practical affairs of life. Giddens describes *reflexivity* as the conscious, monitored dimension of social life that is constantly assigning meaning to the transactions of everyday life (pp. 2-5). Giddens proposes three levels of consciousness: the *repressed consciousness*; the *discursive consciousness*, in which consciousness becomes verbalized in systems of meaning and engages in justification and explanation; and the *practical consciousness*, in which awareness is focused on outcomes (pp. 6-8).

Klaus Bruhn Jensen (1995) uses Giddens' structuration logic as the framework for his theory of mass communication, but suggests that Giddens does not develop sufficiently the practices of signification in the concept of discursive consciousness (pp. 39-40). Jensen argues that social action is not simply a direct duality of human agency and social structures, but has a triadic structure in which "social structures are enacted through human agency with continuous reference to a *medium*, resulting in the 'social construction of reality' (Berger & Luckmann, 1966). Through signs, reality becomes social and subject to reflexivity" (p. 39).

This echoes Wuthnow's (1992) insistence that the primary focus of religious studies is not simply individual internal beliefs reacting directly to social structures such as class systems or social institutions. The individual-society dichotomy needs to be amended with more attention to the role of religious discourse that "lies at the intersection of the individual and the community. [This discourse] . . . individuates convictions . . . but it also reinforces a sense of collectivity at the same time" (p. 48). Wuthnow proposes that the analysis of the organization of meaning in texts, in discourse, and in the media moves the study of religious culture from a "study of the meaning of religious symbolism to the study of the symbolism of meaning" and begins to take seriously Bellah's argument in favor of an approach in the sociology of religion stressing "symbolic realism" (1966; 1970, p. 53).

Many disciplines within the cultural sciences have documented the fact that reflexivity becomes a specialized cultural practice; namely, that certain areas of cultural discourse, practice, and institutional organization are more concerned with exploring the possible developments of culture beyond the existing confines of the social construction of reality, whereas other areas are more concerned with sustaining the already established set of institutions, pragmatic goals, and safe patterns of meaning. Klaus Bruhn Jensen (1995) has formalized this duality of cultural practice as part of his theory of mass communication in terms of what he calls "time-in culture" and "time-out culture," a metaphor taken from the world of sport (pp. 55-58). Time-out culture "places reality on an explicit agenda as an object of reflexivity and provides an occasion for contemplating oneself in a social, existential or religious perspective" (p. 57). Time-in and time-out are not two cultures, but two mutually challenging and supporting dimensions of culture, one *prefiguring* the shape of social action and the other *configuring* social action.

The conception of culture as distinct but mutually interacting and mutually supporting areas of prefiguring and configuring enables us to see the sacred and the secular, imaginative representation and pragmatic action, aesthetic practice and social practice, not as oppositions, but as dimensions that presuppose and address each other. This also highlights the fact that moving back and forth across the "edge" of the social construction of reality and finding an equilibrium between these two dimensions of culture is a central problem of cultures that religious and media studies are attempting to address.

Although the debate between substantive and functionalist conceptions of religion continues (O'Toole, 1984, pp. 10-42), the most common tendency in religious studies is to define the religious as a process of seeking a response to the ultimate, "limit" questions of meaning in life (Bellah, 1970, p. 253; Turner, 1991). This does not assume, as Bryan Turner (1991) notes, that the "'problem of meaning' strikes all members of a society in the same way and with equal force" (p. 246), but it does assume that religious discourse plays a central role in the way societies represent a synthesis of the core symbols. These symbols both integrate the culture around what Victor Turner (1974) has called "root paradigms" and establish the separating boundaries between cultures.

Peter Berger (1967) left a lasting influence on religious studies when he defined the religious as a cultural activity that deals with sustaining the boundaries between the islands of meaning socially established as real, commonsense, and rational, and the areas beyond the boundary that are considered dream, fantasy, aberrant, and insane. The religious endows socially constructed reality "with a stability deriving from more powerful sources than the historical efforts of human beings" (p. 25). Religious discourse deals with the manifestations of an autonomous, fully meaningful, "sacred" order, not constructed by human endeavor, that both guarantees the continued meaningfulness of the humanly constructed reality and wards off the invasions of chaotic meaningless. More important, religious institutions monitor the exploratory forays out of the imperfect and impure world of the secular into the mysterious realm of the sacred sources of meaning, truth, being, and happiness. But the religious also forces the sacred to address and return to the secular.

Likewise, media studies have moved away from a preoccupation with social control through prosocial or antisocial effects, to a focus on the processes of exploring new paradigms of meaning at the boundaries between accepted common sense and the unexplainable. Silverstone (1981) has used Lévi-Strauss's conception of resolution of conflicting cultural meaning through mythic narrative to explain how television news and drama take seemingly irrational, strange, and highly specialized esoteric information and weave the new information into existing, understandable discourses of common sense. Hoover (1988, pp. 101-103), Jensen (1995, pp. 56-58), Newcomb and Alley (1983, pp. 18-45), and many other communication theorists have applied Victor Turner's conception of ritual process to explain the media as a liminal space of cultural freedom that audiences move into to be reinvigorated by a quasi-religious experience of perfect community and then move back to the pragmatic world.

Carey (1977) has been inspired by Geertz's conception of culture to describe media studies as a ritual communion in which all major actors involved in the media reflect on the significance of the meanings that are brought before us in the media's interpretation of social reality (1973, pp. 409-425). Stuart Hall (1977, 1982) and many others in the critical studies tradition argue that the media discourses represent an autonomous arena of social struggle, in addition to the struggle over the political-economic bases of cultural power, in the attempt to resist, subvert, and resignify hegemonic ideological discourse.

Thus, religious studies and media studies share the analysis of different aspects of social reflexivity: (a) the cultural practices sustaining and repairing the integrated pattern of meanings in cultures; (b) the processes of defining the boundaries between the socially acceptable constructions of meaning and translating what is beyond the boundaries of the "rational" into commonsense terms; (c) the practices of constituting the core values as a "test" that can be put on hold as "sacred" and untouchable while the society can explore new cultural formulations and carry out intense debate among many different subcultural contenders (Gonzalez, 1994, pp. 54-182); (d) the constitution of time-in and time-out cultures that can challenge and evaluate each other; and (e) the continual contestation of ideological discourses.

The Differences and Complementarity of Religious Studies and Media Studies in the Reflexive Reproduction of Cultures

If religious studies and media studies share a common ground, quite obviously the two disciplines have very different intellectual histories and bring quite different capacities for analyzing the reflexive prefiguring of cultures. Religious studies have sharpened the concepts of sacred and secular and have developed a phenomenological discourse for detecting continually new and diverse symbolic expressions of the sacred in an immense variety of cultural and social formations. Religious studies have also come to see the sacred and secular not simply as opposites, but as interdependent aspects of the continuing dialogue between the ideal that is "always beyond" and the imperfect that is "always becoming." Where religious studies are weakest, I would argue, is in their lack of a sense of the communicative process through which sacred and secular symbols are created and recreated. There is a tendency to get stuck on the dichotomy of either attributing to religious symbolism a kind of autonomous, substantive existence or reducing religious symbolism to the ephemeral functionalist reflection of sociopolitical processes (Beckford, 1989, pp. xi-8; O'Toole, 1984, pp. 10-42).

Media studies, on the other hand, bring an increasing ability to detect the social processes of creating discourses and texts that articulate a moment of meaning and then continually to challenge and reformulate that definition of meaning. What media studies lack is the ability to distinguish between moments in which the media are "configuring" relations of social power and moments in which commitment to that structure is suspended to "prefigure" a different possible world. Media studies are still stuck on the debate between advocates of the power of the media and defenders of independent interpretation by audiences. Nowhere has this weakness been more evident than in the debates about just how powerful the televangelists are. Their phenomenological analysis of sacred and secular, on the other hand, greatly enriches our understanding of the media in social agency and imaginative representation practices.

Religious studies bring a phenomenological methodology (Wuthnow et al., 1984), exemplified in Peter Berger (1967), Mary Douglas (1966, 1970) and David Martin (1980), for entering into the prefiguring logic of symbolic metaphors experienced in ecstasy, prophecy, dream, rituals, and rallies and for detecting the processes of assigning sacred meaning to objects, spaces, times, and experiences. Once the codes for the sacred world are identified, this phenomenology follows the code through its pathways of transmutation and classification. Most important is the methodology for revealing the many logics through which the sacred and the secular are mutually addressing and challenging each other. The ideal city becomes the symbol of perfection, absolute goodness, the pure, the truly coherent integration of meaning, the all powerful, and the infinite. In contrast, the secular is codified as the realm of the imperfect, the limited, and the disintegrated, the sinful and impure, the mixture of good and evil, the weak and the inconsistent, and the ephemeral, short-term interests in life. Yet the seeds of the sacred, the perfect, and the whole are there in the analogical logic of the *via negativa* and in the symbols of the "already but not yet" (Tracy, 1981).

As the sacred code extends into the area of "governance," there is first a demand of strict justice and order, but immediately the dialectics of mercy, redemption, and restoration enter. The sacred affirms a realm of intolerance and punishment of evil impurity; but as the sacred addresses the secular realm of common sense, pragmatism, predictable explanation, the controllable, a place where one must make compromises with ideals in order to get on with the job of society, the sacred begins to double around, relent, and become loving and compassionate (Martin, 1980, pp. 69-70).

The dialectic of love and redemption transmutes into the dialectic of restoration. In religious experience, the holy is associated with the foundations of reality, the deep-down, unshakable structure of existence, the unchangeable givens of existence, the beginnings, the natural, and the "really real." By contrast, the secular is associated with human construction, the artificial, being severed from the deeper roots, straying away from the inherent order of existence, and destroying the natural sacred destiny of all existence. The secular represents the breakdown of community through structures of social differentiation and power, war, disease, and exploitation. In response to this, the sacred is the restoration of harmony and justice, the rediscovery of the roots of human existence, healing, and ordering one's life in line with the absolute justice of existence.

And here enters the most central logic of religious symbolism: the dialectic of paradox. The image of the sacred began as power, perfection, transcendence, unpredictability, and dangerous mystery; but as it moves into dialogue with the power and artificiality of the human city, the logic of the sacred calls for a return to original community and to humble willingness to serve others. The symbols of the sacred become simplicity, poverty, a childlike existence, the imperfect, the broken, and nothingness. The language of the sacred is rooted in a paradoxical logic—the juxtaposition of opposites (Crossan, 1988; Martin, 1980, pp. 58-70).

The discourse of paradox leads, finally, to the symbolism of religious revitalization (McLoughlin, 1978; Wallace, 1956), personal conversion (Rambo, 1993) and the ritual process of cultural renewal (Turner, 1969). The sacred creates the images of perfection, but then the image becomes an idol; and it is the secular that must enter to smash the sacred image so that it can be reborn and called back to its original holiness.

Thus, the phenomenology of religious studies rescues us from a reduction of all reality to linear, unidimensional, instrumental rationality and reminds us that the construction of culture is not a linear progression toward utopian community, but a paradoxical, continually reversing process of "making and breaking of the image" (Martin, 1980).

▨ Creating a Public Cultural Text—With the Public

Media studies, freed from a narrow administrative preoccupation with effects, are increasingly concerned with the relation of media to the social construction of cultures. As Klaus Bruhn Jensen (1995) argues,

> I take as an initial premise, at the *theoretical* level of analysis, that societies come before media as generators of meaning. Meaning flows from existing social institutions and everyday contexts, via media professionals and audiences, to the mass media, not vice versa. (p. 61)

The media are working in "sacred space" and are a site for the dialogue of the sacred and the secular in three areas: (a) the search for ultimate, consistent patterns of mythic meaning and the integration of the "unexplainable" into the commonsense cultural consensus; (b) the search for perfect community and the confrontation of community with the power structure of social practice; and (c) the search for authentic personal identity and the resolution of the conflicts between personal and social identities. Media studies have come to realize that there is communication only if all the major actors in the signification process see the public cultural text as somehow a reflection of their own identities (Martín-Barbero, 1993, p. 223-228; Wilson, 1993, pp. 126-152). Media studies, perhaps more explicitly than religious studies, are concerned with the different phases or moments of the involvement of the public in the signification of the sacred and in the dialogue of sacred and secular meaning.

The first moment of sacred-secular signification highlights *the context:* the nature of media as a leisure-time activity in which, freed from the constraints of a formal workplace, audiences may let their imaginations and feelings roam free. As Newcomb and Alley (1983) suggest, the media invite us to enter into a time and space apart from the ordinary world, where we can consciously entertain another possible world that we could create (pp. 18-45). Leisure is the time when individuals and communities are free to define their personal and cultural identities (Kelly, 1983), and the media consciously create an ambience of exploration. The media use narrative, symbolic languages, which are cast in archetypal modes connotative of the mythic tradition of the culture, and which project the meaning beyond the everyday routines of life (Silverstone, 1981). Most important, the media are associated with festive times, which are redolent of the calendars of theological and civil religions. The time-out dimension stresses the ritual nature of theater, film, and television in which the person is invited to leave the context of short-term work goals and struggle for hierarchical power in society to contemplate the timeless values and sense of communal origins. The public then returns to everyday life with a kind of mandate to transform the everyday (Turner, 1982).

The second moment in the mediation process focuses on *the capacity of media artists, professionals, and "stars" to articulate the sense of the sacred and formulate this into dramatic symbols*. Newcomb (1978, p. 279) borrows Marshall Sahlins' reference to creators of advertising as "cultural synapses" who have their antennas out to discover the objects and activities in the public imagination particularly charged with emotion in order to transform these objects and activities into symbols of deep streams of value that people can identify with. Media artists do, in fact, live ecstatically in a world beyond common sense, possessing a "gift of the muse" that makes them, relative to the established social construction of reality, somewhat insane. Media professionals are not only dedicated to prefiguring and articulating, but are driven to seek out the audience in order to celebrate the moment of applause when the artist has managed to bring the audience to share deeply her or his own intuitive experience (Newcomb & Alley, 1983, pp. 31-45).

The third moment is *the creation of a text* that makes it possible to "hold" the communicative moment in a form that we can return to repeatedly. This enables us to contemplate the text more deeply to draw out the full meaning in a type of *lectio divina* and preserve this meaning for future generations. The celebratory act becomes a formulaic genre with a format, standardized language, and traditional metaphors that assures publics of a given age, sex, occupation, and educational background that this media will, indeed, be an "entertaining" moment for them (Feuer, 1987). The textual genre also assures the media artists that their gift and their desire will find a community of interpretation. Part of the formula of these genres is the continual recasting in new cultural languages of the archetypal symbols embedded in the foundational religious texts of a religious tradition so that the audience can place in dialogue these references to the primeval sacred with the present secularity of the culture.

Recent audience research has shown that although media producers may tend to use well-known formulas and symbols so that the text will be intelligible to a mass audience without great difficulty, interpretations vary a great deal because each member of the audience is a complex composite of cultural identities and can call on very diverse repertoires of interpretative codes. Media producers know that part of the pleasure of the audience emerges from the sense of independence and power of negotiating the meaning placed upon the text (Fiske, 1987, pp. 95-99). Indeed, the affirmation of personal identity is arguably one of the sites of the sacred in contemporary society (Luckmann, 1967). Thus, the fourth moment of signification is *the implicit invitation to negotiate and recreate the text* from the perspective of personal and cultural identities.

The construction of cultures, especially the signification of the sacred, is always a contested process in which some groups attempt to affirm that their cultural capital is sacred, natural, and beyond question, and other groups attempt to delegitimize and desacralize these symbols of identity. Recent developments in media theory have identified a fifth moment, *the struggle over the symbolism of media texts* (Jenkins, 1992, pp. 24-49). One of the most typical evidences of this struggle is when a particular devoted public (the fans) takes a genre considered "trash" by establishment groups—new popular musics, soap opera (Brown, 1994), sports—and makes the "trash" the symbol of the subcultural identity in much the same way that the primitive Christian community took the cross and inverted its meaning from humiliation to glory.

From contemporary media studies, it becomes apparent that although there is a continual negotiated incorporation of symbols of the sacred into hegemonic cultural formations, the new symbols of the sacred are continually "escaping" from hegemony within new cultural movements to signify countercultural identities. And just as soon as new symbols of the sacred are formed in alternative movements, the media are there articulating these into a media text, and the cycle begins over again.

The Analysis of the Religious in Texts of the Public Media

Having developed some basic conceptions of the dialogue of sacred and secular and how religious studies and media studies enter into this dialogue, we turn now to a central question: the emerging discourses of sacred and secular in the moments of intensive reflexivity.

A first premise is that social systems do, in fact, enter into episodes of more intensive reflexivity. If the Enlightenment project located religious and media studies within an analytic framework and a worldview of unilinear progress of instrumental, efficient rationality, the cultural sciences have helped us to see that there is another, deeper historical current continually reasserting what Geertz (1973) has termed "primordial sentiments of community." If cultures do tend toward innovation, it is also necessary for cultures to continually rediscover the core symbols so that society and culture can return to these constitutive and formative symbols (Geertz, 1973, pp. 255-320; Rambo, 1993, p. 26). Religious studies and media studies in combination not only identify the continual renewal of cultural identities and the resacralization of the cultural environment, but enable us, in a second hermeneutic, to become aware that our social analysis is part of these revolutions of primordial sentiments (Wallace, 1956; Wuthnow, 1992, pp. 1-8).

A second premise is that these intense moments of cultural revitalization and confrontation between sacred and secular may be operative at one level—for example, within a particular denomination—while at a more general national or cultural level there is little sacred-secular dialogue or it is carried on with a completely different set of discursive symbols. One example of this is the apparent anomaly of secularization at the societal level and, at the same time, intense religious revitalization activity in certain movements. Four levels are proposed here, each with quite different discursive strategies of sacred-secular symbolism: (a) sacred-secular dialogue at the level of existential human concerns above any one national/regional cultural tradition; (b) the level of particular cultures, usually a nation or region with a common "civil religion"; (c) sacred or secular revitalization within a particular denominational organization; and (d) the expression of the sacred at the level of individuals in relatively small but intense movements, sects, and cults. Obviously, the wider and more diverse the public addressed, the more abstract and inclusive must be the symbolism and discursive strategies.

A third premise is that different levels can be at quite different moments of quiescence or revitalization, but if there is an intense sacred-secular dialogue at all levels at the same time, this could imply profound changes not only in global religious paradigms but also in cultural paradigms.

A fourth premise is that the sacred is not identified with explicitly religious organizations or institutions and the secular with other types of organizations, but rather that the sacred and secular are interrelated aspects of all institutions (Beckford, 1989, pp. 171-172). For example, the revitalization within a church or denomination might be a move toward a more open, secularized definition (as happened, for example, in the Catholic Church in the movement articulated in the Second Vatican Council). The central question is not whether our societies are becoming more or less sacred or secular, much less whether church activity is growing or diminishing, but rather how the discourses of sacred and secular are addressing each other at this moment.

Finally, a fifth premise is that the meaning of the sacred is not the annihilation of the secular or vice versa, but rather to call each other into dialogue and reform. The analysis focuses on the ways revitalization is generating new symbols of the sacred and the secular and creating new discourses that are putting the sacred and secular into dialogue. We want to identify the sites of struggle over sacred and secular meaning in cultural practice, especially in the genres of mass popular communication. This enables us to see our own personal and collective roles in the construction of social reality without lapsing into hopeless cynicism, replacing one utopian ideology with another, or retreating into a shell of cultural fundamentalism.

Theory in the cultural sciences is most useful for understanding what kinds of cultures we are creating and for discerning whether these are the kinds of culture we want. Theory is also important for explaining the historical process we are living in and for critically examining our reflexive response to this history. The following analysis of the creation of new symbols of sacred-secular interaction at four different levels of revitalization movements illustrates how this methodology might be applied at the empirical level.

▨ Revitalization Movements at the Level of Transcultural, Existential Human Concerns

There is broad consensus in religious studies that the worldwide countercultural movements of the late 1960s and early 1970s marked a "new religious consciousness" (Glock & Bellah, 1976), the formulation of new symbols of the sacred (Martin, 1981), a new phase in religious revitalization (McLoughlin, 1978, pp. 193-216), and new forms of ritual liminality (Turner, 1969, pp. 112-113). This revitalization movement transcends civic religious symbols, symbols within specific religious traditions, and cult symbols because it has been global and because it addresses basic human problems of alienation. Indeed, it has sparked the formulation of theories of religion and globalization of cultures (Beyer, 1994, pp. 97-98; Robertson, 1992, p. 81).

The starting point for analyzing the interaction of the sacred and the secular in a revitalization movement is in the symbols of utopian, transcendent community and the closely associated countersymbols that attempt to delegitimize what are considered to be the sites of alienation from community. The counterculture called to reform the central symbols of the "secular" that modernity held sacred: nationalism, the rationalistic bureaucratic organization of industrial modernization, the mobilization of industrial capitalism, the myth of unilinear evolution, the epistemology of instrumental rationality (Ellul, 1967), socialization structured around graded educational systems, and the print media. The new symbols of the sacred in this movement are well known: the small, interacting, participatory, and expressive community; the return to nature; the symbol of all humankind forming a multicultural family (dropping surnames that may indicate nationality, denomination, race, language, or sex); and the use of symbols of global popular culture to level and unite all humankind. This juxtaposition of contrasting symbols and discourses sets up an atmosphere of reflexivity, freedom to rethink mythic frameworks, and distance from everyday life.

A second site for the creation of new symbols of the sacred is the ritual occasions for ecstatic experience of the transcendent, the creation of a liminal space apart from everyday life, and a space for allowing the "real self" to come forth. As Victor Turner (1982) indicates, liminal space is established largely by creating a symbolic atmosphere. Ritual almost always creates a separate ambiance through music, dance, incense, special clothing and food, and the sacred symbolism of ritual space. Bernice Martin (1981) and others argue that in the countercultural movements, rock music (sometimes combined with trance-inducing drugs), with its ritualized concerts, discotheques, and meetings of small groups of friends in homes, was and continues to be a major ritual site for the new expressive movements (pp. 153-184). Rock music has many symbolisms, but its origins in a combination of Afro-American and occidental country-western music has been a sacred symbol of rejection of modern progress and a return to a primeval existence. An alternative site of ritual symbols was created by the adaptation of Eastern religious traditions to the needs of middle-class Western youth. This borrowing enabled young people to reach out of the decadent mythic tradition of nationalism to something untainted, closer to nature, mystical, communitarian, and nonformal.

A third site for the creation of sacred symbols is the definition of a new mythic conception of history. Some of the central symbols in the counterculture movement have been concerned with a future of restoration of the harmony of nature, the harmony of the person with nature, and the internal harmony of the person—all in direct contrast with the antisymbols of modernizing development.

The reassertion of the sacred eventually must address the secular more directly. A first moment of confrontation with the secular is in the form of paradoxical symbols in which the desire of the realizations of the secular are appealed to, but it is affirmed that the true realizations are in forms quite the opposite of the societal myth. For example, the counterculture recognized that growth and development are good things, but affirmed that "small is beautiful." Symbols such as "flower power" recognize the desire of power in modernization, but assert that power is found in its opposite.

In a second moment of addressing the secular, the prophets of the movement realize that it is not possible to ignore or reject the secular project, but that the sacred must contribute to the secular project. Many of the alternative religious movements, such as the Human Potential groups and the Nichiren Shoshu, attracted more stable adherents with symbols of self-realization, self-fulfillment, and self-improvement or, more directly, by suggesting that one has to have a level of personal attractiveness and interpersonal competence to bring about community and a more personalized society (Hamilton, 1995, pp. 211-213).

In all of the symbol formation, there is a process of interaction with the public cultural expression, that is, in the mass media. One of the first public manifestations of the counterculture was the Berkeley Free Speech movement, which was concerned, typically, with the right to dramatize and project the new sacred symbols into public space and in so doing to catch the attention of the mass media. These symbols were designed with an eye to their ability to catch the eye of the mass media and become *symbols of identification* for millions of other young people on university campuses. Once the media discovered the potential of the counterculture for good mass media, various genres of media began to articulate this and to create a text: the news in terms of the political dramatism (especially to exploit the debate about the Vietnam War), the innovative appearance of the Beatles on the *Ed Sullivan Show,* but especially the development of the rock music genre as a text expressing the countercultural symbols (Martin, 1981, pp. 180-183).

In turn, the youth wing of the movement transformed the varieties of rock music into the symbol of their subcultures to create a series of new texts, a process of interaction of youth identity formation and the mass media that continues today.

From the perspective of the religious institutions identified with modernization, the countercultural movement was antireligious and secularizing. Indeed, from the perspective of many definitions of secularization, this movement did tend to delegitimate the presence of the sacred symbols of "civic religion" in many parts of the culture. On the other hand, one could argue that at the broader existential level, there has been a massive sacralization of cultures evident, for example, in the peace movements, in the collapse of many totalitarian regimes, in the emphasis on decentralization and communitarianism in development, in education and especially in the priority of leisure lifestyles of today.

As we have noted above, this has encouraged the search for new paradigms of interpretation in both religious studies and media studies.

▓ The Civil Religion of the Populist Nation-State

An earlier great religious revitalization movement, which created a highly developed system of religious symbols and involved both religious studies and media studies, was the sacralization of the way of life built around the democratic welfare state from about 1830 to 1970. Although industrialization was identified with the secular by the artistic Romantic movement, the revitalization attempted to discover and rescue the sacred in this new age. Although the symbol system owed much to the French Revolution and the Enlightenment, these symbols needed to be fused with a popular religiosity of the "common man," the origin myths of the folk, and the democratic ideal of the community—local, regional, and national—to take on sacred, transcendent dimensions. This sacralization of the new populist civil community and democratic solidarity provided a strong basis for the Durkheimian tradition of a "sociology" of religion that found its best expression in Bellah's "civil religion"(1967; 1970).

The core of the new system of sacred symbols was centered around the populist movements that exalted the working class man—a notoriously patriarchal set of sacred symbols—and his honest work that made the nation possible. The wisdom, virtue, common sense, and productivity of the laboring man forming a community was irreducible evidence of the presence of the sacred. These symbols quickly developed a set of antisymbols delegitimating aristocracy, which had been the patron of the sacred, the arts, and the order of society for more than a thousand years in Western Europe. The churches with a dissident, antifeudal tradition, or the wing of churches identified with popular movements, became an important force legitimizing the new sacred symbols of the common man and pointing out that the hereditary aristocracies had lost their anointing (Hofstadter, 1955, pp. 23-36). By contrast, the common citizen is pure, just, without guile, the solid foundation of the virtue of the nation, capable of being an instrument of the transcendent through the vote and through education. If once God's wisdom was expressed in kingly anointing, now it was expressed in the voice of the majority.

These symbols were sacred precisely because they were built around paradox: the simple, working-class person was the foundation of education, science, wise government, and a just society. The school, centered around children and youth, became a sacred symbol (Dolan, 1984).

A second site of the formation of sacred symbols was in the formation of the sacred community by discovering the historical origins of the common man in the "folk" and "nation" and the mythic destiny of this folk to form an egalitarian community. The modern industrial nation could find its origins in the folk and the ordinary people. In the new immigrant nations, this far-distant tribal origin was replaced by the origins of the nation in the rural community. In the United States, for example, the symbol of the community of agriculturalists and artisans around the church, the town meetings, the school, the community boosterism, the respect for freedom of expression based on the inherent wisdom of the common man, and the acceptance of participatory decisions became unquestionable symbols of the sacred. As the rural community became more remote, this sense of commitment to community was transformed into universal professionalism based on the sacred oath of the professional to serve society and to serve individual clients regardless of their background. This was grounded in codes of ethics, the responsibility of the professional community, and the guarantees of the nation state (Bledstein, 1976). There was far more resistance to militant labor and farmer communitarianism, but this eventually found sacred legitimacy in the welfare state, largely through the development of the "social gospel" and the "social teaching" of the churches.

What was particularly important in the forming of this set of sacred symbols is that the major churches essentially joined in with the secular project of the nation-state to legitimize its democratic pluralism; and insofar as the churches separated themselves from the aristocracy, they were accorded a role in articulating the sacred symbols of the new order. Part of the price was that the churches had to become simply different "denominations," playing down dogmatic differences and upholding the basic civic religion of progress, democracy, free speech, free association, and human rights (Herberg, 1955, pp. 85-112). Indeed, the religious traditions felt that they could recover their sacredness only by leaving the confines of the churches and dogma and moving out into the secular world, becoming more secular in order to address the secular.

A third site for the elaboration of sacred symbols was the rituals of local and national community. Every public event, from sports contests to political elections, had its moment of sacred reflection symbolized by the national hymn, by the presence of the representatives of the major religious denominations, by taking sacred oaths to serve the nation, and by the ritual exaltation of the rights of the common man. The mobilization for nationalistic wars and for colonialistic expansion—whether overseas or across "frontiers" into "wilderness" territory—were sites of sacred symbols of sacrifice, martyrdom, and tests of faith.

The mass popular media, rooted in the doctrines of freedom of expression and the right to information and education, became another site for the creation of symbols of civic religion. The "mass media" had their origin in the populist movements (Schiller, 1981). The genres of the penny newspaper—editorial comment, comic strips, the popular serial novel, the short story—were formed around the articulation of the sacred symbols of these movements: popular protests, nationalistic wars, and so forth. Once the penny newspapers defined the text of the popular media, these were carried on by film, radio, and television (Tunstall, 1977). Indeed, it became difficult to distinguish theology, religious studies, social philosophy, and social teaching of the religious traditions, journalistic debate, and public philosophies of communication. The criteria for public truth was no longer metaphysics, but rather the objectivity guaranteed by the methodology of the social sciences. Again, the role of the mass media was sacralized by its code of public service and by bringing in the denominations willing to support the civic religion as part of the public service of media to the nation-state. The sects and movements unwilling to support the religion of the liberal democracies were excluded.

Today, the nation-state and the modernist organization of society make less sense to people as an agenda for the construction of cultures. Likewise, the symbols of the sacred associated with this agenda make less sense. But the disappearance of this form of dialogue between the sacred and the secular does not mean that the sacred is simply absent from our lives (Warner, 1993). There are simultaneously other processes of sacralization. The social alienation generated by the civil religion became the foundation for a third kind of contemporary religious revitalization.

The Sectarian Revitalization of Evangelical Fundamentalism

Since the 1950s, the evangelical tradition has been able to mobilize one of the most attractive sacred symbol systems in the world; and it is demonstrating striking growth not only where Protestantism has been traditionally strong, but also in Latin America and Africa. The force of evangelicalism, however, is largely that of a "choice" for revitalization within the Christian faith system.

Whatever may be the social origins of evangelicalism—we deliberately avoid a sociological reductionist explanation—it is a tradition that shares a common devotion to the sacred located in a revelation of the transcendent that is not affected by the passing changes of culture. The most typical symbols are the inerrancy of the revealed word of God preserved in an unchanging written form, a written statement of unchanging theological propositions, an unchanging moral code, a personal asceticism that avoids the vanities of passing fads of popular culture (Rosman, 1984), the unchanging oral wisdom of the elderly, classical conservative and conserving social institutions such as the patriarchal family, and a diffidence regarding modern science and technology (except where it can be considered a pure instrument not contaminating the unchanging word of God; Marsden, 1980, 1991). For the contemporary evangelical movement, the symbols of the secular are the power of late modernity (or postmodernity) to restructure nature itself: ending and shaping human life at will, restructuring sexuality (and socially related aspects of sexuality) at will, and denying in the public cultural forum that reality has any sacred ground whatsoever that is off-limits to human transformative efforts (Hunter, 1987). Thus, unborn life, family-centered heterosexuality, and public manifestations of religiosity have become symbols of the sacred.

The Protestant evangelical tradition has always distrusted any kind of cultural, socially mediated contact with the sacred and has tended to find "salvation" in the direct vertical descent of God's irrepressible miraculous power in their lives. Thus, an important symbolic indication of sacred presence is the prophetic preacher who has received a call directly from God (with little approbation by the institutional church) and who exudes the power to radically convert, to heal, to hold the audience in a motivational trance, and to put together with enormous energy the religious event of the revival (Marsden, 1991, pp. 98-121; Schultze, 1991, pp. 69-96). A secondary sacred symbol is the organization that surrounds the charismatic preacher, helping him to make present the unchanging word of God. Coming in contact with the powerful word of God is enough to transform a person (Bruce, 1990).

Another set of sacred symbols grows up around the experience of the religious revival, where one is swept away by the power of God. Just to enter the revivalist tent or hall is to draw near to the sacred, and the atmosphere itself—the singing, the sonorous preaching, the conversions, and the healings—induces the sacred power of God to operate in quasi-sacramental fashion. The experience of spiritual rebirth, going back to one's childhood and mythic cultural origins, recalls an archetypal symbol of the sacred. Evangelicalism in the United States calls for a return to more primitive values, and Pentecostalism in Latin America also appeals to the desire to a return to pre-Columbian nativist syncretism in countries such as Guatemala (Concha, 1996).

Time and history also assume a sacredness in that the prophet feels an irresistible call to announce the irresistible coming of the kingdom of God at this particular time. There is an urgency to preach the transforming word to the whole world and to call all to respond to the word immediately.

The present evangelical revitalization movement began at the level of interpersonal communication in the new form of urban revival, but radio and television evangelists quickly picked up the new symbols of adaptation to urban society and created the genre of the televangelist (Hoover, 1988; Horsfield, 1984). Once again, the media became an important site for generating the new sacred symbols in the images of Billy Graham and Pat Robertson. Although technology, especially media technology, is part of the secular world, once it is used for announcing the gospel it becomes a site of the sacred. The media are sacred gifts of God given in these "last times," and powerful persuasive rhetoric is just as much a symbol of the sacred. Asking the audience to gain power by touching the TV set in their homes is simply an extension of this symbolism.

Politics become a sacred symbolic action for evangelicals because this is the installation of God's kingdom, and all of the techniques of gaining political power are therefore sacralized.

Interestingly, in facing the dilemma of postmodernism, evangelicalism is tending to take the postmodern "secularity" seriously; and it is the postmodern "new religious consciousness" and radical communitarianism that is entering to smash the idol of evangelical identification with the modernist individualism (Hunter, 1991, pp. 157-186).

The Postmodern Cults of Symbolic Liminality

This analysis would not be complete without at least briefly indicating a fourth type of revitalization movement at the level of the person and small groups. This vague form of cultural and religious revitalization has been referred to as "the new movements" or "the postmodern." A central characteristic is that the conscious creation of culture and symbols has become a site of the sacred. As Melucci (1989) notes in his study of the new movements, the young especially are aware that we have cut our moorings to "nature" and that we can make the world anything we want to. They have studied "communication" and know that symbols are inherently communicating meaning. Creating a symbolic liminal state and then consciously inhabiting that, knowing that it is totally artificial, is a celebration of the sacredness of our own human creativity. We can verify the sacredness of this by just as quickly destroying the edifice of symbols and moving on to create another one. The secular is all that is sane, ordinary, commonsense, permanent, and instrumentally rational. As soon as something begins to be considered rational, the "Nomads of the Present," to use Melucci's (1989) term, quickly move to create a symbolic world that is quite bizarre, alternative, and—"creative"! The texts that articulate this are persons such as Michael Jackson, who resist all sexual or any other definition. Madonna quickly moves beyond any social construction of reality and tells us by the extremely conscious use of sacred symbols that the sacred is always beyond the edge of common sense.

■ An Agenda for Further Research

The present chapter has been more concerned with exploring a new set of questions for research in the area of religion and media than with more definitive conclusions. A summary of these issues for further discussion may be the best way to synthesize this chapter.

First, if the creation of sacred symbols and the "poetic" construction of meaning are too important in the construction of cultures to be excluded from the public sphere as autonomous discourses, then how do we think of their presence in the public sphere, especially at the level of a second hermeneutic? Do practitioners of religious studies and media studies necessarily have to be objective, areligious, and unpoetic people in the act of their study? The introduction of Giddens' concept of reflexivity and Jensen's discussion of time-in and time-out cultures may be starting points, but where do we take this?

Second, it is proposed that there is a considerable variety of modes of creating sacred symbols at sites of meaning and that the different modes of the sacred and the secular are in continual dialogue. To focus on one mode of sacralization to the exclusion of others may lead—mistakenly, I would argue—to affirmations of inevitable secularization or inevitable sacralization. Likewise, to make one mode of creating sacred symbols (e.g., the civic religion) the normative mode negates the variety and shifting importance of the sacred in the construction of cultures. But how do we think of a variety of modes of sacralization interacting with others with equal normative validity? I have suggested that the process in the public media of dialogue between media and audience, continually creating and recreating public texts, implies exchange and negotiation between modes of sacralization. But will a public sphere be sustained if there are, in fact, multiple criteria of "truth"?

Third, this chapter has suggested that the common focus of religion and media studies is the analysis of the emerging symbols of the sacred and how the symbols of the sacred and the secular are continually addressing and evoking each other. The analysis of this dialogue across the edges of our socially constructed realities is part of the reflexive process of understanding what kind of culture we are creating and whether this is the kind of culture we want. This sort of analysis avoids the tendency to reduce the religious in media to issues of control and impact, a tendency that has dominated the study, for example, of the electronic church. The analysis of "impact" is from the "outside" and has generated very little solid theory of religion and media.

Does this approach respond to the issues of hegemony and ideological co-optation of the search for religious meaning? I would argue that research, conceived as a reflexive double hermeneutic, is also a process of continually feeding back to religious groups the symbols of the sacred they are creating in order to ask if this is the expression of the sacred that they sense in their own personal and cultural identities.

The central question posed at the outset of this chapter remains: How are we to conceive of the presentation of the religious and the sacred in the public sphere in an era of radical pluralism that is suspicious of civil religions and equally suspicious of denominational revivals and other cultural revitalization movements? Part of the answer lies, I think, in the new self-conception of the media as a ritual space in which various actors are dramatizing their sacred symbols. Elsewhere (White, 1990), I have described the key importance of the media as public cultural rituals and as a process of cultural negotiation (White, 1995). Increasingly, we are overcoming the high-culture/low-culture dichotomy and are willing to see the "popular" as the common language of all. The media invite all cultural fronts to be present in a time-out context when our dogmatic, purist identities are most permeable and we are in festive mood, ready to discover something of our common sacred archetypes in the sacred symbols of all. The media experience is a moment more open to the immense variety of sacred symbols being generated, and audiences are less ready to dichotomize the sacred and the secular. Thus, both media studies and religious studies are coming together to create a new understanding of the media as cultural negotiation.

References

Beckford, J. (1989). *Religion and advanced industrial society.* London: Unwin Hyman.

Beckford, J., & Luckmann, T. (Eds.). (1989). *The changing face of religion.* London: Sage.

Bellah, R. (1967). Civil religion in America. *Daedalus, 96*(1), 1-21.

Bellah, R. (1970). *Beyond belief: Essays on religion in a post-traditionalist world.* Berkeley: University of California Press.

Bellah, R. (1975). *The broken covenant: American civil religion in time of trial.* New York: Seabury.

Berger, P. (1967). *The sacred canopy: Elements of a sociological theory of religion.* Garden City, NY: Doubleday.

Berger, P. L., & Luckman, T. (1966). *The social construction of reality.* Garden City, NY: Doubleday.

Beyer, P. (1994). *Religion and globalization.* London: Sage.

Bledstein, B. (1976). *The culture of professionalism: The middle classes and the development of higher education in America.* New York: Norton.

Brown, M. E. (1994). *Soap opera and women's talk: The pleasure of resistance.* Thousand Oaks, CA: Sage.

Bruce, S. (1990). *Pray TV: Televangelism in America.* London: Routledge & Kegan Paul.

Carey, J. W. (1977). Mass communication research and cultural studies: The American view. In J. Curran, M. Gurevitch, & J. Woollacott (Eds.), *Mass communication and society* (pp. 409-425). London: Edward Arnold in association with Open University Press.

Concha, J. (1996). *Los movimentos pentecostales en América Latina como parte de los procesos de la cultura popular Latinoamericana.* Unpublished doctoral dissertation, Gregorian University, Rome.

Crossan, D. (1988). *The dark interval: Toward a theology of story.* Sonoma, CA: Polebridge.

Dolan, J. (1984). *Catholic revivalism: The American experience, 1830-1870.* Notre Dame, IN: Notre Dame University Press.

Douglas, M. (1966). *Purity and danger: An analysis of the concepts of pollution and taboo.* New York: Pantheon.

Douglas, M. (1970). *Natural symbols: Explorations in cosmology.* New York: Pantheon.

Ellul, J. (1967). *The technological society.* New York: Vintage.

Feuer, J. (1987). Genre study and television. In R. C. Allen (Ed.), *Channels of discourse* (pp. 113-133). Chapel Hill: University of North Carolina Press.

Fiske, J. (1987). *Television culture.* London: Routledge & Kegan Paul.

Geertz, C. (1966). *Religion as a cultural system.* In M. Banton (Ed.), *Anthropological approaches in the study of religion* (pp. 1-46). London: Tavistock.

Geertz, C. (1973). *Interpretation of cultures.* New York: Basic Books.

Giddens, A. (1984). *The constitution of society: Outline of the theory of structuration.* Cambridge, MA: Polity.

Glock, C., & Bellah, R. (1976). *The new religious consciousness.* Berkeley: University of California Press.

Gonzalez, J. (1994). *Más (+) cultura(s): Ensayos sobre realidades plurales.* Mexico: Consejo Nacional para la Cultura y las Artes.

Hall, S. (1977). Culture, the media and the "ideological effect." In J. Curran, M. Gurevitch, & J. Woollacott (Eds.), *Mass communication and society* (pp. 315-348). London: Edward Arnold in association with the Open University Press.

Hall, S. (1982). The rediscovery of "ideology": Return of the repressed in media studies. In M. Gurevitch, T. Bennett, J. Curran, & J. Woollacott (Eds.), *Culture, society and the media* (pp. 56-90). London: Routledge.

Hamilton, M. (1995). *The sociology of religion: Theoretical and comparative perspectives.* London: Routledge & Kegan Paul.

Herberg, W. (1955). *Protestant, Catholic, Jew.* Garden City, NY: Doubleday.

Hofstadter, R. (1955) *The age of reform.* New York: Vintage.

Hoover, S. (1988). *Mass media religion: The social sources of the electronic church.* Newbury Park, CA: Sage.

Horsfield, P. (1984). *Religious television: The American experience.* New York: Longman.

Hunter, J. D. (1987). *Evangelicalism: The coming generation.* Chicago: University of Chicago Press.

Hunter, J. D. (1991). *Culture wars: The struggle to define America.* New York: Basic Books.

Jenkins, H. (1992). *Textual poachers: Television fans and participatory culture.* New York: Routledge.

Jensen, K. B. (1995). *The social semiotics of mass communication.* London: Sage.

Kelly, J. (1983). *Leisure identities and interaction.* London: Allen and Unwin.

Luckmann, T. (1967). *The invisible religion.* New York: Macmillan.

Marsden, G. (1980). *Fundamentalism and American culture: The shaping of twentieth-century evangelicalism, 1870-1925.* New York: Oxford University Press.

Marsden, G. (1991). *Understanding fundamentalism and evangelicalism.* Grand Rapids, MI: Eerdmans.

Martin, B. (1981). *A sociology of contemporary cultural change.* Oxford, UK: Basil Blackwell.

Martin, D. (1980). *The breaking of the image: A sociology of Christian theory and practice.* Oxford, UK: Basil Blackwell.

Martín-Barbero, J. (1993). *Communication, culture and hegemony: From the media to the mediations.* London: Sage.

McLoughlin, W. G. (1978). *Revivals, awakenings, and reform.* Chicago: University of Chicago Press.

Melucci, A. (1989). *Nomads of the present: Social movements and individual needs in contemporary society* (J. Keane & P. Mier, Trans.). London: Hutchison Radius.

Morley, D. (1992). *Television, audiences & cultural studies.* London: Routledge & Kegan Paul.

Newcomb, H. (1978). Assessing the violence profile: Studies of Gerbner and Gross, a humanistic critique and suggestion. *Communication Research, 5*(3), 264-282.

Newcomb, H., & Alley, R. (1983). *The producer's medium: Conversations with creators of American TV.* New York: Oxford University Press.

O'Toole, R. (1984). *Religion: Classic sociological approaches.* Toronto: McGraw-Hill Ryerson.

Rambo, L. (1993). *Understanding religious conversion.* New Haven, CT: Yale University Press.

Robertson, R. (1992). *Globalization: Social theory and global culture.* London: Sage.

Rosman, D. (1984). *Evangelicals and culture.* London: Croom Helm Ltd.

Rowland, W. (1983). *The politics of violence: Policy uses of communication research.* Newbury Park, CA: Sage.

Schiller, D. (1981). *Objectivity and the news.* Philadelphia: University of Pennsylvania Press.

Schultze, Q. (1991). *Televangelism and American culture: The business of popular religion.* Grand Rapids, MI: Baker.

Silverstone, R. (1981). *The message of television: Myth and narrative in contemporary culture.* London: Heineman Educational Books.

Tracy, D. (1981). *The analogical imagination.* London: SCM Press.

Tunstall, J. (1977). *The media are American.* New York: Columbia University Press.

Turner, B. S. (1991). *Religion and social theory* (2nd ed.). London: Sage.

Turner, V. (1969). *The ritual process: Structure and anti-structure.* London: Routledge & Kegan Paul.

Turner, V. (1974). *Dramas, fields and metaphors.* Ithaca, NY: Cornell University Press.

Turner, V. (1982). *From ritual to theater: The human seriousness of play.* New York: Performing Arts Journal Publications.

Wallace, A. F. C. (1956). Revitalization movements. *The American Anthropologist, 58,* 264-281.

Warner, R. S. (1993). Work in progress toward a new paradigm for the sociological study of religion in the United States. *American Journal of Sociology, 98*(5), 1044-1093.

White, R. A. (1990). Cultural analysis in communication for development: The role of cultural dramaturgy in the creation of a public sphere. *Development, Journal of the Society for International Development, 2,* 23-31.

White, R. A. (1995, June). *The conditions for cultural negotiation in civil conflicts.* Unpublished paper presented at the meeting of the International Association for Mass Communication Research, Portoroz, Slovenia.

Wilson, T. (1993). *Watching television: Hermeneutics, reception, and popular culture.* Cambridge, MA: Polity.

Wuthnow, R., Hunter, J. D., Bergesen, A., & Kurzwell, E. (1984). *Cultural analysis: The work of Peter L. Berger, Mary Douglas, Michel Foucault and Jürgen Habermas.* London: Routledge & Kegan Paul.

Wuthnow, R. (1989). *The struggle for America's soul: Evangelicals, liberals, and secularism.* Grand Rapids, MI: Eerdmans.

Wuthnow, R. (1992). *Rediscovering the sacred: Perspectives on religion in contemporary society.* Grand Rapids, MI: Eerdmans.

Chapter 4

Technology and Triadic
Theories of Mediation

Clifford G. Christians

Martin Heidegger's philosophy of technology best accounts for the unprecedented conditions in which religion as a symbolic universe is mediated today. Within Heidegger's tradition, contemporary industrial culture is an instrumentalist order of amoral means and technocratic efficiency, in opposition to the religious imagination. From his perspective, the cultural turn in our understanding of the media and religion must go through technology to have long-term credibility. A paradigm shift away from the functional approach to communications and religion requires a philosophy of technology that comes to grips with the structure of technology itself. For Heidegger, that means understanding technology in terms of being, and our human habitat as technoculture.

▨ Aristotle's Legacy

The traditional conception of technology as means originated with Aristotle. "Technology is a human arrangement of technics—tools, machines, instruments, materials, and science—to serve human ends. . . . It is not thought to have any meaning in itself. It is, as commonly said, neutral" (Hood, 1972, p. 347). Technology is not an end, but a means to something else. It is extrinsic to a person's being and society's character. Its value derives from nontechnological goals. What it produces is not necessary or innate. Rabbits or bushes grow according to their natural form, whereas through technics we arbitrarily build a plastic stool from minerals. The meaning of technological products is found in the human purposes they serve, even as, in Aristotle's terms, "the end of the medical art is health, that of shipbuilding a vessel, that of strategy victory, that of economics wealth" (*Nicomachean Ethics* I, 1, 1094a5-10).

Of all possible ends, technology serves human life (cf. *Metaphysics* I, 1, 98161-35; also *Politics III*, 9, 1208a32). Tools are needed to meet necessities—shelter, clothing, food, and medicine. Only after securing freedom from organic needs is technology beyond human survival possible. Musical instruments are for enjoyment, and scientific tools in astronomy expand human knowledge. But in all cases, technical activities and products receive their justification from the uses to which they are put. Technology is one of the lower human actions. Through philosophy and politics, humans contemplate and reflect the intelligible order of things. Because reason, more than anything else, makes the human species distinctive, politics and philosophy are to be pursued in their own terms. "Technology is subordinate to practical wisdom, to moral and intellectual activities" through which humans realize their essence and stabilize society (Hood, 1972, p. 349; cf. *Nicomachean Ethics* X, 6, 1177a 20-21).

It is a placid, clean, and congenial model, giving religious sensibilities a role in articulating ends. In Aristotle's framework, religion as a symbolic universe of ultimate values is needed more than ever for directing sophisticated technology to appropriate purposes. Religious rituals celebrate food production rather than military equipment. Television technology can be used for salvation rather than for political propaganda or commerce. Public transportation moving the masses to jobs is emphasized instead of yachts and sports cars for the elite. A knife in a surgeon's hands saves lives; among criminal gangs it kills.

Mainstream engineers and philosophers have embraced the Aristotelian tradition as well. For the inventor of cybernetics, Norbert Wiener, instrumentalism compels politicians and social theorists to fret over

technology's impact, while allowing engineering efficiency in the labora-
tory. For Shannon and Weaver, it provides a framework for mathematical
models of media transmission that inspire our inventions from 60,000 bits
per second in telephone wires to 100 billion bits per second in light-based
fiber optics. In Buckminster Fuller's synergetics, data can flow in comple-
mentary patterns following the harmony of nature rather than the contradictions of political ideology.

But even if one grants the validity of Aristotle's two-tiered model for
the premodern age, how defensible is it now? Since the 1890s, technological development has multiplied so rapidly in industrial societies that little
viable space remains for setting limits and proper direction. In the face of
technology's complexity and dominance, in the traditional view, "we are
abandoned to a haphazard scattering of goods and evils, of productive
and destructive tendencies, and the structure of technology escapes us"
(Hood, 1972, p. 352).

Given the intricacies of 20th-century technology, social impact can
rarely be calculated anymore. In agriculture and transportation, what
meets a basic human need in one context is often counterproductive
overall and in the long term. In fact, the French sociologist, Jacques
Ellul—from his first major book in 1954, *The Technological Society*, to his
death in May 1994—demonstrated that the instrumentalist approach is
not merely limited, but historically and sociologically bankrupt. The
technological enterprise is value-centered throughout—in invention, design, manufacture, and distribution. It involves choices of energy use and
resources. True to the character of machineness, the values of productivity,
power, and efficiency direct the technological process. Thus the principle
of self-augmentation begins to rule, pushing technology toward greater
speed and larger size, marginalizing small-scale activities and taking on
a life of its own, no longer subject to human control. Instead of the
elementary view that technological products are a means to transtech-
nological ends, Ellul identifies a process of ever-expanding means that
finally overwhelm all ideals worthy of human allegiance. We can no
longer assume that technological problems can be fixed by appealing to
an arena outside technique. The situation now is completely different. In
the traditional triad, people use a lever to move a stone. The prevailing
paradigm is no longer humans using tools to cultivate nature and build
civilization, but a technological order that engulfs us, a technocratic
artifice that isolates everyday life from the natural realm.

In a similar manner, Martin Heidegger (1889-1976) connects 20th-century technological practice in the West with its classical Greek origins. In his view, technology's modern manifestations are a culmination of the traditional dualism of means and ends. As with Ellul, pleading for more concern about ends is futile. Aristotle's epistemology is wrong, his social philosophy bankrupt. To establish a systematic critique, a fundamentally different approach to technology is needed. The instrumentalist world-view must be turned on its head and inside out. The whole phenomenon ought to be called into question, and not just some of its features. By examining the ontological ground of technology, Heidegger destroys the instrumentalist paradigm.[1]

▒ Heidegger's *Dasein*

Along with John Dewey and Ludwig Wittgenstein, Martin Heidegger is typically cited as one of the most influential philosophers of the 20th-century West.[2] From his early classic *Being and Time* in 1927 through his last major book in 1958 (*What Is Philosophy*), the fruitful soil and presupposition of philosophical inquiry was Being. As a student and later successor of Husserl at the University of Freiburg, Heidegger pursued his existentialist agenda through a phenomenological method.[3] For him, technology was the primary mode of givenness for contemporary culture, and therefore a central arena for coming to grips intellectually with human existence.[4]

In contrast to the traditional conception, technology for Heidegger is an ontological issue. Humans do not stand in external relation to it, but technology is intertwined with the existential structure of human being. The character of technology can be understood only by coming to terms with the human species. The foundations of the technological enterprise are rooted in human life. The meaning of technology is known through the way it works into our humanness, along with the characteristics it receives from such a grounding.

In Heidegger's existentialism, human beingness differs radically from objects or things, though it can be properly known only in its concreteness. Heidegger calls human being *Dasein* (literally meaning "therebeing") to indicate that intentional existence distinguishes people from all other entities. The human species actualizes the presence of

Being, and Being can show itself only through humanity. Humans alone are the beings to whom all the things in the world can reveal themselves as meaningful. Phenomena disclose their is-ness through the human opening. Human beings are "the clearing of Being" (Heidegger, 1947/1962b, p. 277). Humans are in the peculiar position of raising the problem of Being through their unique self-consciousness. Human beingness is not a static substance, but a situated existent receiving and expressing the significance of things. There is no subject-object dichotomy; "the disclosure of things and the one to whom they are disclosed are co-original" (Hood, 1972, p. 353).

The traditional view equates technology with tools or artifacts, reducing the technological enterprise to products. In Heidegger, technology is not a noun, but a verb, a cultural process in which human existence is established in relation to natural reality. Technology and human beings stir through one another like a giant food mixer. Technology is not merely the application of science, but an artistic mode of social construction. "Techne reveals or brings to presence something which is possible. . . . Techne belongs to bringing forth, to *poiesis*; it is something poetic" (Heidegger, 1977, p. 13).

How is technology grounded ontologically? According to Heidegger, our active relation to the world is motivated by human concern (*Sorge*). The concept of concern is our "relation to things insofar as this takes such forms as using, handling, producing, and so on. . . . This concern for entities . . . is manifested in a very particular way by technology" (Hood, 1972, p. 354). The meaning of technology is not rooted in the satisfaction of human needs, but in the concern of the human species for the Being of specific entities. Rather than *homo faber* (humans as tool makers to meet basic needs such as food and shelter), technological activity for Heidegger is our attempt to overpower death. The struggle for mastery "embodies the interrelated principles of utility and consumption which lie at the heart of technological consciousness" (Taylor, 1984, p. 14). Heidegger's Being is defined by mortality. "We now call mortals mortals—not because their earthly life comes to an end, but because they are capable of death as death. . . . Rational living beings must first become mortals" (Heidegger, 1971b, p. 179). "Being can only presence itself through death" (Fry, 1993, p. 88).

In Heidegger's framework, the ontic dimension and Being as the foundation (the ontological) are not to be identified. These two concepts, the ontic and the ontological, are the two main dimensions of Being (Heidegger, 1927/1962a, secs. 3-4). Humans exist simultaneously in both arenas. Although the ontological is structurally prior to the ontic, it is disclosed on the ontic level.

> Insofar as man *is*, exists in the ontological dimension, he is already oriented toward an ensemble of entities in the ontic dimension—that is, things of such and such a character, quantity, quality, relation, and so on. Both the background of man's ontological dimension provided by his basic orientation to Being and the horizon of his ontic dimension which emerges from his discovery of entities are revealed together. (Hood, 1972, p. 353)

Being is not an essence as Western philosophers have traditionally assumed. In fact, only through the ontic or phenomenal can the ontological be understood. The electromagnetic spectrum was concealed until radio and television unveiled it. A house reveals something of woodenness, and a ship discloses the character of water (Heidegger, 1977, p. 13). But the ontological dimension is in turn the set of conditions that founds the ontic. Technology, as Heidegger sees it, is ontic and ontological in an organic whole. He locates what is ontological through a phenomenological analysis of what appears as "the ready-to-hand." A praxical engagement with actual entities becomes primary instead of a cognitive struggle over ends or an engineering wizardry with techniques and materials. Thus, technology is not mere means or an ensemble of things, but "a mode of revealing, that is, of truth. . . . [It] comes to presence in the realm where revealing and unconcealment take place, where *aletheia*, truth, happens" (Heidegger, 1977, p. 13).

For Heidegger, technology cannot be grasped in its ontic dimension alone—that is, in the human activity of producing things with tools. This is the mistaken approach of instrumentalism, and unless we overcome it, we cannot hope to understand the technological order.

> We are delivered over to technology in the worst possible way when we regard it as something neutral, for this conception of it, to which today we particularly like to do homage, makes us utterly blind to the essence of technology. (Heidegger, 1977, p. 4)

To get beyond the traditional conception, we must grasp how humans ground technology and how technology "takes on its determination in such a grounding. The problem, then, is to see how the ontological dimension of man makes possible the ontic determination of technology" (Hood, 1972, p. 354).

Heidegger asks the philosophical question: "What are the conditions which make technology possible?" "Modern technology . . . is not merely human doing" (Heidegger, 1977, p. 19). Technology has an ontological "structure which . . . is the particular form of its set of possibilities which [ground] what we take as contemporary technics. The name for this shape of technological truth, Heidegger calls *Gestell*" (Heidegger, 1977, pp. 19-21; Ihde, 1979, p. 107). In Heidegger's use, *Gestell* is enframing,[5] and it is similar for him to Michael Polanyi's tacit knowledge and Raymond Williams' structures of feeling. Our revealing of technology is always bounded by its horizons. The human response to technology is located and limited. Human action is not self-originating, but guided by a historical play of language and concepts not under any one person's control.

> Man can indeed conceive, fashion, and carry through this or that in one way or another. But man does not have control over unconcealment itself, in which at any given time the real shows itself or withdraws. (Heidegger, 1977, p. 18)

"Beings or entities thus appear only against, from and within a background or opening, a framework. But the opening or clearing within which they take the shapes they assume, is itself structured" (Ihde, 1979, p. 105). Technology is not an individual invention, but emerges within the claims that the natural and cultural worlds lay on us. Beings as such are never simply given; they come to presence in a definite way that depends on the total field of revealing in which they are situated. Technology appears ontically in terms of civilizational givens that are taken for granted. The technological mode of truth has specific features, deriving from an era's pretheoretical commitments, "something like deeply held, dynamic but enduring traditions, historical but no more easily thrown over than one's own deepest character or personality" (Ihde, 1979, p. 102). In the contemporary age, the disclosure of technology takes place under conditions of scientific and commercial prowess, rationalism, and secularism. As interpretive agents, we find ourselves in a new interpretive situation—a life-world of technological texture that stipulates for us what is true (Ihde, 1983, p. 11). In Heidegger's terms, the modern epoch of Being is technological. Thus, penetrating its "essence or shape becomes a central philosophical concern if we are to understand our era and prepare a response to it" (Ihde, 1979, p. 107).

One of the civilizational givens in a technological world is defining the earth as standing reserve (*Bestand*). Nature is understood in one-dimensional terms as a field of energy or power that can be captured and stored. "The earth now reveals itself as a coal mining district, the soil as a mineral deposit" (Heidegger, 1977, p. 14). We look at forests and see paper products. The river Rhine is a water power supplier for a hydro-electric plant (p. 16). Only on the margins are there alternative claims "which, for instance, regard the earth as mother and to which one does not even put a plow" (Ihde, 1979, p. 108). "Everywhere everything is ordered to stand by, to be immediately at hand, indeed to stand there just so that it may be on call for a further ordering" (Heidegger, 1977, p. 17). Unrelenting technological development depends on our viewing nature as a storehouse for the engineer. The world is on hand for human inter-action, and "whatever stands by in the sense of standing reserve no longer stands over against us as object" (Heidegger, 1977, p. 17). "Hidden behind modern physics is the spirit of technology, technology in its ontological sense as world-taken-as-standing-reserve. . . . Nature appears, within enframing, as standing reserve" (Ihde, 1979, pp. 111-112).

This selective way of seeing the world contains a direction or destiny.

> We shall call the sending that gathers, that first starts man upon a way of revealing, destining. . . . Man is endangered by destining. The destin-ing of revealing is as such, in every one of its modes, and therefore necessarily, danger. (Heidegger, 1977, pp. 24, 26)

In the technological mode of revealing, we may forget the concealing. We could mistake the part for the whole. The world may appear totally or ultimately as standing-reserve. "Nature becomes a gigantic gasoline sta-tion, an energy source for modern technology and industry" (Heidegger, 1966, p. 50).

> When destining reigns in the mode of enframing, it is the supreme danger. . . . As soon as what is unconcealed . . . concerns man exclusively

as standing reserve, then he comes to the brink of a precipitous fall, that is, he comes to the point where he himself will have to be taken as standing-reserve. (Heidegger, 1977, p. 27).

The danger in revealing, though unnoticed, is the pre-empting of human existence in the technological process. For something "to be" means it is material for the self-augmenting technological system.

Media technologies are especially powerful mechanisms for reconstructing an inauthentic humanness. For Ellul, this mediated process of enculturation is sociological propaganda, in which commonplaces and conformity bubble up from below to homogenize rather than inform. Viewers and readers are cast up as purchasers; private and confidential data become commodities for digital information banks. In Tony Fry's (1993) application of Heidegger,

> The power of television in many ways stems from the synthesis of technology and culture as it is projected and thereafter fills and forms the space in which the viewing "viewer" subject is monologically made in knowledge. (p. 8)

In genetic engineering, humans are raw material, fodder for scientific experimentation. We use human resources like a styrofoam cup—throwing it away as soon as the task is finished (Dreyfus, 1995, p. 99). In the classic case of the tomato picker designed by the University of California-Irvine, a new hybrid tomato had to be developed—tomatoes with tough skins so they would not break, that ripened at the same time, with chemical color added as necessary, and that were square or oblong so they moved on feeding trays better. Adapting the tomato to the machine is an analogue of Heidegger's concern with destining. Relentlessly and overwhelmingly, the technological process pre-empts nature and human existence for itself.

Heidegger rejects the presumption that human freedom is independent of technological necessity. But he is not a determinist. There is human agency in Heidegger's model through *poiesis* and revealing, but without subjectivism; nature and instruments are not at our behest:

> The coming to presence of technology gives man entry into that which, of himself, he can neither invent nor in any way make. For there is no

such thing as a man who, solely of himself, is only man. (Heidegger, 1977, p. 31)

Only in its essence does Heidegger consider technology dangerous. "The threat to man does not come in the first instance from the potentially lethal machines and apparatus of technology. The actual threat has already afflicted man in his essence" (Heidegger, 1977, p. 28). What counts as real has been leveled and reduced. The technological revolution has dazzled us into accepting and practicing "calculative thinking as the only way of thinking" (Heidegger, 1966, p. 56). As a result, our authentic humanness is closed down.

▓ Triadic Communication Theory

For Heidegger to be taken seriously when articulating the relation among media, religion, and culture, a triadic theory of communication is necessary. Stimulus-response models and information systems theory are not stitched deeply enough into actual human experience to be relevant. Heidegger's radical contextualism requires the social construction of a Berger and Luckmann or cultural approaches in which "we first produce the world by symbolic work and then take up residence in the world we have produced" (Carey, 1989, p. 30). The phenomenological world humans are said to produce and inhabit anchors the symbolization process without which social relations are impossible.

However, even semiotic and sociological theories do not necessarily incorporate the technological dimension of culture into their frame of reference. Ernst Cassirer's (1953-1957) philosophy of symbolic forms puts our various symbolic universes on a level playing floor; scientific knowledge as a symbolic formation is no longer superior in principle to such symbolic domains as music and religion. But Cassirer's symbolic frontiers do not explicitly account for technological practices. In a dyadic cultural theory of communication such as Cassirer's, the symbolic world within which humans are constituted accounts for the process of meaning-making, but without incorporating the physical world explicitly. As Wayne Woodward (1995) concludes regarding the semiotic legacy of Charles Peirce (1940/1955) and Walker Percy (1975), language interconnects the sociological aspects of community, but the "constraints of the physical/material/technological environment are essentially omitted from consideration" (Woodward, 1996, p. 158).

Rooting our understanding of religion and the media in culture is a significant advance, but itself begs the question whether our cultural approaches account for technology adequately. If our theories of mediation do not reflect Heidegger's complexity, they actually reproduce an instrumental approach to technology rather than an ontological one. In Cornel West's critique of the cultural studies tradition rooted in pragmatism, as represented in this case by Richard Rorty,

> [It] only kicks the philosophical props from under liberal bourgeois capitalist societies; it requires no change in our cultural and political practices. What then are the ethical and political consequences of his neopragmatism? On the macrosocietal level, there simply are none. (West, 1989, p. 206)

Within the cultural studies tradition are dialogic constructions that are explicitly triadic. George Herbert Mead, for example, "situates human symbolic practices within the structures and constraints of the bio-physical environment in which these practices occur; . . . [he does not] resort to separate terminologies to analyze multiple levels of practices and constraints—mind, self, society, and bio-physical environment" (Woodward, 1996, p. 160; Mead, 1934). In Majid Tehranian's (1991) reconstruction of Mead's field of meaning, the world and social reality are symbolically connected through an "established or emerging stock of signals (technology) and knowledge (culture)" (p. 57). Mead's shared symbolic world directs us away from the production of meaning solely through language, toward "the physical and artifactual constraints within, and by means of which, all communication materially occurs" (Woodward, 1996, p. 160). In Martin Buber's variation, our mode of existence includes both Thou and It in the relational moment.

The medium-oriented Canadian tradition is explicitly triadic also.[6] Originating with Harold Innis at the University of Toronto, this cultural theory of communication argues that social change results from media transformations, that changes in symbolic forms alter the structure of consciousness. Instead of ignoring the material, within this triadic paradigm the distinguishing properties of particular media technologies are considered the most productive venue for understanding cultural patterns and human perception.

In dyadic theories of communication and culture, technology is ignored or underdeveloped, and religious sensibilities can be assumed to prosper in symbol making. However, triadic approaches oppose technocratic culture to religion, and contradict naive instrumentalism. They strip us clean of the assumption that religious symbols are definitive or that they can be mediated in salvific terms through global information technologies.

▓ Prophetic Witness

When religion is understood in functional terms and technology reduced to neutral means, the sacred domain can presume for itself an explicit rationale. As the harbinger and catalyst of ultimate values, religious rituals can be said to participate with Aristotle's philosophers and literateurs in vivifying social ends. In the functional model, the visual media are hailed as the savior of religious education.

However, in concert with cultural studies as a whole, Heidegger's philosophy of technology destroys this instrumentalist paradigm. Given his argument that the current epoch of Being is technological in character, Heidegger takes away our presumptions that religious worldviews can actively participate in contemporary meaning-making. Even more pointedly, Heidegger contradicts dyadic communication theories in which symbolically negotiated worlds are devoid of material structures. He challenges the cultural turn to take technology seriously. But he makes no proposals for getting "technology under control so it can serve our rationally chosen ends" (Dreyfus, 1995, p. 97). While getting us on the right track, an ontological view of technology makes the task even for culturalists immeasurably more difficult.

There is no technological problem that needs fixing, but an ontological condition from which we need emancipation. The crisis we face is not technology, but a technological understanding of Being. In Heidegger's view, because our beingness is situated today in technological conditions radically opposed to human freedom, there are no oases in which the moral imagination can prosper undisturbed. The best we can manage is ongoing struggle without guarantees of success. Pockets of resistance may be possible, though always unstable and marginalized. At least in theory, the technological process is not determined and linear, but a dialectical revealing of the concealed.

In fact, should some version of Heidegger's technoculture seem warranted, prophetic witness is the only strategic option for the religious community. When mediation is understood in triadic terms—and technology, therefore, becomes a constituent element in cultural formation—religion's territory is prophetic appeals for authentic Being.

In Abraham Heschel's (1962/1969-1971) monumental study, the prophet is not a doomsayer or self-righteous moralizer. Prophets constantly portray divine participation in the human predicament. History is not a derelict arena where a lonely species struggles on its own for survival. Evil has no independent life of its own; it is a parasite living off an originally good creation. Thus prophets speak to the oppressiveness of technocratic culture, but with a constructive ambience. Their purpose is empowerment, not flagellation for its own sake.

Prophets often react fiercely; they carry a burden on their souls and are stunned at people's blatant greed and their plundering of the poor. The prophet feels compelled to condemn society's complacency and waywardness, but always with the aim of reconciling the human species to God. Judgment is not absolute, but conditional. Disaster will strike only if there is no turning back. The prophetic aim is not to reject history wholesale, but to redirect it. Prophets speak with pathos, with an unquenchable concern for justice. They insist on taking "tragic action in an evil-ridden world" through critical consciousness and moral vision (West, 1989, p. 232).[7] History is no blind alley; God offers a way out.

Within an ontological paradigm, Jacques Ellul is the most distinctively prophetic. Dale Brown (1976) in a typical statement applauds his "Amos-like ministry to the technological society" (p. 37). Ellul's *Judgment of Jonah* is a specific attempt to develop the prophetic motif as a counterpoint to mass media propaganda. *Hope in the Time of Abandonment* and the *Ethics of Freedom* are inspired by his theistic worldview. However, while rejecting disillusionment and refusing to believe history is blind will, Ellul opposes cheap solutions and middle-level bargains. He confronts the industrial era without a hint of compromise. He smashes our modern idols, exposes false claims, insists on demythologizing today's illusions, and stands us squarely before the bloody face of history.

Ellul does not reject technological products themselves, but attacks our sacralizing of them. He witnesses against technicism as an unacceptable worship of an elfin god. We imbue the technological enterprise with an aura of holy prestige, and Ellul as prophet desacralizes the grandiose claims. Prophets in his mode go after the civilizational givens—what Ellul calls *la technique*; they cut through the idolatrous attitudes, intentions, and desires which are driving technology forward.

Given Heidegger's longstanding interest in the philosophy of language (1962b, 1971a, 1971b, for example), he sees a glimmer of hope in another direction. He believes that through a basic revival of *techne* as art, we can broaden and enrich technological revealing. This move is familiar throughout the Heideggerian emphasis on the primal role of the poet: "Poetically man dwells upon this earth" (Heidegger, 1977, p. 34). "Art is technological as *techne*, but its mode of revealing opens new ways of 'saying Being' as Heidegger puts it" (Ihde, 1979, p. 115). "Art is essentially anti-reductive in its imaginative fecundity. Its 'worlds' are effectively endless" (p. 129).

Heidegger chooses this alternative strategically against the totalizing closure of our humanity. Art is *techne*, similar in kind to all praxical dealings with the world. It is thus already related to technology. "Confrontation with [technology] must happen in a realm that is, on the one hand, akin to the essence of technology, and on the other, fundamentally different from it" (Heidegger, 1977, p. 35). "Technology and art belong to the danger and possible salvation of the same epoch of Being" (Ihde, 1979, p. 115).

Heidegger takes the "Greek temple as his illustration of an artwork working. The temple held up to the Greeks what was important, and so let there be heroes and slaves, victory and disgrace, disaster and blessing, and so on" (Dreyfus, 1995, p. 105). If art as handiwork and craftwork can open a nontechnological understanding of being, then artifacts and tools of some sort would continue to exist, but they would no longer constrain our horizon of understanding.

Consistent with triadic theories of communication and culture, richer technological revealing is not limited to message but revolutionizes the medium as well. Reordering the size, shape, and speed of technological products is imperative for enabling a critical consciousness to prosper. As a response to hyperindustrialism, Ivan Illich (1973) insists on alternative technologies—on responsibly limited tools that respect the dignity of human work, are generally accessible, and emphasize personal satisfaction and creative ingenuity. Such democratized technologies, owned by the people themselves and in the vernacular tongue, nurture communities of resistance against the technological mystique (cf. Ganley, 1992; Riaño, 1994; Sreberny-Mohammadi & Mohammadi, 1994). In local settings, they are incubators of nonviolent civic transformation.

However, the task is finally not ontic but ontological, and therefore a prophetic witness is disruptive and extraordinarily painful. We confront deep resistance when we insist on moving beyond new machines and methods to the restructuring of Being.

> *Dasein's* kind of being thus demands that any ontological interpretation which sets itself the goal of exhibiting the phenomena in their primordiality, should capture the being of the entity, in spite of this entity's own tendency to cover things up. Existential analysis, therefore, constantly has the character of doing violence whether to the claims of the everyday interpretation, or to its complacency and its tranquilized obliviousness. (Heidegger, 1927/1962a, p. 359)

The struggle is not over technological devices per se, but over the civilizational givens that undergird the technological enterprise. These underlying values, this instrumental worldview, must be revolutionized for our beingness to be redefined in nontechnocratic terms. Working the trenches has little glamor, but only a prophetic witness matters.

Notes

1. The traditional view, in Heidegger's perspective, has a subjectivistic variant—that is, technology as a human activity. "The two definitions belong together. For to posit ends and procure and utilize the means to them is a human activity. The manufacture and utilization of equipment, tools, and machines, the manufactured and used things themselves, and the needs and ends they serve, all belong to what technology is. . . . The current conception of technology, according to which it is a means and a human activity, can therefore be called the instrumental and anthropological definitions of technology" (Heidegger, 1977, p. 5). These two definitions reflect different aspects of the subject-object dualism on which Aristotle's definition is built.

2. Heidegger's stellar reputation has been sullied by his commitment to German national socialism prior to and during World War II (cf. Lyotard, 1990; Wolin, 1993). As Rector of the University of Freiburg in 1933-1934 and as a prominent intellectual during the war years, he

refused to condemn Nazism and offered no apology before his death in 1976 at age 87. While recognizing the importance of his philosophical project for hermeneutics, postanalytical philosophy, critical theory, poststructuralism, and deconstructionism, Otto Pöggler's question is unavoidable: "How do we come to terms with the fact that perhaps the greatest philosopher of the twentieth century was a Fascist?" (Fry, 1993, p. 16). Since Georg Lukacs first exposed this grotesque failure, explanations that Heidegger distinguished Nazism as it occurred from the inner truth of national socialism have not been satisfactory. Rather than crass indifference, Heidegger's contempt of media-dominated publicity may have motivated his silence; but that rationale seems simplistic even to those who do not want him silenced for his silence.

Rockmore (1995, pp. 128-144) at least provides a plausible account intellectually: Heidegger's transpersonal conception of Being differs radically from the democratic subject and therefore tolerates within itself an anti-democratic politics. From this perspective, a Heideggerian analysis, if connected to prophetic witness, will not "tolerate . . . an anti-democratic politics." For purposes of this chapter, Aristotle and Heidegger are both understood as intellectual forebears of distinctive philosophies of technology. Feenberg (1991, pp. 5-13) labels them the instrumentalist and substantive theories respectively. Even as Aristotle's legacy extends to, and is modified by, a wide range of 20th-century thinkers, so an ontological philosophy of technology is reconstructed by Jacques Ellul, Ivan Illich, Arnold Pacey, and Jean Baudrillard. Although the conceptual focus that follows is Heidegger's for the sake of compactness, it is obviously not presented as Heideggerian existentialism per se, but as a substantive philosophy of technology rooted primarily in Heidegger's *Question Concerning Technology*.

Jean Paul Sartre was Heidegger's most famous student, along with Georg Gadamer and Hannah Arendt. The smaller scale controversy over his four-year affair with Arendt has also complicated an assessment of his philosophical stature (cf. Ettinger, 1995).

3. The phenomenological method for approaching technology is developed in detail by Ihde (1983); see especially chapter 8, "Phenomenology and the Later Heidegger," and chapter 3, "The Technological Embodiment of Media."

4. The major concepts were introduced in *Being and Time* (1927/1962a). After World War II, his philosophy of technology was explicitly developed in four lectures before the Club at Bremen (December 1949). The first two were presented later at the Bavarian Academy of Fine Arts in the series, "The Arts in the Technological Age." These are published as *The Question Concerning Technology*, along with the fourth Bremen lecture ("The Turning," pp. 36-49). For an exposition of how *Being and Time* and *The Question Concerning Technology* are related, see Don Ihde (1979, ch. 9).

5. *Gestell* means in ordinary German, 'frame, bookrack, or skeleton.'

6. For a historical review of Canadian social communications that situates Innis and his successor, Marshall McLuhan, within a trajectory from the 18th century to Michel Foucault, see Heyer (1988).

7. For elaboration against the background of West's "disenchantment with intellectual life in America and . . . demoralization regarding the political and cultural state of the country" (p. 7), see his chapter 6, "Prophetic Pragmatism," pp. 211-239, and West (1988).

References

Brown, D. (1976, November). Critique: *New demons. Sojourners, 5,* 37.
Carey, J. W. (1989). *Communication as culture.* Winchester, MA: Unwin Hyman.

Cassirer, E. (1953-1957). *The philosophy of symbolic forms* (3 vols.) (R. Manheim, Trans.). New Haven, CT: Yale University Press.

Dreyfus, H. L. (1995). Heidegger on gaining a free relation to technology. In A. Feenberg & A. Hannay (Eds.), *Technology and the politics of knowledge* (pp. 97-107). Bloomington: Indiana University Press.

Ettinger, E. (1995). *Hannah Arendt/Martin Heidegger.* New Haven, CT: Yale University Press.

Feenberg, A. (1991). *Critical theory of technology.* New York: Oxford University Press.

Fry, T. (Ed.). (1993). *R U A TV? Heidegger and the televisual.* Sydney, Australia: Power Publications.

Ganley, G. D. (1992). *The exploding political power of personal media.* Norwood, NJ: Ablex.

Heidegger, M. C. (1962a). *Being and time [Sein und zeit]* (J. Macquarrie & E. Robinson, Trans.). New York: Harper & Row. (Originally published in 1927).

Heidegger, M. C. (1962b). Letter on humanism. In W. Barrett & H. D. Aiken (Eds.), *Philosophy in the twentieth century* (vol. 2, pp. 290-302). New York: Random House. (Originally published 1947)

Heidegger, M. C. (1966). *Discourse on thinking.* New York: Harper & Row.

Heidegger, M. C. (1971a). *On the way to language.* (P. D. Hertz, Trans.). New York: Harper & Row. (Originally published in 1959).

Heidegger, M. C. (1971b). *Poetry, language, thought* (A. Hofstadter, Trans.). New York: Harper & Row.

Heidegger, M. C. (1977). *The question concerning technology and other essays* (W. Lovitt, Trans.). New York: Harper & Row.

Heschel, A. J. (1969-1971). *The prophets* (2 vols.). New York: Harper Torchbooks. (Originally published 1962)

Heyer, P. (1988). *Communications and history: Theories of media, knowledge and civilization.* Westport, CT: Greenwood.

Hood, W. F. (1972). The Aristotelian versus the Heideggerian approach to the problem of technology. In C. Mitcham & R. Mackey (Eds.), *Philosophy and technology: Readings in the philosophical problems of technology* (pp. 347-363). New York: Free Press.

Ihde, D. (1979). Heidegger's philosophy of technology. In *Technics and praxis* (pp. 103-129). Dordrecht, The Netherlands: D. Reidel.

Ihde, D. (1983). *Existential technics.* Albany. State University of New York Press.

Illich, I. (1973). *Tools for conviviality.* New York: Harper Colophon.

Lyotard, J. F. (1990). *Heidegger and the Jews* (A. Michel & M. S. Roberts, Trans.). Minneapolis: University of Minnesota Press.

Mead, G. H. (1934). *Mind, self, and society.* Chicago: University of Chicago Press.

Peirce, C. S. (1955). *Philosophical writings of Peirce.* New York: Dover. (Originally published 1940)

Percy, W. (1975). *The message in the bottle.* New York: Farrar, Straus & Giroux.

Riaño, P. (Ed.). (1994). *Women in grassroots communication: Furthering social change.* Thousand Oaks, CA: Sage.

Rockmore, T. (1995). Heidegger on technology and democracy. In A. Feenberg & A. Hannay (Eds.), *Technology and the politics of knowledge* (pp. 128-144). Bloomington: Indiana University Press.

Sreberny-Mohammadi, A. , & Mohammadi, A. (1994). *Small media, big revolution: Communication, culture, and the Iranian revolution.* Minneapolis: University of Minnesota Press.

Taylor, M. C. (1984). *Erring: A postmodern a/theology.* Chicago: University of Chicago Press.

Tehranian, M. (1991, February). Is comparative communication theory possible/desirable? *Communication Theory, 1*(1), 44-59.

West, C. (1988). *Prophetic fragments*. Grand Rapids, MI: Eerdmans.

West, C. (1989). *The American evasion of philosophy: A genealogy of pragmatism*. Madison: University of Wisconsin Press.

Wolin, R. (Ed.). (1993). *The Heidegger controversy: A critical reader*. Cambridge, MA: MIT Press.

Woodward, W. (1996, June). Triadic communication as transactional participation. *Critical Studies in Mass Communication, 13*(2), 155-174.

Part III

Media, Religion, and Culture:
Contemporary Society

The Re-Enchantment of the World
Religion and the
Transformations of Modernity

Graham Murdock

The sea of faith
Was once, too, at the full, and round earth's shore
Lay like the folds of a bright girdle furl'd
But now I only hear
Its melancholy, long, withdrawing roar
> —Matthew Arnold, *Dover Beach*

The world may well have been disenchanted by the rise of science
and reason, but scold as the enlightened ones may, people still
yearn for re-enchantment.
> —Wright, 1995, p. 19

One night in 1867, the poet and critic Matthew Arnold stood on Dover
Beach looking out over the English Channel. Behind him was a country

transformed by industrial manufacture; beyond him, Paris, capital of the Enlightenment and the rule of reason. In the dull roar of the sea pulling away from the shingle, he heard the melancholy echo of religious faith ebbing out of people's lives, leaving them buffeted, exposed, and alone. His lament expressed a sense of loss that many people had come to feel as the century began to move toward its close. By then, the future seemed clear. Spiritual authority had been undermined by science, and materialism and religion had retreated from the centers of institutional and imaginative life. The pins manufactured in Adam Smith's ideal factory had no space on their heads for angels to dance. They were objects in an orderly system of exchange created by the hidden hand of the capitalist market, not by the handiwork of God. Mystery had been displaced by measurement and calculation, the infinite by the tangible. People were struggling to come to terms with what the great German sociologist Max Weber was to call "the disenchantment of the world."

Weber saw this process as the key to understanding the distinctiveness of a modern culture that set out to subsume all natural and social events "under orderly, symmetrical, precisely articulated generalizations and explanatory models" (Gellner 1987, p. 153). Adam Smith was happy to share with Newton the "pleasure to see the phenomena which we reckoned the most unaccountable all deduced from some principle." The intention was not simply to explain, but to manipulate and control. This totalizing project, Weber argued, created a cosmos in which there was no room left for "mysterious incalculable forces" (Gerth & Mills, 1974, p. 139). Its aim was to calibrate the messiness of the world so that "Nature could be 'tamed,' workers made more docile, books balanced, and complexity contained" (Lyon, 1994, p. 24). To this end, the champions of modernity waged an unceasing war to defend the sovereignty of reason against mystery, magic, and faith. "At stake was the right to initiative and authorship of action, the right to pronounce on meanings, to construe narratives. To win the stakes, to win all of them and to win them for good, the world had to be *de-spiritualized*" (Bauman, 1992, p. x).

At first glance, the advance of disenchantment looked unstoppable. Its generals shared an unshakable conviction that the ever-widening application of scientific rationality would lead to cumulative and irreversible gains, an aspiration that found attractive expression in the idea of "progress," modernity's master narrative. People wanted to believe, and many did. They saw steady improvement in the physical and material conditions of everyday life—sanitation, street lighting, vaccination against disease—and new opportunities for mobility and choice—the railway system, mass education, department stores. But as Weber recognized, the dynamics of modernity were also constructing an "iron cage" of bureaucracy and routine based around "an incessant drive to eliminate the haphazard and annihilate the spontaneous" (Bauman, 1992, p. xi). Modernity had made a Faustian pact with the future. Securing the cognitive, administrative, and technical mastery offered by purposive rationality involved giving up a premodern world that had often been "menacing and capricious" but was also "meaningful, humanely suffused, humanly responsive" (Gellner, 1987, p. 153). In contrast, the emerging world of disenchantment appeared "icy, impersonal, abstract, technical, devoid of warmth and magic" (p. 164).

This sense of an unlooked-for ending, of values slipping away, was reinforced by the new science's failure to provide a coherent system of meaning comparable to those offered by religion. Because all scientific propositions are by definition provisional and open to refutation, they can offer no certainties, no anchorage points—only a view of human order as "vulnerable and devoid of reliable foundations" (Bauman, 1992, p. xi). All "truths" become contingent. Matters of "fact" are rigorously separated from judgments of value, and the language of dispute comes to center on questions of evidence. Science rebuilt our view of the cosmos around notions of natural causality; but, as Weber noted, it could not "answer with certainty the question of its own ultimate presuppositions" (Gerth & Mills, 1970, p. 355). This inability to address the meaning of life, as opposed to its mechanisms, generated a growing "disenchantment with modernity" (Smart, 1993, p. 86).

This sense of disappointment was bound up, in turn, with an increasing ambivalence toward the "creative destruction" being carried out in the name of progress. Conservatives had always felt that more was being lost than gained and had fought doggedly in defense of tradition and faith. But even "progressives" began to have doubts. Their sense of exhilaration at the opening up of new possibilities was increasingly suffused with anxiety. The "modern pursuit of mastery over all things . . . seemed destined to remain unfinished, incomplete, and frustrated" (Smart, 1993, p. 87). It manufactured perpetual disillusion. As Weber (quoted in Gerth & Mills, 1974) put it, "the individual life of civilized man, placed into an infinite progress . . . catches only the most minute part of what the life of the spirit brings forth ever anew, and as such is meaningless" (pp. 139-40).

This discontent was reinforced by a growing awareness that the gains of "progress" were balanced by costs, that the continual refinement of calculating and instrumental forms of rationality generated problems as well as improvements. Modernity was becoming increasingly "vulnerable to the recognition of 'inconvenient' facts, the identification of unfulfilled promises, and the continuing existence of problems and dangers, if not exacerbated risks and threats" (Smart, 1993, p. 86). Progress was seen to be devouring itself as "more and more, the advances of science and technology" had "as their principal objective the correction of the harmful consequences of previous innovations" (Lévi-Strauss, 1995, p. 17). Disenchantment found potent expression in popular fiction, beginning with Mary Shelley's cautionary tale of *Frankenstein*. In the world of the gothic, it was not the sleep of reason that bred monsters, but its application.

These two strands in the growing disillusionment with modernity—the confrontation with the dark side of progress and the evacuation of meaning—left a gap in popular structures of feeling through which religion could reenter people's lives. Weber (Gerth & Mills, 1974) understood this very well and argued strongly that the old gods were about to "ascend from their graves" and resume their struggle "to gain power over our lives" (p. 149). The time was ripe for a re-enchantment of the world. But what forms could it take in a world indelibly marked by the experience of modernity?

In medieval Europe, Catholicism had spread a "sacred canopy" (Berger, 1969) over the whole of social and mental life and defended its exclusive control of spiritual services with an impressive range of deterrents and punishments. The Reformation broke this monopoly and introduced competition into the religious marketplace. The Protestant "licensing of private judgment led to a ransacking of tradition and . . . fostered a narcissism of small sectarian differences" as proliferating religious groupings all "claimed the right to authoritative pronouncement in religious matters" (Archer, 1988, p. 200). With the collapse of orthodoxy, heresy was transmuted into dissent.

But in common with most markets, the terms of competition in this new religious field varied considerably depending on the role that emerging nation-states chose to play. In England, at an early point in the state's formation, a particular version of Protestantism, the Church of England, was adopted as the established religion and played a central role in supporting the monarchy and the other central institutions of secular power. As a result, it came to be seen by many people, particularly within the working class, as belonging to "them" rather than to "us." As Richard Hoggart (1959) remembered from his childhood in Leeds between the Wars, people "might still believe, underneath, in certain ways" and would probably draw on "religious institutions at the important moments of life"—birth, marriage, death—(p. 88) but they saw the local churches and chapels as institutions apart, "brooding presences, standing judgment on the pubs" (p. 124). This pattern of *believing without belonging* (Davie, 1994, p. 94) is perfectly caught in the ruminations of one of David Lodge's (1995) contemporary fictional characters:

> I've never regarded myself as a religious person. . . . I have a sort of faith that we survive after death. I respect Jesus as an ethical thinker . . . but I wouldn't call myself a Christian. My Mum and Dad sent me to Sunday School when I was a nipper—don't ask me why because they never went to church themselves except for weddings and funerals. (pp. 87-88)

As the sociologist David Martin reluctantly concluded, "We in England live in the chill religious vapors of Northern Europe, where moribund religious establishments loom over populations that mostly do not enter churches for active worship even if they entertain inchoate beliefs" (quoted in Davie, 1994, p. 189).

This view of religion as a weak and waning presence in popular experience is the principal reason why British Cultural Studies has paid it so little attention. In a seminal article, Raymond Williams (1980) had no hesitation in including it among the "residues—cultural as well as social—of some previous social formation" (p. 40). And because the supporters of the new field had nominated the study of *contemporary* culture as their defining project, "residual" practices held few attractions. Interest focused instead on the "emergent" cultures forming around youth, gender, and ethnicity. But because the intention was to debunk the commonsense labels and explanations of these formations offered by conservative politicians and the popular news media, cultural studies found itself adopting their hierarchy of concerns. This meant that much was left out.

There was a great deal of work on the subcultures that attracted public-ity—the Mods, Hippies, Football Hooligans, and the rest—but very little on the new religious subcultures grouped around the resurgence of evangelism. This selective inattention was shared as much by critics of cultural studies as by its principal proponents. As Roxy Harris (1996) has pointed out, the mostly male writers who struggled to move Britain's transition from an imperial to a postcolonial polity into the center of cultural studies' concerns tended to focus on masculine street styles (Rastas, Rude Boys, Rappers) and to pass over in silence the cultures of the black churches in which women, many of them middle-aged or elderly, played a central role. As foci of interest, such churches had multiple disadvantages. They were law-abiding rather than deviant, vibrant but not spectacular, taken-for-granted rather than publicly visible.

If religion appeared "residual" in the inclement climate of Northern Europe, elsewhere it clearly remained central to both popular culture and everyday life. This was true not just of the Catholic countries of Southern Europe and Latin America and of the Islamic World, which could be seen as still partly premodern or incompletely modernized. It was also true of the most modern country of all, the United States.

Though Protestantism stood at the heart of official American culture, it was not the established religion. On the contrary, the churches were disestablished, separated from the state, at an early point in the country's history. This guaranteed religious freedom in general, but gave no special privileges to any particular faith. "For the people, there was freedom of worship. For the churches it was sink, or swim" (Warner, 1993, p. 1051). They found themselves in an open marketplace, competing for people's time, money, and allegiance. Their vigorous efforts to sell themselves promoted a consumerist relation to religion, in which denominations took on the appearance of brands. The identities they offered could be tested, tried for a time, and discarded. According to polls, between a third and a half of all those asked had changed their religious affiliation in the course of their lives (Warner, 1993, p. 1075).

Many commentators (e.g., Berger, 1969) have seen this as a relatively recent phenomenon, reinforced by the postwar rise of a mass consumer society in which "consumption becomes the main form of self expression and the chief source of identity" (Waters, 1995, p. 140). But this is overly simple. The relations between consumption and Protestantism have a longer, more complex, history.

In his best-known book, *The Protestant Ethic and the Spirit of Capitalism,* Max Weber (1958) argued that the moral imperatives of Puritanism had provided an essential cultural support for the practices of accumulation that fueled the rise of capitalism. But as Colin Campbell (1987) has pointed out, this was only half the story. There existed, from the outset, not one but "two major strands of thought within Protestantism, and even within that especially harsh and vigorous branch of it known as Puritanism" (p. 219). One evolved into the instrumental rationalism that supported capitalist production, the other developed into the Romantic sensibility that fed into the consumer system. Consequently, "the cultural logic of modernity is not merely that of rationality as expressed in the activities of calculation and experiment; it is also that of passion and the creative dreaming born of longing." Its dynamism and energy arise out of the permanent tensions "between dream and reality, pleasure and utility" (p. 227). The shifting relations between these two sides of Protestant culture is especially marked in America, where the consumer society and the religious marketplace are both most advanced.

From the Second Great Awakening, between 1790 and 1830, to the present revival of evangelism, American Protestantism has shown a consistent fascination with being "born again" and with the possibilities of personal transformation. This exaltation of "a more fluid sense of self than was available under the strict Calvinist dispensation" and the "mystic dream of spontaneously flowing spiritual abundance" that accompanies it, fitted neatly with the new language of the marketplace (Lears, 1994, p. 47-48). The emerging consumer system had its own cathedrals, rites, and litanies. The department stores, with their aura of light and abundance, provided spaces for new kinds of communion; and advertising, modernity's "magic system," (Williams, 1980), wrote stirring hymns of "deprivation and desire" (Lears, 1994, p. 49). Consumerism threw a new "sacred canopy" over everyday life, promising that the mundane could be instantly transformed, even transcended, by the alchemy of possession. Those in pain would find relief from their sufferings; the dull hair and blemished skin of the lonely and unloved would shine and glow; the hungry would be fed.

As production became more mechanized and the iron cage of bureaucracy more extensive, the attractions of consumption appeared ever more seductive as industrial organization moved toward the atomization of Henry Ford's assembly line. Work progressively lost its ability to provide a center for identity. It was no longer possible to believe with Zwingli and his early Protestant successors that "in the things of this life, the laborer is most like to God." Living was increasingly identified with "the hours spent away from the stool, the machine, and the plow" and leisure became the major arena in which to search for the "meaning and justification of life" (Durant, 1938, p. 18). And at the center of leisure stood the consumer system, nourished and orchestrated by a rapidly expanding promotional culture.

As a major medium for advertising, the popular commercial press played a pivotal role in this emerging culture of consumption; but in the editorial pages, it also provided spaces where the worldviews of tradition and modernity jostled for hearts and minds. At first sight, news was squarely on the side of modernity. It claimed to offer a daily demonstration of the "objectivity" that underpinned positivist science and purposive rationality. Reporting was presented as an almost mechanical process, recording a picture of contemporary events uncontaminated by personal convictions and partisanship. The modern journalist aspired to be a human camera, dealing with facts not judgments, with the here-and-now not the hereafter. But news reports were also stories; and those printed in the popular press, particularly if they dealt with crime, offered powerful narratives of good and evil, loyalty and betrayal, saints, devils, and redeemed sinners. They drew on older forms of popular storytelling—chapbooks, almanacs, the true confessions of condemned criminals—whose manichean moral universe was firmly rooted in religion. Other sections of the papers were even more strongly inflected with premodern worldviews. Advice columns had elements of the confessional. Astrology columns walked the "borderland of superstition" (Harrison & Madge, 1986, p. 222) reaffirming ideas of fate and predestination. And, as Richard Hoggart (1959) remembered, the conventional wording of the *in memorium* notices—"gone before," "released from work here below"— were a daily reminder of the possibility of a life to come (p. 89).

Within the two central media of modernity, photography and film, the coexistence of religious and realist sensibilities was rather more problematic, however. Because they claimed to offer an objective picture of whatever was in front of the lens at the time, representations of sacred subjects that could not normally be seen appeared to believers as blasphemous, or at the very least, highly offensive. Religious lobbies had some early success in controlling the circulation of filmed images. In the first

British system of cinema censorship, for example, "materialism of Christ or the Almighty " was one of only two absolute grounds on which a film could be banned (Christie, 1994, p. 120). At the same time, other religious leaders, particularly in the United States with its open market in beliefs, were quick to see the proselytizing potential of the new medium. In 1897, two years after the Lumiere brothers had mounted the first public cinema performance in Paris, the American evangelist Colonel Henry Hadley argued that, "These moving pictures are going to be the best teachers and the best preachers in the history of the world. . . . Mark my words, there are two things coming; prohibition and moving pictures" (quoted in Christie, 1994, p. 121). He was correct on both counts, but whereas Prohibition came and went, the movies became a major medium for popularizing biblical stories and "lessons."

The contradiction between realist representation and religious conviction was initially resolved by filming reenactments of sacred dramas staged by the faithful. The first major success was a film released in 1898 claiming to be a documentary record of the most famous vernacular performance of Christ's passion: the Oberammergau Passion Play. The fact that it was actually made on a rooftop in New York City did little to dent its popularity, and it initiated a long line of biblical epics. Indeed, the story of Christ played a central role in establishing cinema as a new kind of spectacle, providing the subject matter for the first American feature-length film, Kalem's *From the Manger to the Cross*, which lasted 80 minutes and was released in 1912 to great acclaim. Depictions that break with received notions of idealization can still provoke violent reactions, however. Performances of Martin Scorsese's recent film, *The Last Temptation of Christ*, for example, have been disrupted by demonstrations, damage to cinema screens, and bomb incidents. To understand why, we need to examine the current crisis of modernity and the range of religious responses it has prompted.

Over the last 15 years, an increasing number of commentators have come to view the culture of modernity as "exhausted" (Lyon, 1994, p. 6). They point to signs that the conceptual scaffolding that supported its structures of meaning is cracking and buckling. They see contemporary institutions laid open to the "inherently critical, restless, unsatisfied, insatiable 'drive to inquiry' originally deployed against the old order" (Bauman,1992, p. viii). The optimism promoted by the legitimating narrative of "progress" has collapsed, burned to ashes in the ovens of the

Nazi death camps and the firestorms of Hiroshima, Nagasaki, and Dresden. The patient application of scientific inquiry and calculating rationality produced manufactories of slaughter beyond the darkest gothic imaginings. Even the dividends of peace were increasingly soured as the environmental and human costs of economic growth were added up. And confronted with the AIDS epidemic, science could offer no cure, no consolation. Into this vacuum flowed apocalyptic visions of a new plague, a divine punishment for "unnatural" acts and sexual permissiveness. The limitless horizons of "progress" were replaced by an acute awareness of limits. The runaway expectations of improvements ran into a wall. The absence of meaning at the heart of modern culture, which Weber had identified as its fatal flaw, was exposed to full view. As David Harvey (1989) has argued, "The moral crisis of our time is a crisis of Enlightenment thought. . . . [T]he affirmation of 'self without God' in the end negated itself because reason, a means, was left, in the absence of God's truth, without any spiritual or moral goal" (p. 41).

The secular theology of consumption was increasingly unable to address this lack. Consumerism had always promised "something which it can't deliver" (Bauman, 1992, p. 225). Tangible improvements in well-being and the quality of life depend not only on personal possessions, but on the infrastructure of public goods, paid for out of taxation and equally available to all—clean air, drinkable water, libraries, parks. These amenities were fought for and won over the same period that saw the rise of consumerism. Consequently, the consumer system did not have to meet the full range of people's wants and desires. In the last two decades, however, the relentless rise of neoliberal economic policies has radically altered the balance between the public and market sectors in a number of advanced industrial societies. Public utilities have been sold to private investors, and commercial institutions have been urged to become more market-oriented. People have been exhorted to behave as consumers rather than citizens. They have been discouraged from thinking of themselves as members of moral and political communities, and invited instead to assert their rights to choice in the marketplace. But as the underpinnings provided by public goods are dismantled, the pleasures of possession are left to bear a greater and greater responsibility for delivering contentment and confirming personal identity and self-worth.

In the era of high modernity, consumption was inextricably bound up with the pleasures of immersion in the spectacle, diversity, and constant movement of the modern city. Window-shopping, browsing, and buying were integrated into a flow of unexpected juxtapositions and chance encounters. Now for many people the streets are sites of fear, and shopping has moved into the monitored spaces of the mall and the hypermarket. Security guards and video surveillance guarantee a safe and predictable experience. Differences and eccentricities are carefully controlled. Anyone who does not fit is expelled, leaving a space peopled entirely by shoppers.

But as Richard Sennett (1993) has argued, "The essence of developing as a human being is developing the capacity for ever more complex experience. If the experience of complexity is losing its value in the environment, we are threatened 'spiritually'" (p. 131). This process of "hollowing out" consumption is reinforced by major changes in working life. The emerging computerized technologies of production and control frequently de-skill workers, turning them into caretakers of machines that carry out the complex tasks they once performed themselves. "More brutally . . . large numbers of people are set free of routine tasks only to find themselves useless or, at best, under used" (Sennett, 1995, p. 13). In the callous lexicon of efficiency and "downsizing," they are blamed for their own redundancy. They have failed to make themselves of value. We have entered the age of the "dispensable self." Consumption could offset the boredom of the assembly line, but it cannot easily compensate for this deep loss of dignity and self worth.

Nor are those in professional and managerial jobs untouched by economic restructuring. For many, the prospect of a lifelong career has been replaced by permanent insecurity. "The corporate 'downsizing' of the 1980s [has] wiped away legions of bean-counting place-keepers, sweeping them into new jobs, unemployment or tightly marginalized 'consultancy' work" (Kane, 1995, p. 39). As material and job success become more difficult to guarantee, the task of constructing a viable self becomes more problematic (Pahl, 1995).

These three trends—the loss of faith in "progress," the intensified sense of meaningless at the heart of modernity, and the consumer system's increasing inability to compensate—have enlarged the space through which religion can reenter the mainstream of private and public life. The tide of history seems to have turned. As Rocco Buttiglione, a Catholic theologian, has put it, the present pope has not attacked the major secular philosophies of the 20th century because "they are the wave of the future" but because "their time has already passed" (quoted in Harvey, 1989, p. 41). Karol Wojtyla's election as pontiff in 1978, and his vigorous defense of conservative theological positions, can be seen as part of a wider fundamentalist current within Christianity.

Fundamentalism speaks to a popular "desire for impregnable certainty" and simplification in the face of the social dislocations and moral ambiguities of late modernity (Armstrong, 1995, p. 37). It sets out to explain and counter the confusion and disorder people experience, first, by "breathing fresh life into the vocabulary and categories of religious thought" (Kepel, 1994, p. 191), and second, by moving the expression of religious identity from the private sphere to the public domain and the policy agenda, sometimes with considerable success. In the United States, the Christian Coalition, an assembly of evangelical and fundamentalist groups that took control of the country's largest Protestant denomination, the Southern Baptist Convention, a decade ago, is currently the dominant force in the Republican Party in some 18 states (Bell, 1995, p. 17). Its influence is evident in the shift to the right on issues such as abortion, gay rights, and artistic freedom. Battles over these areas have been fought across all the major spaces of public culture, including the most central site: television.

Fundamentalists drew on the long American tradition of aggressive proselytizing and mobilized the style of the tent meeting and the revivalist crusade to launch a wave of televangelism, selling salvation through donation. They sought to reassure congregations drenched in consumerism that affluence is a sign of godliness. As a later disgraced evangelist on a local channel in San Diego, put it, in her signing-off phrase: "Remember, prosperity is your divine right."

These televized performances, with their carefully orchestrated interplay between preacher and congregation, beckoned viewers to join an extended community of believers. The continually revolving counter in the top corner of the screen, showing the money being pledged over the telephone, calibrated their sincerity.

The same search for meaning, certainty, and belonging in the face of a disintegrating culture of modernity also underpinned one of the other major religious reactions: the proliferation of sects and cults. Whereas televangelism mobilized virtual communities, they sought to build more durable solidarities. Some, like Scientology, offered routes to self-improvement, promising that their program of reorientation would enable adherents to reenter the mundane world better equipped to cope with flux and change. In return, they demanded total obedience and loyalty, construing any form of dissent or criticism as heresy. Other movements, such as the Unification Church (popularly known as the Moonies), took these demands a stage further. They are total institutions that completely envelop converts, requiring "a radical curtailment of privacy and personal choice" in return for a clear structure of community and security, based on absolute rules and values and explicit hierarchy (Martin, 1981, p. 223). This exchange of subservience for belonging finds its most visible and potent symbol in the mass Moonie weddings staged in sports stadiums, at which couples marry partners chosen for them by the church's leader, the Reverend Sun Myung Moon. As the father of one convert recounts in Don Delillo's (1992) novel *Mao II*:

> They are grouped in twos, eternal boy-girl they assemble themselves so tightly, crossing the vast outfield, that the effect is one of transformation. From a series of linked couples they become one continuous wave. . . . Karen's daddy watching from the grandstand, can't help thinking "this is the point. They're one body now." (p. 3)

Although the Moonies and a number of other fundamentalist sects have international followings, their support is primarily a response to the crisis of late modernity.

Institutionally, late modernity is built around two major axes: the nation-state and capitalist economic relations. But in many countries, these formations have only developed relatively recently. Political independence and full nationhood were frequently gained only after a long and bitter process of decolonization, but the full force of capitalism was often checked by substantial commitments to state planning, public ownership, and restrictions on foreign investment and enterprise. The past two decades, however, have seen a gathering crisis in this system of late-arriving modernity. The terminal problems and eventual collapse of the Soviet system and the introduction of "open door" economic policies in countries such as India and China, which had previously pursued strongly protectionist measures, has massively extended the reach of Western capitalism and consumerism. The construction of a more globalized culture has the effect of revitalizing meaning systems by promoting new and more intensive points of comparison (Waters, 1995, pp. 125-126). This movement, in turn, has reinforced the dissatisfaction with indigenous elites that has been gathering momentum for some time among the generation that grew up after independence and had no memory of the old corruptions. From the mid-1970s onward, this rising tide of discontent fed into a resurgence of fundamentalism "aimed no longer at adapting to secular values, but at recovering a sacred foundation for the organization of society" (Kepel, 1994, p. 2).

It would be a mistake, however, to see the growing strength of fundamentalist strands within Islam, Judaism, and Christianity in areas of the world that have only recently encountered the full force of capitalist modernity as a simple assertion of religious values. It is more useful to see them as a response to the crisis of late-arriving modernity that speaks to a range of anxieties through the rhetorics and rituals of faith. As the Japanese commentator Shoichi Inoue (1994) has put it, "Religions absorb anxiety and feed upon it. In plain terms, this is a new magic, paradoxically brought about by the 'liberation from magic'" (p. 221). Within fundamentalism, the division between sacred and secular is superimposed on a number of other dichotomies—pure/profane, tradition/modernity, national/imported, indigenous/Western—to construct a comprehensive, layered, and self-reinforcing worldview. The links among fundamentalism, nationalism, and anti-Americanism are particularly strong. As an ultra-Orthodox Jew who works as a kosher inspector of Jerusalem restaurants told a British journalist, "When a Jew, a pure soul, eats an impure animal, it destroys his soul, and he becomes a jungle man, an evil animal. . . . It's worse than Hitler. McDonald's is contaminating all of Israel, and all of the Jewish people" (Lancaster, 1995, p. 8).

The resurgence of fundamentalism in the three great religions of the Book aims to intervene in the process of capitalist modernity and the existing social and moral order "so as to bring it into line with the commands and values" of the holy texts (Kepel, 1994, p. 191). This necessarily involves a protracted struggle within the major institutions of public culture, to drive out or marginalize secular and "ungodly" views and values. Because of its centrality as a focus for modern identities, consumerism is a particular target. As the Catholic writer David Birch has observed, "Once powerful symbols of 'love,' 'grace,' 'charity,' 'wonder,' 'offering,' 'sacrifice,' 'light' and 'fellowship' are as much part of the advertiser's lexicon, his vocabulary, as they are of the liturgist, as such their meanings in relation to the church degenerate" (quoted in Martin, 1981, p. 229). Fundamentalism sets out to reclaim the language of devotion for the faithful and to reduce the reach of promotional culture, often resorting to coercion and censorship. In January 1995, for example, the Iranian parliament passed an order banning people from having satellite dish receivers on their roofs. The aim, as the interior minister Ali Mohammed Besharati explained, was to "immunize the people against the cultural invasion of the West" ("Tehran Detunes," 1995, p. 6).

Iran stands at one end of a continuum of relations among church, state, and communications, with the state sponsoring and drawing its legitimacy from a particular version of Islam and using the national communications system to promote this officially approved religious system. At the other end stands the United States, where there is no established church and where denominations and sects struggle for visibility and support in a commercialized communications system. Historically, many of the countries of Europe have stood somewhere in the middle, with an established church enjoying certain privileges within a public service broadcasting system. In England, for example, in the early days of BBC radio, there was no secular entertainment on Sundays. The airwaves were taken up with church services, sermons, and morally uplifting fare. This rigid separation between the religious and the mundane softened as time went on, but the church retained its favored position, with weekly relays of services from around the country and news stories of members of the royal family at worship serving as insistent reminders of the links among church, state, and national tradition.

The triangular relations between religion, the state, and the communications system can thus be usefully thought of as organized along two main dimensions: the degree of religious disestablishing (as measured by the relative prevalence of government subsidy or interference in religion) (Iannaccone, 1991, pp. 160-163), and the relative balance between public enterprise and commercial entrepreneurship, and national and transnational cultural forms, within core sectors of the communications system. This classification system offers a serviceable basic starting point for a comparative study of the shifting relations between religion and communications in the contemporary world, but it falls some way short of what is needed for a comprehensive analysis.

Most research to date has concentrated on the established media: the press, broadcasting, cinema. There has been comparatively little work on emerging media such as video, satellite television, broadband networks, and virtual reality systems. At one level, these innovations continue the process begun by established media, extending religious observance and participation further in space and time as with the huge audiences around the globe reached by established religious figures by satellite. But they also offer the prospect of new kinds of religious rallies and rituals. A devout Jew can send a fax to Jerusalem and have a prayer said for him or her at the Wailing Wall. Dispersed believers may follow the lead provided by Paternal, the World Wide Web site established by the disgraced Catholic bishop, Jacques Gaillot, and come together over the Internet but never meet physically. Participants in virtual reality systems may step into a biblical story and "navigate" their way around it, using a variety of routes and personae. Vernacular, unofficial expressions of religious conviction and belief can be widely reproduced and circulated on videotape and audio cassette. These developing possibilities have an uneasy, and as yet largely unexplored, relation to the institutionalized relations between the religious and media systems of individual nation-states. On the one hand, they offer a powerful new ensemble of mechanisms for extending the reach of the major religious organizations. On the other, a number also provide channels for grassroots initiatives that bypass official structures.

Exploring the shifting interplay between established and emerging communication systems and the contemporary forms of the religious life they are constructing is a major task for future research. But as I have argued, it must be seen not as a specialized topic in media studies or the sociology of religion, but as part of a wider effort to understand the institutional and cultural transformations of modernity and the dynamics of re-enchantment. To understand the present and to make informed guesses about the near future, we need to return to the central themes of inquiry and speculation that lie at the core of the human sciences' long struggle to make sense of the contemporary world.

References

Archer, M. S. (1988). *Culture and agency: The place of culture in social theory*. Cambridge, UK: Cambridge University Press.
Armstrong, K. (1995, July 21). Spiritual Prozac. *New Statesman and Society*, pp. 37-38.
Bauman, Z. (1992). *Intimations of postmodernity*. London: Routledge & Kegan Paul.
Bell, D. (1995, June 9). The disunited states of America. *Times Literary Supplement*, pp. 16-17.
Berger, P. (1969). *The sacred canopy: Elements of a sociological theory of religion*. Garden City, NY: Anchor.

Campbell, C. (1987). *The romantic ethic and the spirit of modern consumerism.* Oxford, UK: Basil Blackwell.

Christie, I. (1994). *The last machine: Early cinema and the birth of the modern world.* London: British Film Institute.

Davie, G. (1994). *Religion in Britain since 1945: Believing without belonging.* Oxford, UK: Basil Blackwell.

Delillo, D. (1992). *Mao II.* London: Vintage.

Durant, H. (1938). *The problem of leisure.* London: Routledge & Kegan Paul.

Gellner, E. (1987). The rubber cage: Disenchantment with disenchantment. In *Culture, Identity and Politics.* Cambridge, UK: Cambridge University Press.

Gerth, H. H., & Mills, C. W. (Eds.). (1974). *From Max Weber—Essays in sociology.* London: Routledge & Kegan Paul. (Originally published 1948)

Harris, R. (1996). Openings, absences and omissions: Aspects of the treatment of "race," culture and ethnicity in British cultural studies. *Cultural Studies, 10*(2), 334-344.

Harrison, T., & Madge, C., (Eds.). (1986). *Britain by mass observation.* London: Cresset Library.

Harvey, D. (1989). *The condition of postmodernity.* Oxford, UK: Basil Blackwell.

Hoggart, R. (1959). *The uses of literacy.* Harmondsworth, UK: Penguin.

Hoggart, R. (1988). *A local habitation: Life and times. Vol. 1: 1918-1940.* London: Chatto & Windus.

Iannaccone, L. R. (1991). The consequences of religious market structure. *Rationality and Society, 3,* 156-177.

Inoue, S. (1994). Religions old and new. In A. Ueda (Ed.), *The electric geisha: Exploring Japan's popular culture* (pp. 220-228). Tokyo: Kodansha International.

Kane, P. (1995, November 10). Not by bread alone. *New Statesman and Society,* pp. 39-40.

Kepel, G. (1994). *The revenge of God: The resurgence of Islam, Christianity and Judaism in the modern world.* Oxford, UK: Polity.

Lancaster, J. (1995, August 3). Big Macs and Jacko Rock Israeli culture. *The Guardian,* p. 8.

Lears, J. (1994). *Fables of abundance: A cultural history of advertising in America.* New York: Basic Books.

Lévi-Strauss, C. (1995, September 1). The river of sorrows. *Times Higher Education Supplement,* pp. 15-17.

Lodge, D. (1995). *Therapy: A novel.* London: Quality Paperbacks Direct.

Lyon, D. (1994). *Postmodernity.* Buckingham: Open University Press.

Martin, B. (1981). *A sociology of contemporary cultural change.* Oxford, UK: Basil Blackwell.

Pahl, R. (1995). *After success: fin-de-siécle anxiety and identity.* Oxford, UK: Polity.

Sennett, R. (1993). *The conscience of the eye: The design and social life of cities.* London: Faber and Faber.

Sennett, R. (1995, September 22). Something in the city: The spectre of uselessness and the search for a place in the world. *Times Literary Supplement,* pp. 13-15.

Smart, B. (1993). *Postmodernity.* London: Routledge & Kegan Paul.

Tehran detunes Western culture. (1995, April 18). *The Guardian,* p. 6.

Warner, R. S. (1993). Work in progress toward a new paradigm for the sociological study of religion in the United States. *American Journal of Sociology, 98,* 1044-1093.

Waters, M. (1995). *Globalisation.* London: Routledge & Kegan Paul.

Weber, M. (1958). *The Protestant ethic and the spirit of capitalism.* New York: Scribner.

Williams, R. (1980). *Problems in materialism and culture.* London: Verso.

Wright, P. (1995, March 3). Rooting in the greenery, *The Guardian,* p. 19.

Chapter 16

Mass Media as a Site of Resacralization of Contemporary Cultures

Jesús Martín-Barbero

In recent years, I have become increasingly aware of the profound changes in the way people come together socially and how they relate to each other when they are together. I think that this constitutes, at the deepest level, the object of the study of human communication. What does, in fact, bring people together socially? This is connected, I would argue, with the study of the media as the locus of the constitution of identities and as a space for configuration of communities. The media are, above all, a factor in the differentiation of various types of communities. This implies, of course, that the media are not just economic phenomena or instruments of politics. Nor are the media interesting simply as one more instance of rapid technological change. Rather, the media must be analyzed as a process of creating cultural identities and of bringing individuals into coherent publics that are "subjects of action." To conceptualize the relations of modernity, religiosity, and media, one must see the media as a central factor in the constitution of social actors.

▓ The Disenchanted Modernity

I begin this chapter with the affirmation that modernity has not lived up to many of its promises of social, political, or cultural liberation. But there is one promise that it has fulfilled: the disenchantment of the world.

Modernity has drained off the sense of the sacred, in large part, because it has rationalized the world. The reduction of values to instrumental efficiency has left the world without magic and without mystery. Today one finds a whole generation of young people who are living, in their daily experience, what Weber (1947, 1958) has called the disenchantment of the world. I think that it is almost impossible for many people to comprehend what it means for the young to live the dizzy pace of today or the ecstasy of drugs if one does not see this in relation to the profound loss of awe and fearful reverence that pervades contemporary cultures. Every aspect of our experience reflects this disenchantment, from our blind faith in empirical science to insensitivity to environmental pollution, but especially the superficiality of social relations. In virtually all of us, especially in those who have drunk in the rationality of formal education, the disappearance of the holy has changed the way we see the world.

And yet modernity, for all its power of control over nature, has left its sense of emptiness. Few people have learned to live without some form of enchantment, mystery, mythic vision, and some ritual moments. Strangely enough, we continue to seek ways to re-enchant the world, bring back the magic, and clothe our lives with mystery.

One of the most lucid social analysts of our time, Daniel Bell (1994), a sociologist ready to declare the end of utopian thinking, has argued that the real problem with modernity is a kind of crisis of spiritual vision. The old foundations of our culture are now buried and the new have turned out to be illusory. Such an affirmation is interesting because Bell by no means holds a brief for religious apologetic. And in Latin America, Beatriz Sarlo (1994) writes in one of her recent articles that in the last twenty years, where once people were inspired by socio-political movements, today the new religions are advancing.

Closely linked to this pervasive rationalization of the world are the phenomena of fundamentalist, sectarian, and integralist movements that are once again implanting themselves on our planet precisely when we thought we had risen above all that. This is in part a reaction against the forces of modernization and in part filling the void—especially at the level of popular religiosity—of the sense of unchanging absolutes. In the midst of rapid cultural changes, people look for foundations beyond human construction where they can anchor their personal and social identities. In some cases, such as the case of former-Yugoslavia, these fundamentalisms are a mixture of religion and ethnic nationalism. In other cases, the fundamentalist anxiety strikes back in the form of violent, racist hatred, such as the skinheads in Germany who see the immigrant Turks as so threatening that they feel they have the right to kill them as "invaders." In virtually all forms of fundamentalism, the media play a central role in this search for identity and in the attempt to affirm that the religious and the sacred can be the basis for significant social actors in a modernizing world.

I would like here to explore the phenomenon of disenchantment primarily in the Latin American context. It is not easy to give an account of the relations of modernity, religion, and media on this continent because secularization has such a different connotation here. In cultures that have experienced an ongoing confrontation between Catholicism and the liberal Enlightenment, the extreme ideological polarization has colored the concept of secularization with layers of misunderstanding. Indeed, one can say that Latin Americans, caught between poles of integralisms, have lived the relation between religion and modernity in a quite schizophrenic manner. On the one hand, modernity is synonymous with the triumph of reason, equality, democratic participation, and progress. For persons who think in this manner, religion is simply a matter of the past: irrational obscurantism and the remnant of an uneducated peasant society.

In contrast, those with religious commitment have tended to identify modernity with atheism. Dating from the condemnation of "modernism" by Pius X, modernity has been associated with a society abandoned to the forces of evolution and to beliefs in naturalistic determinism that destroy values of tradition. For those with this perspective, modernity means secular humanism and an individualism that makes a communitarian commitment impossible. Thus, in Latin America, our lived perception of secularization is characterized by this radical split of worldviews and a Manichean polarization. One is supposed to make a choice between becoming modern or remaining a believer. Whereas, in countries such as the United States, modernity not only is equivalent to being religious or has its foundations in religious belief (Bellah, Madsen, Sullivan, Swidler,

& Tipton, 1985), in Latin America we have faced an irreducible opposition of worldviews.

To understand this radically polarized conception of secularization, one must go back to the explanation of secularization suggested by Max Weber (1958). First, for Weber, a secular, modern world is not only a world without gods, but a world completely rationalized, a world guided by a scientific reasoning that destroys the foundations of a magico-mysterious perception of human existence. Second, Weber understood the secular world to be a world in which experience is without an ultimate meaning. No longer are there realities that have meaning in themselves and that can be a starting point "outside our constructed reality." What guides the world, in this explanation, is a type of instrumental rationality that Weber called, with a very apt metaphor, "a cage of iron." Persons now come to live in a world that is so entirely constructed by human logic that it becomes for them an inescapable cage because the reasoning that guides human destiny is concerned only with instrumental means, without reference to any ulterior ends.

Finally, the secular means the breaking apart of the old certainties that have supported the communitarian integration of the city. Because we can no longer assume the existence of community, we have to make enormous efforts to somehow find the kind of sociability that we have associated with community.

I have found Gellner's (1989) rephrasing of the position of Weber a particularly apt one:

> What Weber meant by disenchantment is the Faust-like acquisition of cognitive, technological and administrative power. We have acquired diabolical capacities by trading off our world full of meaning, a meaning humanly experienced even if risky and threatening, for a world that we can manipulate. We have abandoned that insecure world for a world that is predictable and much more manageable, but a world that is coldly indifferent and insipid.

This is the matrix of the concept of secularization. It is a world ruled by instrumental rationality—cold, pragmatic, and functional. To this, one would have to add, from the tradition of the sociology of religion, two other elements. First, as Hegel emphasized, a secular world is an entirely human project, created out of our images and desires, an objectivation of the consciousness and creativity of humans. Second, a secular world is an autonomous world, a world in which the state, society, culture, and art have made themselves more and more independent of religion and have created their own bases of social power. This is a world that has progressively won its cultural, ideological, and cognitive freedom and that no longer needs justification from beliefs, creeds, and religious institutions. Once cultures cut their ties to religious institutions they become diverse and complex, no longer following univocal paths of evolution. Consequently, this kind of culture does not provide a substratum of meaning that can be linked with any form of religion or any form of church (Rahner, 1969).

▨ How Secularization Has Been Lived and Thought From the Perspective of Latin America

In a very schematic way, I would like to sketch out two Latin American conceptions of secularization. The first is what I would call a *historicist* perspective, represented, for example, in the work of the Chilean, Pedro Morande (1984), a sociologist for whom modernity in Latin America is characterized by the secular politicization of faith. By this, Morande means that the history of these peoples, which was once identified with religious institutions, has become identified with their nation-states. In Latin America, he would argue, the conception of history, through influences as diverse as textbooks and political rhetoric, has gradually found its principle of unity in its sociopolitical project and in the development of the nation-state. Whatever may have been its origins, the history of the peoples has become identified with the history of the states. It has been forgotten that there were once other symbols around which community was formed, other cultural syntheses and other mediating institutions through which these peoples expressed the richness and the tragedy of their own history. Among these other social contexts, there was, above all, the church. According to Pedro Morande, the history texts of Latin America have lost the memory of the profoundly important role of the church as a specific space for social meeting and a place for cultural synthesis. More concretely, the histories of Latin America have forgotten what was called *barroco*. The Latin American baroque, one of the periods of greatest creativity and cultural synthesis, has been covered over to make way for a political-economic unity that allows us to find our identities in the nation-state.

The historicist conception of secularization in Latin America has also tended to rewrite the religious history in a way that popular religiosity and the formal rationality of ecclesiastical institutions conflates as one thing. Fortunately, according to Pedro Morande, this mistaken conception never gained much importance because popular religiosity is still, in Latin America, the strongest link of cultural continuity in these countries. Popular religiosity, never absorbed by the institutional church, is precisely what enables Latin American culture to respond so differently to the abstract universalism of modern functionalist rationality. Popular culture is a form of resistance, and popular religiosity is one of the major cultural resources that helps Latin America to resist the instrumental rationality of modernity.

Another current of thought about secularization in Latin America is the *populist* conception. The theologian Díaz-Alvarez (1978) presents an example of this view quite clearly when he argues that atheism, as a type of secularization that denies any meaning to religion, is something that has affected only a small minority among the dominant elites. The great mass of people, especially the popular classes, constitute the true cultural memory and moral strength of these countries. Díaz-Alvarez argues that for the majority of the people, religion has continued to be the source of meaning in life and a powerful influence for the preservation of moral integrity.

At the same time, Díaz-Alvarez recognizes that the popular religiosity carries strong elements of fatalism, ritualism, and blind devotion to saintly patrons that dilute the strength of the humanity and moral intuition inherent in this religious culture.

Díaz-Alvarez also admits that many important social sectors of Latin America, such as intellectuals and educators, are being absorbed into a secularized culture. He is concerned about the fact, and I think rightly, that the historical churches, especially the Catholic Church, have not been able to develop a discourse that captures the interest of young people. As young people become increasingly indifferent to religious and moral commitment, we are seeing a slow but important growth of secularization.

It is quite significant, however, that both the historicist and populist conceptions of secularization sidestep the question of the power of the

churches over social and cultural institutions. For Latin America, secularization has not been a question of atheistic rationalism, but rather of a
desire for autonomy from the church in the areas of politics, the state,
sexuality, and artistic culture. One still finds countries where the state is
strongly tied to the church, where the church feels it has the right to
manage and manipulate the field of education and blackmail the area of
culture. I think that in questions of autonomy from ecclesiastical imposi-
tion, the Enlightenment project of secularization is still very much alive.
As Alan Touraine (1992) has put it, a modern society is not indifferent to
religion or liberated from religion. Modern society is one that defends the
separation of the temporal and spiritual spheres, without the disappearance of the spiritual. With modernity, we have found a way to maintain
simultaneously the affirmation of the personal subject with the various
freedoms and rights that this entails: the freedom of conscience, the
freedom of convictions, and the right to resist the destruction of collective
identities.

▓ The Re-Enchantment of the World

How is the world being re-enchanted? I would say that this leads to
still another question: What remains of ritual in public performance and
entertainment? (Baudrillard, 1993). Or, better put, What remains of ritual
in the mass media?

My premise is that the mass media are not just a phenomenon of
commercial or ideological manipulation, but are, rather, a cultural phenomenon to be understood by anthropology and other cultural sciences.
The mass media are the places where many people—indeed, an increasing number of people—construct the meaning of their lives. The media
offer the opportunity for people to come together to understand the
central questions of life, from the meaning of art to the meaning of death,
of sickness, of youth, of beauty, of happiness, and of pain. Thus, I am
suggesting that we should look for the processes of re-enchantment in the
continuing experience of ritual in communitarian celebration and in the
other ways that the media bring people together. We must ask what
remains of ritual and community celebration in the Olympic Games, the
political rally, rock concerts, and the huge television contests. This will
help us understand the phenomenon of the electronic church.

The electronic church has its roots in the popular religiosity of the United States, but it has extended into Latin America through the Pentecostal churches and the intensive use of the mass media (Assmann, 1988). The electronic church has been part of a veritable cultural revolution in Latin America: the conversion of millions of people to the Protestant sects and, in particular, the passing of millions of Catholics to the world of the most fundamentalist churches such as the Pentecostals.

This phenomenon has occurred both in the world of rural, indigenous peoples in areas such as Chiapas in Mexico—I am thinking of the splendid study of Gilberto Jimenez (1989) describing the presence of the evangelical churches in Chiapas—and in the more urbanized parts of Latin America, such as Argentina and Brazil, where millions of Catholics have entered the Protestant churches.

The electronic church has a far more profound meaning than most people suspect. It is not simply that some churches have used the media to project their sermons to a larger audience or have used a variety of media and genres to reach many new sectors of the public. Rather, in my opinion, the significance is that some churches have been able to transform radio and television into a new, fundamental "mediation" for the religious experience. That is, the medium is not simply a physical amplification of the voice, but rather adds a quite new dimension to religious contact, religious celebration, and personal religious experience. To demonstrate this, I quote from an article by an Argentinean, Pablo Seman (1993), describing a Pentecostal ceremony in Buenos Aires recently:

> Today we are going to create a "holy scandal," the pastor proclaims to thirty thousand people in the middle of a massive revivalist meeting that has lasted eight hours. A feminine voice is humming in the background, rising above the deep counterpart of the drums and the sound of guitars falling away. Now the preacher, his voice swelling to a crescendo in a commanding tone, drowns out the woman as he exhorts, "You are the spouses of the Lord." While the evangelist prays and preaches, the voice-over of the television anchorman provides a plaintive counterpart of "Amen!" "Yes, Lord!" "Come now, Jesus!" in the foreground. Now the choir comes in with its part, "Raise me up, Lord! Break me up, Lord! Lord, consume me with your love!" Then the huge chorus pleads, "Oh come, Holy Spirit" with trembling body and voice. Now the sound dies away, and a kind of silence falls over the crowd. In this scene, there may be particular actors who stand out, but the coming of the Holy Spirit in

a trance-like experience is the customary high point that the mass seeks and feels together as one body.

This is not simply a time of worship, but a media event. From time to time, gospel rock groups take the stage, leading the people in an intense dance, some people swirling by themselves, others twisting and turning in unison. Some walk around with home video cameras to catch some of the action for later showing in their local assemblies. There are dozen of counselors circulating among the masses of people with walkie-talkies. A preacher dances frenetically before a huge screen that projects the words of the hymns.

Nothing of this seems to be coordinated. It appears to emanate from the urban cultural experience which the cultural process of the cult seems to know how to take into account as if all were planned.

To me, this account shows that the electronic church is supplying the magic that established religions have intellectualized, made cold and disenchanted. The electronic church has taken hold of the technologies of the image and of the sentiments to capture the messianic, apocalyptic exaltation of the feelings. This gives a face and a voice to the new tribal cults, the new sects, and the new communes. For these communities, ritual and moral norms are far more important than theological doctrine.

Thus, as the Catholic Church and some historical Protestant churches grow rational and intellectualized, the Pentecostals, charismatics, and other apocalyptic groups are making ritual and celebration the focal point of religious experience. And these movements are carrying this experience out of the churches into homes and circles of friends through the mass media. Radio—FM, short wave, and, increasingly, local stations—is by far the most important medium at present. Television, however, is finding ways not only to broadcast religious worship but to intensify and magnify the religious experience itself. Through the use of media, the fundamentalist churches have learned to transform the media into a mediation that is fundamental to the new forms of religious experience; and these churches are now in tune with the popular sectors of Latin America. The Catholic Church has somehow lost the wave length of the masses, especially the young people, in part, I think, because this Protestant tradition has understood that the media are a way to re-enchant the world. The media are the way to transform the everyday life of the people into magic.

For intellectuals, there remains little magic in the world. But for the great majority of people, the media are mysterious, magic, exciting, and enchanting with the melodrama, the star system, the ability to create the drama of the Olympic Games, the frenzy of gigantic sports contests (more real than the actual sports contests), and the spectacle of televised religious revivals. Somehow the media have eliminated the distance between the sacred and the profane. The walls around the sacred that the religions have protected so jealously have been broken down by the media. Television, especially, has introduced magic into the realm of the profane and has made secular what once was sacred. Without doubt, the sacred has undergone a trivialization, but at the same time, the sacred is penetrating into the recesses of everyday life. I am thinking, for example, of how advertising spots make enchanting even the most humble and routine tasks of daily life. Even the simple activities of washing, scrubbing, cleaning, and ironing have been transfigured, made poetic, and somehow raised to transcendence. Just think of how advertising makes a bottle of Coca-Cola a magic source of energy, beauty, and wisdom—the source of life and youth itself.

Television is the place for the visualization of our common myths. I refer to myth, not in the sense of R. Barthes (1974) (a form of ideology), but in the deeper anthropological interpretation: myths as the source of cultural unity, the myths that cause and remove deep anxieties, the myths that protect us from the terror of chaos, and the myths that save us. We find our motivating symbols in our myths, from the myths that give meaning to the life of the poor to the myths that sustain our poor life. It is television that is articulating and catalyzing the integrating myths of our societies. What are the myths of our countries if not our football stars, our rock groups, our champion boxers? The people live their deep identification with their idols and their stars in television.

As trivial and superficial as these symbols may seem, television has a deep resonance with the capacity and necessity of the people to be "someone." And people feel themselves to be someone to the degree that they identify with *Someone*—someone on whom they can project their fears, someone capable of assuming and silencing these fears.

For those of us who for years now have been studying the cultural meaning of *telenovelas*, this discussion of re-enchantment leads to important reflections. Why do drama programs occupy such a large part of Latin American television, and why is drama continuing to be ever more important? Is it not because drama is the basic form of ritual? Is it not because the people find in television drama a way to ritualize their fears, their joys, and the tasks of their daily lives? Despite the limitations of the *telenovelas*—the bad acting, the reactionary themes, the poverty of aesthetic expression—there is, in the dramatization, a poetic moment, an almost frightening poetic mysteriousness, that permits people to break out of the monotonous cocoon of their daily routines and re-enchant their lives.

If, indeed, the media and religion are coming together, then perhaps it is because they are fundamental cultural mediations of the need felt by the people to transform them into magic, into mystery, and into the seduction of the world. We would find, then, that something very curious has happened. Despite all the promise of modernity to make religion disappear, what has really happened is that religion has modernized itself (Gil-Calvo, 1993). Religion has shown itself capable of eating modernity alive and making modernity an important ingredient for its own purposes. What we are witnessing, then, is not the conflict of religion and modernity, but the transformation of modernity into enchantment by linking new communication technologies to the logic of popular religiosity.

Three Questions About Religion, Media, and Society

The Catholic Church and the religiosity of the Catholic Church have been central factors in the development of Latin American culture. Today, there are three contradictory questions that one must confront in understanding the religious transformations in Latin America. As a form of conclusion, I would like to address these questions.

1. *Is not the religiosity of the less-favored classes—whether this be the popular religiosity of Catholicism or the new forms of Pentecostalism—a factor influencing subordination to the dominant classes?*

It is very difficult to deny that there is, in religious beliefs and practices, an element of alienation, of conformism, and of the uncritical acceptance of an unjust order. But it would be unjust and false to reduce religiosity to this. No one will deny that on continents such as Latin America, religion has been associated with power. Indeed, popular religiosity has often been seduced into being an accomplice of power, domination, and subjugation and has lost the capacity to make an independent criticism of power.

Religion and the church have also been a fundamental element in the historical memory of the people. Religion enables many to discover the meaning of life, to create a cultural synthesis, and to develop indigenous cultures. It is necessary to look at both faces of such a complex and contradictory phenomenon—both the complicity with totalitarian religions and inquisitions, and the sense of cultural identity of the popular classes.

2. *Why have the historical churches in Latin America—especially the Catholic Church—seemingly lost their capacity to challenge and inspire the urban masses, the youth, and the popular classes?*

In fact, the historical churches, particularly the Catholic Church, have been deeply involved in the liberation struggles of Latin America in the past 40 years. For the Catholic Church, the Second Vatican Council set in motion a great deal of self-criticism regarding its complicity with structures of power. There have been powerful currents of honest examination of the manipulation of popular credulity (for example, the devotion to the saints) and the superficiality of the experience of religious commitment.

The theology of liberation went far beyond self-criticism and not only stimulated a questioning of complicity with dominant classes on the part of the churches but also released a spiritual energy to nourish revolutionary movements. To see this side of the church, we must examine the meaning of the movement of the base communities in Brazil and the role of the Catholic Church in Chile in the darkest days of the people's struggle with the Pinochet dictatorship. In these and other contexts, the churches have been a support and a source of energy to sustain the memory and values of a civil society. The theology of liberation awakened energies that have shown the possibility of a religiosity that not only is not alienating and does not numb revolutionary aspirations, but that instead has been an important inspiration to transform, diversify, and revitalize societies.

It is my view, however, that the churches still retain too much social power in Latin America. If the church wishes to rebuild its links with the popular sectors and with the young people, it must renounce any pretension of imposing its cultural power. In some countries, the Catholic Church still attempts to gain a privileged position over other confessions and to retain its ability to manipulate political processes. As long as the church attempts to impose a cultural monopoly and sustain its position by cooperating with the most reactionary power groups of these countries, church leaders will not understand what the popular classes are suffering and will not be able to comprehend the discourse of the younger generations.

3. *What is the significance of the renaissance of shamanism, spiritualism, and other forms of traditional indigenous religion in the cities of Latin America?*

The paradoxical rebirth of religious and magical practices from our rural past in the midst of our great Latin America cities is an aspect of the "ruralization" of our societies that can be traced back, in my view, to the political economic policies of our times.

In a period of little more than 40 years, many Latin American countries have changed from being largely rural, with some 75% of the population in agriculture or in small villages, to being largely urban, with more than 70% in huge cities. But at same time, we are witnessing the impoverishment of the lower-middle classes and the working classes due to the neoliberal policies that discourage social investment and favor high-technology employment. This means that the majority of the people in the cities are learning to survive on the basis of a kind of urban subsistence economy that mixes rural solidarity and traditional practices with the new skills of the city. This affects all aspects of urban life among the lower-middle and popular classes. For example, people are once again learning to get by with a mixture of indigenous herbal medicine and modern medicines. This cultural and socioeconomic context is also affecting the religious practices in that a curious mixture of urban secularization, importation of oriental cults, New Age lifestyles, and rural magic and spiritualism is taking shape.

This new urban religious culture is such a widespread phenomenon that forms of it may now be found in all social classes of the city. Among young people of the professional classes, for example, one finds the attractions of New Age and oriental religions linking up with traditional shamanism and "re-semanticizing" even the traditional religiosity inherited in Catholic families. We are witnessing a kind of new foundational religious logic growing up in the urban areas.

▨ The Tribalization of Modern Cultures

In the background of this re-enchantment of modern cities is a profound change in the way young people construct their social life. The youth of today are very much like nomadic tribes.

The new diversity of our cultures is lived by young people as a source of wealth. Although adults still fear this diversity and pluralism, young people love to move from one cultural identity to another. Identification with the cultures of media, especially the culture of popular music, is strikingly important in discovering and experimenting with new identities. For young people, music is not just entertainment, but a language, a way of expressing their dissatisfactions, their anger, their confusion, and their search. The diversity of this music gives birth to a multitude of tribes and communities. There is not just rock music, but plastic rock, authentic rock, rock of the 60s, rock of the 90s, and an endless invention of other musical styles. In all of their searching, young people take to this diversity with an energy and force that enables them to rapidly identify, disidentify, and reidentify with cultures and thus escape the pressure to any one commitment.

Why is this like nomadic tribes? There is no attachment to one particular place. Identity does not come from any place, but rather young people give identity to places, at least for a short, passing moment. Their identities are temporary. This is in striking contrast to older conceptions of identity for a whole life and attachment to a particular place that is semi-sacred, not for religious reasons, but because the place has such affective and symbolic importance (Herlinghams & Walter, 1994). Young people do not live in such a relationship with a defined territory. Rather it is the tribe, the group that in a given moment decides to convert a discotheque, the street corner of a neighborhood, or a village square into "our" place. For this moment, the youthful tribe marks the place with their graffiti; they put up their symbols there and take possession of it. Nation-states now have far less power of attracting identification than does the terrain of the cities. People now live close to the landmarks of their cities, but from a global, transnational perspective. People have developed such a global vision, in large part, because the globe is brought to them by the media. They thus feel at home in just about any part of the globe or in any world, real or imagined.

The patch of soil, the native village, the consecrated church and temple have ceased to have a power of enchantment. Instead, the mass media create symbols of the sacred; and the youthful nomadic tribes, identifying with these totems, have learned how to make holy and enchanted any place they decide to inhabit.

References

Assmann, H. (1988). *La iglesia electrónica y su impacto en América Latina*. San José, Costa Rica: D.E.I.

Barthes, R. (1974). *Mythologies*. London: Cape.

Baudrillard, J. (1993). *La illusión del fin*. Barcelona: Anagrama.

Bell, D. (1994). La Europa del siglo XXI. In *Claves de razón práctica*, No. 44. Madrid.

Bellah, R., Madsen, R., Sullivan, R., Swidler, A., & Tipton, S. (1985). *Habits of the heart: Individualism and commitment in American life*. Berkeley: University of California Press.

Díaz-Alvarez, M. (1978). *Pastoral y secularización en América Latina*. Bogotá: Ediciones Paulinas.

Gellner, E. (1989). La jaula de goma: Desencanto con el desencanto. In *Culture, identidad y política*. Barcelona: Gedisa.

Gil-Calvo, E. (1993). Rituales modernos de salvación. In *Claves de la razón práctica*, No. 38. Madrid.

Herlinghams, H., & Walter, M. (Eds.). (1994). *Postmodernidad en la periferia*. Berlin: Langer Verlag.

Jimenez, G. (1989). Nuevas dimensiones de la cultura popular: Las sectas religosas en México. In *Estudios de culturas contemporâneas*, No. 7. Colima, México.

Morande, P. (1984). *Cultura y modernidad en América Latina*. Santiago, Chile: Univ. Católica de Chile.

Rahner, K. (1969). *Secularización y ateismo*. Madrid: Ediciones Paulinas.

Sarlo, B. (1994). *Escenas de la vida postmoderna*. Buenos Aires: Ariel.

Seman, P. (1993) Pentecostales: Un cristianismo inesperado. *Punto de vista*, No. 47. Buenos Aires: Ariel.

Touraine, A. (1992) *Critique de la modernité*. Paris: Fayard.

Weber, M. (1958) *The Protestant ethic and the spirit of capitalism*. New York: Scribner.

Chapter 7

Escape From Time
Ritual Dimensions of Popular Culture

Gregor Goethals

In contemporary American society, religion is a personal, highly individual matter. Yet throughout popular culture, particularly in sports and entertainment, communal values and dreams effervesce and form themselves into public mythologies and rites. During the recent baseball strike, many commentators noted that something important was missing in the American psyche. The rhythm of the "boys of summer" was cut short; the accustomed entry and exit into the ball park—real or televised—was not there for us as an escape from ordinariness. We could not, to use A. Bartlett Giamatti's (1989) phrase, "take time for paradise."

For many years now, scholars have used *ritual* as a metaphor to understand the unifying vitality of some events in popular culture (Goethals, 1981). In this chapter, I would like to reexamine this paradigm. First, I will look at formal elements used to make connections between ancient ceremonies and contemporary happenings in sports and entertainment, focusing particularly on traditional rituals' exterior boundaries—space and time. A closer look at these may point up both similarities

117

and differences. Following this, I will turn to the interior dimensions of traditional religious rites, particularly the experience of transcendence. Here our comparisons may become more strained, causing us to qualify our basic metaphor further. A reexamination of these two foci—the external formal dimension and the internal spiritual transformation—may indicate how we can say both "yes" and "no" as we use religious rituals to illuminate aspects of popular secular culture.

▥ Exterior Boundaries: Time and Space

Scholars frequently draw attention to the formal properties of carefully orchestrated actions framed in units of time and space. Ritual essentially constitutes, in Victor Turner's (1977) words, "formal behavior," an ordered process in time, distinct from ordinary routine. These patterned actions in time and space are, he notes, generally oriented to "mystical beings or powers." Barbara G. Myerhoff (1977) has similarly emphasized the importance of the morphological elements of ritual, observing that ordering is often that aspect which most obviously sets ritual apart from other activities. A wedding, for example, is a special framing of time and space in which a man and a woman make marriage vows. For Sally F. Moore and Barbara G. Myerhoff (1977), ritual is "a container, a vessel which holds something" (p. 8). In another context, Myerhoff (1977) writes,

> The most salient characteristic of ritual is its function as a frame. It is a deliberate and artificial demarcation. In ritual, a bit of behavior or interaction, an aspect of social life, a moment in time is selected, stopped, remarked upon. (p. 200)

This framing, she says, may be secular or religious in nature.

Previously, philosopher Ernst Cassirer (1956) wrote that among the earliest constructed symbolic forms, space was paramount. He analyzed the basic action taken in the creation of sacred space, the establishment of boundaries that set apart a special place:

> Hallowing begins when a specific zone is detached from space as whole, when it is distinguished from other zones and one might say religiously hedged around. (p. 99)

Citing a classical scholar, Heinrich Nissen, Cassirer pointed out that the root of the Greek word for *temple* means "to cut," signifying that an area has been spatially set apart from ordinary terrain. Moreover, Cassirer maintained that every mythically significant content and each extraordinary experience that takes us out of commonplace situations has its own "ring of existence, a walled-in zone separated from its surroundings by fixed limits" (p. 103). Through this separation, the space achieves an individual religious form.

Bounded spaces could be sheltered or open. Historian Walter Burkert (1985) has written that for the living religious cult in Greece, the outdoor altar was critical to defining the sacred space. It was the altar space at the east that formed the sacred boundary, not the interior space of the temple. Great religious festivals took place in the open air, where people could parade around the temple. While the sacrifice took place at the altar, the participants, like the temple itself, looked toward the east. "So the pious man stands, as it were, beneath the eyes of the deity; but it's not the inner space of the temple which draws him in" (p. 92).

Historian of religion Jonathan Z. Smith (1987) also underscored the importance of place. For him, ritual is fundamentally a "mode of paying attention" or "a process of marking interest." A temple, he says, functions as a "focusing lens." Within the marked-off space, ordinary objects and actions become "sacred" by being there. Nothing, he says, is inherently sacred or profane; for these are not substantive categories, but "situational ones." Sacredness is essentially a category of emplacement (pp. 103-104). Thus ritual derives its power from the fact that ordinary activities occur in an extraordinary setting without which there would be no sense of difference between the "now" of ritual place and the "now" of everyday experience (p. 110).

Temporal boundaries, like spatial ones, are essential to ritual. Cassirer (1956) pointed out that long before human consciousness developed basic definitions of number, time, and space, the simplest people showed a subtle sensitivity to the periodicity and rhythm of existence. Their mythical-religious "sense of phases" applied to all the occurrences of life, especially to age and status transitions. Critical points of change were marked by special rites or ceremonies:

> Through these rites, the monotonous course of existence, the mere "flow" of time, undergoes a kind of religious stamp that gives it a specific

meaning. Birth and death, pregnancy and motherhood, puberty and marriage—all are marked by specific rites of initiation. (p. 109)

Cassirer also observed that the consciousness of rhythmic biological time preceded the intuition of cosmic patterns and periodicity. The regularity of the motions of the heavenly bodies and the earth's seasons were understood through life's processes. Such perceived reciprocity enabled early people to connect subjective human rhythms to the more distant, objective forces and movements of nature.

In his study of Greek religion, Burkert (1985) also brings together the marking off of space and the measuring of time: "[A]s the sanctuary articulates space, so the festival articulates time." Particular days are set aside and distinguished from the everyday motion of time:

[W]ork is laid aside and customary roles are dissolved in a general relaxation, but the festive program holds new roles in readiness. Groups come together, setting themselves apart from others. The contrast with normality may be expressed in mirth and joy, in adornment and beauty, or else in menace and terror. (p. 99)

Festivals were occasions for dancing and hymns, masking, banquets, contests, and processions. One festival procession can be seen, for example, in the Parthenon frieze, where one sees carved images of the citizens of Athens—mounted horsemen, chariots, sacrificial animals—in the great Panathenaic Procession.

Even in today's societies, which are predominantly secular or religiously differentiated, such as the United States, traditional religions continue building sanctuaries and marking off liturgical times. At the same time, however, the sacred calendar and symbolic spatial forms of any one religion do not work for all. Sociologist of religion Bryan Wilson (1982) has indicated that with increasing secular and religious diversification, the latent functions of religion, particularly the formation of shared cultural symbols, are taken over by secular institutions (p. 36). In the United States, for example, the most widely recognized bounded or "cut out" spaces and times are found in popular culture. Various sports—basketball, baseball, football—and entertainment events provide a series of familiar liturgical calendars and sacred sites. Entering the portals of the baseball stadium, for example, we, like the ancients, enter into a different world and temporal rhythm.

Most people recognize the plan of a baseball diamond and understand the central importance of individual teams for local communities. Even the sport's language has filtered into ordinary speech. We describe some individuals as "out in left field" or "off base." Others may be called "home free." Great success is "hitting a home run." An official layout of a playing field shows carefully measured spaces with special areas for the major actors, the boundaries of their play, and a spatial hierarchy of seats for spectators. Just as fans leave ordinary space behind as they enter the stadium, they begin an ebb and flow of time not measured by the clock, but by the order of the game itself. The space/time of innings is punctuated by a personal, preferential choice of refreshment: hot dogs, popcorn, sodas, and beer. There is also the rhythm of "spring training," followed by the ceremonies of the opening game. Thereafter comes the essence of the liturgical season, the continuous flow of competitive games until, finally, the playoffs and World Series.

Ritual space and time of all professional sports have been markedly affected by the unprecedented communications revolution. As we make analogies between popular sporting events and ritual, we acknowledge that television has irrevocably modified our comparisons. This medium has stretched the boundaries, using technology to "transport" sacred time and space anywhere in the world at any time. Great plays can be rerun as sports commentators highlight and summarize the game. Many ballparks have even installed huge TV screens. Those in attendance, and even the players themselves, may take part in two levels of time and space: the one that is lived and the other that is re-presented. Moreover, technology has now introduced some interactive features so that viewers may manipulate the time and space of the game. Eventually the representations may be rendered in holographic or virtual reality forms. Yet for many, television viewing is no substitute for *being there*, enclosed within extraordinary boundaries of space and time.

Although spatial and temporal demarcations allow for some analogies between primitive rituals and contemporary cultural events, premodern mythologies of space and time differ radically from our own. Such differences shake up formal comparisons. In *Before Philosophy* (1964), historian of religion Henri Frankfort contrasts mythopoeic and modern concepts of space and time. For ancient people, spatial experience was inclusive in ways we cannot possibly comprehend. Space, for example, encompassed the world of dreams, hallucinations, and the dead; distinctions between appearance and reality dissolved. Frankfort notes that unlike modern concepts, the spatial system of archaic peoples was based on values:

> Day and night give to east and west a correlation with life and death. Speculative thought may easily develop in connection with such regions as are outside direct experiences, for instance, the heavens or the nether world. (p. 30)

In such a system, sacred space is ambiguous, capable of multiple manifestations. Frankfort cites the importance in Egypt, for example, of the primeval hill from which creation began. This hill was traditionally located at the sun temple at Heliopolis, and yet the holy of holies of every temple was equally sacred. These multiple manifestations of a sacred site are illogical to modern persons expecting unambiguous locations and specific spatial coordinates.

Frankfort has also analyzed archaic people's radically different concepts of time, understood concretely as periodicity, following the cycles of the human and natural order. These successions and rhythms, however, were not viewed as "natural," but were instead related causally to supernatural beings or to a conflict of forces. Distinctions between past and present disappear:

> Each morning the sun defeats darkness and chaos, as he did on the day of creation and does, every year, on New Year's Day. These three moments coalesce; they are felt to be essentially the same. Each sunrise, and each New Year's Day, repeats the first sunrise on the day of creation; and for the mythopoeic mind each repetition coalesces with—is practically identical with—the original event. (p. 33)

Thus in archaic societies, the symbolic action of ritual "reverses" time, or in Mircea Eliade's (1963) words, it "abolishes Time and recovers the sacred Time of myth" (p. 140). By contrast, contemporary persons typically live in an irreversible, flowing continuum, broken down into linear, abstract, quantifiable segments.

Frankfort's distinctions are an unmistakable reminder that our analogies of exterior boundaries must always be modified by each culture's mythologies. Yet, however qualified, the persistent temporal and spatial demarcations of significant events in ancient and modern societies identify the enduring, compelling role that ritual has played: an escape from ordinary, often dreary, day-to-day realities into an extraordinary world. But how do we characterize such an "escape"? And does one differ from another?

▓ Interior Boundaries: Transcendence

Exterior boundaries that establish the context for ritual are more readily identified than pathways of the spirit. In breaking out of their everyday world and entering an extraordinary time and space, participants experience some kind of transcendence. In reexamining our paradigm, we look now at the interior processes of transformation or self-transcendence.

Building on Arnold van Gennep's analyses, Victor Turner (1982) described the phases of ritual activity—separation, transition, incorporation. Separation sets participants apart in space and time; but more than that, it involves them in symbolic behavior that detaches them from their previous social status. In the transition or transformative stage, the subjects pass through a period of ambiguity, "a sort of social limbo." The third stage, incorporation, includes symbolic actions that enable participants to return, taking on a "new, relatively stable, well-defined position in the total society" (p. 24).

Turner was among the first to suggest that residual traces of tribal rituals are found in various forms of entertainment, as well as in the high and popular arts. Drawing on his fieldwork and observations of contemporary culture, he documented and analyzed qualities of mind and action that characterize ritual experience. His studies of the liminal behavior in the second, or transitional, phase of ritual are especially important for analogies between popular culture and traditional ritual.

Turner observed an inversion of normal reality in the transitional stage. Participants undergo a leveling process, he said, in which their previous roles or positions are destroyed. This puts the participants in a "topsy turvy" world, a kaleidoscopic mixing of natural and supernatural, grotesque and benign, terrifying and redemptive forces. Because this phase is irreducible and mysterious, Turner refers to it as the essential *antisecular* component of ritual, whether it be labeled "religious" or "magical" (p. 80). This essentially antisecular element of traditional religious ritual established the boundaries of the human and the holy, opening up the experience of transcendence or the revelation of an Other. To explore these dimensions, we would need to turn to writers, ancient and modern, who are concerned with the category of the holy and the distinctions between the sacred and profane. Turner, however, while identifying the "antisecular" quality of ritual's liminal phase, nevertheless speculated that some aspects of this mysterious sacred element had become dispersed into secular spheres. Contemporary persons, unable to participate meaningfully in a religiously structured, multi-ordered liminal state, may become involved in the *liminoid*—a term the anthropologist invented to describe symbolic activity that resembles, but is not identical with *liminal.*

Turner found that tribal ritual framed both the serious and the playful, combining elements frequently split asunder in an industrialized society. Today, people divide their lives into on-the-job time and leisure or play time, and the residue of liminal ritual activity, he says, is located in our playing. Leisure offers a freedom to enter into, even generate, new symbolic worlds in entertainment, sports, games, theater, film, the arts. More than in tribal and agrarian rites and ceremonies, "the ludic and the experimental" are paramount. Through our games and our arts, we momentarily transcend social structures to play with ideas, fantasies, words, paint, and social relationships.

The contemporary researcher Mihaly Csikszentmihalyi and his colleagues also studied leisure activities, sport, and arts to better understand their "anti-secular" elements and self-transcendence. Through empirical studies—interviews and questionnaires—this team of scholars attempted to document and identify specific instances of the "flow" experience: the "peculiar state ... that is not accessible to 'everyday life' ..." (Csikszentmihalyi, 1975, pp. 21-23). The researchers based their studies on experiences they describe as *autotelic,* essentially defined as "an activity in which one loses oneself or becomes totally engrossed, regardless of the external rewards" (pp. 21-23).

Researchers compiled concrete data from athletes, performers, and artists, constructing a constellation of elements they called the "flow experience." These include:

1. The merging of action and awareness.

2. A centering of attention on a limited stimulus field, leading to a merging of action and a sense of pure involvement.

3. A sense of at-oneness, described in various ways: "loss of ego," "self-forgetfulness," "loss of self-consciousness," "transcendence of individuality," "fusion with the world."

4. Control of one's actions and of the environment. Skills are adequate to meet the demand, and there is a positive concept of the self, often seen as a victory over one's limitations.

5. Artists and athletes also reported that the flow experience generally contained coherent, noncontradictory demands for action and offered clear, unambiguous feedback to them.

6. The flow experience was for some "autotelic," that is, without goals or rewards other than participation in the activity itself. (pp. 38-47)

These studies of performing artists and athletes gave human voice to some of the abstract speculations of psychologists and anthropologists. For example, one composer described his state of mind:

> You yourself are in an ecstatic state to such a point that you feel as though you almost don't exist. I've experienced this time and again. My hand seems devoid of myself, and I have nothing to do with what is happening. I just sit there watching it in a state of awe and wonderment. And it just flows out by itself. (Csikszentmihalyi, 1975, pp. 42-44)

Those persons interviewed have described something akin to the ecstatic moments of religious experience. To extend these comparisons, we will turn to William James' classic study, *The Varieties of Religious Experience* (1971). James called attention to "the hot place in a man's consciousness, the group of ideas to which he devotes himself . . . *the habitual center of his personal energy.*" This means, says James, that when a person is "converted," some religious ideas that were previously peripheral in consciousness now take a central place (p. 165).

In exploring these shifts of emotional center, James drew on the work of E. D. Starbuck, a psychologist of religion, and constructed two basic types of regenerative change: one that is voluntary and conscious, and another that is involuntary and unconscious. In a voluntary shift of consciousness, change is gradual, consisting of building up, "piece by piece," a new set of moral and spiritual habits. On the other hand, the subconscious or subliminal shifts involve a kind of letting go, a self-surrender. Yet to James, the difference between the two is not radical. Even with the most voluntary type of regeneration, he says, a partial self-surrender is imposed. When the will has done its utmost to bring about unification, "it seems that the very last step must be left to other forces and performed without the help of its activity" (p. 174). To illustrate this, James chose an example, cited by Starbuck, that shows the interplay of voluntary and involuntary activity experienced by athletes and artists:

> An athlete . . . sometimes awakens suddenly to an understanding of the fine points of the game and to a real enjoyment of it, just as the convert awakens to an appreciation of religion. If he keeps on engaging in the sport, there may come a day when all at once the game plays itself through him—when he loses himself in some great contest. In the same way, a musician may suddenly reach a point at which pleasure in the technique of the art entirely falls away, and in some moment of inspiration he becomes the instrument through which the music flows. (pp. 173-174)

James, of course, was interested not only in the dynamics of the conversion experience, but also in the transformation that follows. One of the significant characteristics of the religious experience for him was the objective change the world itself seems to undergo: "An appearance of newness beautifies every object." There is a sense of clean and beautiful newness both within and without (p. 202).

In writings of Turner, Csikszentmihalyi, and James we have seen how play, self-surrender, and "flow" are associated with self-transcendence. But now another question emerges: Are all experiences of self-transcendence the same? Are there different levels of symbolism? In the conclusion of his essay, "Liminal to Liminoid," Turner (1982) raises this same issue. "I have left out," he says, "both from communities and 'flow' an essential feature—the *content* of the experience. This is where the analysis of symbols begins. . . . Surely, the processes of communities and flow are imbued with meanings of the symbols they either generate or are channeled by. Are all 'flows' one and do the symbols indicate different kinds and depths of flow?" (p. 59).

Turner's question leads to writers who are concerned with the symbolism of transcendence. Sports historian Allen Guttmann (1978) has shown in his book, *From Ritual to Record* how Greek athletic events were part of religious festivals, having a purpose beyond themselves (p. 23). In industrialized societies, he says, the record has replaced the ritual. We are concerned with "minute discriminations between the batting average of the .308 hitter and the .307 hitter." We no longer run to appease the gods, but to achieve a uniquely modern form of immortality, to set a record (p. 55).

In his book *Take Time for Paradise* (1989), Bartlett A. Giamatti, Renaissance scholar, former president of Yale University, and later Commissioner of Major League Baseball from April 1, 1989, until the time of his death, differed with Guttmann. The idea that sports' sacred connections are radically lost in the modern world, he says, "misperceives leisure, the condition of being in which sport, or athletics, plays merely a part" (p. 26). Leisure offers time for *autotelic* activities to be pursued for their own sake, providing a condition for the freedom of human spirit to express itself. An art or game, Giamatti writes, "stimulates what is promised, or provided, by religious experience—a state of contemplation, vigorous and expansive, of the highest force conceivable. The result is to be careless, or carefree. It is to be happy" (p. 28).

The religious quality of the activities of our leisure time, whether in the arts or games, is manifested in the seriousness with which we follow or participate in them, according to Giamatti. Moreover, we invest in professional or amateur sports certain transcendent values. For the fan, the religious quality of sport "lies first in the intensity of devotion brought to the game" (p. 23). On the other hand, the athlete, like the painter, sculptor, poet, architect, composer, and actor, "is basically driven to express what begins as a gnawing hunger and becomes a rage for perfection." It could be called, he said, a rage to "get it right" or "make things fit as they never have before." Like actors, musicians, singers, and athletes must have impeccable control and understand split-second timing. There must be a near-absolute concentration. As an athlete or actor brings all skills into focus, he or she will "achieve that state of complete intensity and complete relaxation—a total coherence between what the performer wants to do and has to do. This achievement transforms an individual; and we too, are recreated. Giamatti writes,

> The individual's power to dominate, on stage or field—and they are versions of the same place and are only by analogy altars—invests the whole arena around the locus of performance with his or her power....

> Power flows in a mysterious circuit from performer to spectator . . . and back, and while cheers or applause are the hoped-for outcome of performing, silence or gasps are the most desired, for then the moment has occurred—then domination is complete, and as the performer triumphs, a unity rare and inspiring results. (pp. 41-42)

The preeminent value Giamatti finds in the perfection of athletes and performers is an extraordinary spiritual freedom. Sport, like the arts and religion, represents our artistic and imaginative impulse to stretch beyond ourselves and to achieve an indescribable sense of liberation. Thus the transcendent power of sport parallels that of religion and the arts in its capacity to awaken in both athlete and spectator what Giamatti identifies with the Judeo-Christian notion of a paradise lost: "[B]etween days of work, sports or games only repeat and repeat our effort to go back, back to a freedom we cannot recall, save as a moment of play in some garden now lost" (p. 44).

In his book *The Denial of Death* (1973), psychologist Ernest Becker wove together insights of Eastern and Western religion as he reflected on transcendence. Following the writings of the Danish theologian, Søren Kierkegaard, Becker pointed out how awareness of one's finitude and ultimate death becomes a catalyst for self-transcendence (p. 88), a truth he found in Zen Buddhism as well as in an Augustinian-Lutheran tradition. After the total destruction of the emotional armor with which we protect ourselves, a new order of reality appears. The self, Becker writes, must be "brought down to nothing, in order for self-transcendence to begin," thrashing around in its own finitude in order to see beyond itself. "See beyond to what?" Becker gave Kierkegaard's answer: "To infinitude, to absolute transcendence, to the Ultimate Power of Creation which made finite creatures" (p. 89). One's being is opened to the "horizon of unlimited possibility, of real freedom" (p. 90). A liberating transcendence, says Becker, goes beyond cultural achievement and mastery of everyday things to infinity, to the possibility of cosmic heroism:

> He links his secret inner self, his authentic talent, his deepest feelings of uniqueness, his inner yearning for absolute significance, to the very ground of creation. . . . This invisible mystery at the heart of every creature now attains cosmic significance by affirming its connection with the invisible mystery at the heart of creation. (p. 91)

Thus, out of an experience of destruction and an absolute aloneness comes a transformation that presents a different level of experience: "the adventure in openness to a multidimensional reality" (p. 92).

Along with Otto Rank, Becker believed the artist's gift is "always to creation itself, to the ultimate meaning of life." A creative person, he said, faces a particular problem of personal transformation: "How to develop a creative work with the full force of one's passion, a work that saves one's soul, and at the same time, to renounce that very work because it cannot by itself give salvation." Artistic individuals, writes Becker, live in a tension, balancing the "eros" of self-expression with an "agape" of self-surrender (pp. 173-174).

Becker could have found in the diaries of the artist Paul Klee (1964) thoughts similar to his own. One entry reads,

> Art is like Creation: it holds good on the last day as on the first. . . . Everything Faustian is alien to me. I place myself at a remote starting point of creation, whence I state a priori formulas for men, beasts, plants, stones, and the elements, and for all the whirling forces. A thousand questions subside as if they had been solved. Neither orthodoxies nor heresies exist there. The possibilities are too endless, and the belief in them is all that lives creatively in me. . . . In my work I do not belong to the species but am a cosmic point of reference. My earthly eye is too far sighted and sees through and beyond the most beautiful things. (pp. 344-345)

Earlier in this entry, Klee had written that he sought only to relate himself to God. Thus Klee's words seem to confirm the close connections Becker found between self-transcendence and creative action of the artist.

We turn now to a theologian, Hugo Rahner, who used play as a prime metaphor for understanding God, creation, and the continuous interaction between the human and the divine. In his book *Man at Play* (1972), Rahner acknowledges his indebtedness to Johann Huizinga, whose *Homo Ludens* inspired many scholars to examine play as a formative element in various spheres of cultural activities—the arts, war, religion, philosophy.

For Rahner, all creation—past, present, and future—is caught up in the playing of a divine game. His mystical view envisions a creator God who freely calls all levels of being into the game. Everything in creation proceeds from the One that initiates the ultimate game, extending from the "round of the stars and atoms to the gravely beautiful play" of human beings (1972, p. 12).

> Whoever has, even for a moment, caught sight of this vast cosmic game will thenceforward at all times know that the little life of man and all the seriousness thereof is only a vanishing figure in this dance. (p. 25)

Only when we catch a glimpse of a playing God, a *Deus vere ludens*, Rahner writes, can we truly understand ourselves as a *homo ludens*, a creature who plays in an awesome game.

Rahner's perspective, like Becker's, includes an emphasis on the tragic dimension of human life and its importance in the ultimate meaning of play and ritual. Humans can only be truly playful, he said, when "poised between gaiety and gravity, between mirth and tragedy." Drawing on the richness of biblical and classical literature, as well as on the writings of the early church fathers, Rahner paints a vivid portrait of the "grave-merry" person who grasps the sobering but liberating truth that life at all levels participates in a great cosmic game. A genuine lightness of heart is inextricably bound together with a darker vision of human frailty. Existence is fundamentally joyful because it is secure in God, but our actions are also tragic. In our self-centeredness, even creative actions become destructive and perilous. Playing in the game involves suffering, created and endured. Our game time is "a mixture of joy and sorrow, a comedy and a tragedy" (Rahner, 1972, p. 29). There is no play, writes Rahner, that doesn't have something profoundly serious at the bottom of it, even the play of children. "They come, with all the compulsion of characters in a myth, under the spell of absolute obligation and under the shadow of the possibility that the game may be lost" (p. 27).

Although Rahner's formulation of the "grave-merry" player owes much to classical philosophy, Christ's passion is critical to Rahner's theology and his concepts of ritual and play. The Creator God is also one who has suffered. In the divine game, suffering and redemption take their place alongside creation. Thus human players cannot fully play or understand the game unless they grasp—however dimly—the mystery of both creation and suffering. Rahner's Christian player thus lives in an unrelieved tension of merriment and gravity, ultimately ignorant of the final outcome of the game, but spiritually compelled to play it. An internal combustion of profound sorrow and joy sparks a mysterious burst of energy, empowering frail creatures to dance with death and to pirouette with atoms and stars.

These last three writers—Giamatti, Becker, and Rahner—suggest that there may be a continuum of meanings ascribed to self-transcendence in ritual experience, from human heroism to participation in the cosmic play of a Creator-Redeemer God. Needless to say, one can well imagine criticism of the continuum metaphor by both the orthodox humanists who do not acknowledge the metaphysical end of the spectrum and religionists who draw a sharp line between the sacred and the profane. What seems clear, however, is that ritual is a springboard for self-transcending, for an escape from time that cannot be denied to those who play the game—human or divine—with passion.

There is more to the meaning of transcendence, however, than the solitary escape of individuals through sports, the arts, or religious liturgies. Turner's question "Are all 'flows' one and do the symbols indicate different kinds of depths and flow?" will eventually have to be seen from another perspective if we want to do it justice. To examine further the question of levels of meanings, we would need to look carefully at various communities of individuals who share experiences of transcendence. What are their loyalties and responsibilities? How is the community perpetuated? Such an inquiry would, I believe, lead to an awareness that, in fact, we take part in many rituals and thus identify with many communities of believers. Through participation, we discover in ourselves substantially different types of flow and levels of meaning—from being a sports fan, to serious creative activity, to playing in an ultimately mysterious cosmic game whose rules are unknown.

References

Becker, E. (1973). *The denial of death.* New York: Free Press.

Burkert, W. (1985). *Greek religion* (J. Raffan, Trans.). Cambridge, MA: Harvard University Press.

Cassirer, E. (1956). Mythical thought. In *The philosophy of symbolic forms,* Vol. 2 (R. Manheim, Trans.). New Haven, CT: Yale University Press.

Csikszentmihalyi, M. (1975). *Beyond boredom and anxiety: The experience of play in work and games.* San Francisco: Jossey-Bass.

Eliade, M. (1963). *Myth and reality.* New York: Harper and Row.

Frankfort, H. (1964). *Before philosophy: The intellectual adventure of ancient man.* Baltimore, MD: Penguin.

Giamatti, A. B. (1989). *Take time for paradise: Americans and their games.* New York: Summit.

Goethals, G. (1981). *The TV ritual: Worship at the video altar.* Boston: Beacon.

Guttman, A. (DATE?) *From ritual to record.* New York: Columbia University Press.

James, W. (1971). *The varieties of religious experience: A study in human nature.* New York: Collier.

Klee, P. (1964). *The diaries of Paul Klee, 1898-1918.* (Felix Klee, Ed.). Berkeley: University of California Press.

Moore, S., & Myerhoff, B. (Eds.). (1977). *Secular ritual.* Amsterdam: Van Gorcum.

Myerhoff, B. (1977). We don't wrap herring in a printed page: Fusion, fictions and community in secular ritual. In S. Moore & B. Myerhoff (Eds.), *Secular ritual.* Amsterdam: Van Gorcum.

Rahner, H. (1972). *Man at play.* New York: Herder and Herder.

Smith, J. Z. (1987). *To take place: Toward theory in ritual.* Chicago: University of Chicago Press.

Turner, V. (1977). Variations on a theme of liminality. In In S. Moore & B. Myerhoff (Eds.), *Secular ritual* (pp. 36-52). Amsterdam: Van Gorcum.

Turner, V. (1982). *From ritual to theater: The human seriousness of play.* New York: Performing Arts Journal Publications.

Wilson, B. (1982). *Religion in sociological perspective.* Oxford, UK: Oxford University Press.

Chapter 13

The Dispersed Sacred
Anomie and the Crisis of Ritual

Gabriel Bar-Haim

Oh, who can divide dream from reality, day from night,
night from dawn, memory from illusion?
  —Danilo Kis, *The Encyclopedia of the Dead*

As Durkheim so brilliantly demonstrated, it is the group and the relationship between the individual and the group that generate sacred symbols and transcendental sentiments. The very fact that modern Western groups have increasingly failed to produce religious feelings was central to Durkheim's work. Since his book *The Division of Labor in Society* was first published in 1893, some of his analyses have become crystallized and have even surpassed his predictions, whereas others have not materialized.

The present crisis of the ritual in postmodern society (a term chosen to distinguish between Durkheim's time and our own contemporary one) is the result of the intensification of an ongoing problematic relationship between the individual and the group (a term employed here generically), a trend that Durkheim foresaw.

The growing difficulty faced by Western welfare states in coping on the one hand with the multitude of unprecedented demands placed on them, and on the other hand with the disintegration of geographical communities no longer capable of providing social cohesion and support, has led many to believe that a "civil society" seems to be transpiring from the current impasse. A civil society, as a social organization displaying no hegemonic ideological virtues, but able to restore a qualitative relationship between individuals and structures and consequently to recover the ritual, may be a solution. How, nonetheless, can this type of nonhegemonic society be capable of persisting without forcing a common consciousness, or posing a common vision? And furthermore, how are these possible without the support of certain forms of sacredness?

Any future model of social organization, be it a civil society or something else, that attempts to redefine an individual-group relationship, and thus to determine the nature of the sacred, will have to confront the central problem of *anomie*. It is this acute state of intrinsic and permanent anomie that primarily characterizes the present individual-group relationship. Merton's (1968) interpretation of Durkheim's term as the process "whereby people prefer technically efficient over morally prescribed means" (p. 189) provided only a limited understanding of the meaning of anomie without examining the significance, thus reducing the concept to a mere lack of normative guidance.

By the mid-1980s, new theoretical research on Durkheim's usage and understanding of anomie was suggesting novel and wider ramifications. These interpretations centered around the idea that Durkheim basically regarded anomie as a state of social withdrawal, not only as a consequence of a structural imbalance, but also as a disposition of an individualistic consciousness, a subjectively inclined frame of mind. Typically, Hilbert (1986) observed that, "Anomie is the absence of our objective experience of reality" (p. 19). Hilbert concluded that Durkheim perceived anomie as an excess of individuality. The objective experience of reality is not the result of a mere cognitive order, but is fundamentally a moral one. Mestrovic (1985) thus correctly concluded that Durkheim used the concept of anomie as the secular counterpart of sin, "which is to say, as an incorrect arrangement of individual and collective representations, as the treatment of the sacred as if it were profane and vice versa" (p. 124). He went on to specify that "if the gulf between the sacred and the profane is an unbridgeable abyss, anomie is any tendency to mingle the two opposites, even reverse their relationship" (p. 133).

Durkheim's conception that it is the individual who represents the profane, whereas society represents the sacred, has become blurred in postmodern society. Contemporary groups are increasingly amorphous in their composition, having a temporary and uncommitted existence and being too weak to provide solace and reassurance. Only rarely do groups display a sui generis reality forceful enough to mobilize and impose persistent patterns of behavior. In short, groups no longer leave their imprint on individual consciousness. The once intersubjective reality of the group has given way to interindividuality of the functional network; that is, the individual has become a self-contained unit, gravitating in a space filled with ever-changing networks that the individual initiates or to which he attaches himself for certain periods of time and for specific utilitarian or cultural purposes. Only occasionally are permanent social contracts established within a network, and even these only bind individual persons.

The *network*—a better term to characterize the increasing postmodern social organization—is the creation of the individual, providing services, including emotional ones, and facilitating contacts with other individuals and with adjacent networks. Traditional groups have centers and sacred collective representations, whereas networks established to fulfill individual goals are incapable of representing anything but individual aspirations and desires; thus, having no sacred collective representations, networks are little preoccupied by ritualizations.

Networks are made up of autonomous subjects drawn into certain temporary contacts or fragmentary relationships, and centered around one specific individual. Having little or no historical memory, common mythology, and opportunities for self-reflexivity, networks seem to possess no collective consciousness and therefore no need for common mechanisms to maintain social solidarity and to revitalize the society's sacred representations and symbols. The result is a kind of blurred distinction between individual and group-network representations; that is, a hybrid representation of both individual and network that reflects the individualization of social relationships, a state that weakens a transcendental process. Lefebvre (1968) commented on "the profane displacing but not replacing the sacred" (p. 59), as he characterized the nature of everyday life, neatly encapsulating the situation.

Durkheim (1893/1964) focused on the main issue when he asserted that "it is first affirmed that the sphere of the social grows smaller and smaller to the great advantage of the individual" (p. 204). Observing that Durkheim's concept of anomie was fundamentally connected to an excess of individuality, Mestrovic (1985) argued that "anomie requires a veneration of the individual to such an extent that it is believed that the individual is capable of choosing a state of moral transgression" (p. 129). To go one step further, it is reasonable to assume that anomie exists when society is predominantly perceived as vulnerable and too "transparent" and individuals are all too aware of this, when the myths of society are cynically regarded by individuals whose insecurity prevents their comprehending a total social entity beyond their own limited personal experience. Furthermore, in such a state, whatever falls beyond the individual's experience is doubted, challenged, and debated, not only because society is vulnerable and therefore little is taken for granted, but also because concomitant with the loss of one type of sociality, an intense search occurs for a new one. Lefebvre's (1968) observation concerning contemporary society is highly relevant in this case: "Thus we have a society that is obsessed with dialog, communication, participation, integration and coherence, all the things it lacks, all the things it misses" (p. 185).

The notion of acute awareness of society's vulnerability was also discerned by Bauman (1992), for whom this alarming sign was followed by the advent of modernity:

> The kind of Society that, retrospectively, came to be called modern, emerged out of the discovery that human order is vulnerable, contingent and devoid of reliable foundations. The discovery was shocking. The response to the shock was a dream and an effort to make order solid, obligatory and reliably founded. It prompted an incessant drive to eliminate the haphazard. (p. xi)

The discovery that human order is vulnerable preceded both modernity and postmodernity. The only distinction is that the response of modernity was a certain kind of sociality that feverishly experimented, especially with rationality, whereas the response of postmodernity is a kind of sustainable disorder, living in one's own ruins, making anomie not a warning sign, but a permanent condition; even trying to exploit it, as Martin (1983) observed: "embracing anomie for the sake of the expounded creative possibilities it can offer" (p. 51).

The perception of a vulnerable social order, either as a warning sign for an imminent new order, as Bauman claims, or as a newly permanent condition (Bar-Haim, 1996) underlies the structure of contemporary culture, which perceives the sacred either as "too far away" and therefore irrelevant unless it can be reduced to as many familiar tokens and identifiable icons as possible, or as a man-made myth, lacking in mystery and for just this reason highly nostalgic as well as rife with various genres of incredulity.

It is on these grounds that the megaspectacles thrive. The grand spectacle has become the epitome of contemporary celebration. With its large-scale technical wizardry and stunning effects, logistical complexity and vast publicity, it attempts to compensate for the loss of mythology and the absence of a metaphysical presence. Spectacles, especially— although not only—the large ones, are planned as events intended to impress and entertain; they are desacralized occasions that bring together individuals who are generally unacquainted and seldom encounter one another after the spectacle or perhaps only on a few other rare occasions. These are events of passive consumption, with a self-imposed discipline supervised by the custodians of the social order.

As far as the ritual, especially the ritual celebration, is concerned, it is likely to become a certain derivate of spectacle—a ceremonial spectacle. This is the only apparent option when what is left of the sacred is exposed as a man-made mythology. Thus, the disintegration of traditional, small communities, and with them the gradual disappearance or transformation of religious and agricultural rituals, has left a void that is gradually being filled by mostly secular celebrations along with some civic rituals.

There are three prevalent categories of secular celebrations, all of which can be characterized as being organized from above by specially assigned experts. First, there are the state rituals and celebrations orchestrated by governmental agencies, such as the Fourth of July in the United States. Individuals participate mostly in the shape of family celebrations, in addition to a central, state-organized event arranged as a media spectacle with the participation of politicians and celebrities. Government ceremonies, such as on Memorial Day, as well as historic events, such as the 50th anniversary of D-Day, have become special media spectacles, rather than days of mass participation.

The second category is the ethnic or ethnic/regional festival, such as St. Patrick's Day, the Chinese New Year, Mardi Gras, or Oktoberfest in the United States or Folklorama in Manitoba, Canada, which are organized by local authorities and regional ethnic organizations. The parades, the folk dancing, the merrymaking centered around ethnic food are painstakingly organized spectacles, controlled and supervised by the police, the organizers, and especially by the ubiquitous TV cameras.

In the third category are the cyclic commercial entertainment festivals organized by entrepreneurs with some assistance from the local cultural authorities. These include musical events such as rock, country, and jazz festivals, but also classical music festivals, such as Tanglewood in Massachusetts, U.S., or theater festivals, such as Stratford in Ontario, Canada; the annual theater festival in Edinburgh, Scotland; the Jerusalem Arts Festival; or the Berlin Film Festival. All of these festivals are broadly publicized events and, in most cases, annual media opportunities that transform them into class cultural spectacles, generally perceived as respectable middle-class events.

In all three categories the connection between the individual and the gathering is ephemeral, weak, and insignificant, involving some recreational catharsis and sociality, but not coalescing into any major collective sense of strength and togetherness, and consequently not leaving any imprint on the individual's consciousness. Similarly inconsequential are most current political rituals and rites of passage. If ritual, including celebrations, is a mechanism that synchronizes and bridges between individual aspirations and collective ideals, as well as between self-reference and collective symbols, then the omnipresent state of anomie that assumes a crisis of credibility in the collective mythology renders such a mechanism superfluous.

Because individuals can no longer experience that primordial and authentic state of powerful togetherness except during such extraordinary times as war, natural disasters, or epidemics on the one hand, and exceptional moments of achievement on the other, rituals now only evoke and remind collective history of former periods of strength and glory, albeit mostly incongruously in regard to present patterns of social significance. Happy are the few for whom in our present age of disjunction and rupture, the present is in fact a remembered past that has the capacity to appease the present experience of angst with the joy and strength of time immemorial.

By overrepresenting the past collective mythology, while for the most part not having a current social referent, contemporary ritual becomes an overbearing occasion for vacuous nostalgia, devoid of any meaningful inspiration for the majority who cannot relate to it. In general, a tendency to overrepresent reality may be an indication of the stress on ritual as a cultural, autonomous mechanism with no social base underlying its representations. Culture has a propensity to overrepresent when the social is weak, whereas the social side tends to be overrepresented when the culture is less relevant. But because both culture and the social are interconnected, culture cannot continue to overrepresent without the support of an intense social life, nor can the latter make much sense of its actions without underpinning them through cultural symbols and commentaries.

Durkheim (1912/1965) argues that sacredness is the representation of collective ideals generated during times of intense social life transcended into sacred symbols (whereas rituals are, among other things, mechanisms of evocation of these). Following Durkheim's line of thought, one can argue that when the social life is intense, the ritual symbols are either a part of hegemonic ideology or in competition with it. If co-opted by the dominant ideology, the ritual is meaningful only as a positive instrument legitimizing and reconciling the social order through metaphysical symbols; and if in competition, it is meaningful only if it can suggest the path to an alternative vision.

It is also possible that when social life functions at ordinary intensity, then ritual is perfunctorily received as part of the effort intended to maintain the belief in collective strength. By providing a compelling opportunity to bring people together for a common purpose, ritual in itself, regardless of the symbolism (though it is difficult to separate between the two facets) might contribute to the continued flow of collective energy. In such a case, ritual is seen as an accepted but independent cultural practice, its symbols coexisting side by side with the dominant social symbols.

At other times, when the social life disappoints, ritual holds the possibiity of becoming both the vehicle and the occasion to revitalize confidence in the group and consequently to revive social ideals. Under such circumstances, ritual is significantly under pressure to evoke those shared moments of collective strength and glory; and by doing so, it is viewed as a possible mechanism to renew belief in the power of the group. In this case, ritual is regarded as a dramatic event, although its significance and symbolism may be debatable and problematic for some, while providing a source of spell-binding belief for others.

Furthermore, to revitalize confidence in the group or to evoke earlier and more fortunate times of collective heritage demands the prerequisite of an appropriate structural relationship to provide organic conjunctions between the individual and the collective with its center and representations. Such structural appropriateness prepares people for a comparison between the collective past and the present, between "those times" and "these times." However, when there is a loosely defined collective with an amorphous identity, shifting centers, and unauthoritative symbolic representations, as is characteristic of the emerging contemporary group-network, then the sacred becomes feeble and the ritual that is supposed to serve it becomes insignificant.

In other words, a certain historical social time that succeeded in producing an event of collective solidarity that further underwent a process of divinization and consequently created a sacred collective mythology, however atemporal and universal, cannot be currently embraced without a meaningful appropriation of its content; that is, no past reference can become relevant as long as it cannot be sustained by the present social arrangements. Furthermore, the continuing acceptance of past mythology as a sacred symbolic system depends on the fundamental supposition that this sacred symbolic system continues to reflect a collective destiny beyond concrete social circumstances and specific individuals in addition to perception of a supernatural metaphysical dimension.

The group-network's main features—such as temporal and fragmented relationships, stress on individuality and everyday life, all in a general anomic context that regards social order as vulnerable and weak—are not conducive to preserving past sacred mythology and its symbols. Hence, the crisis becomes inherent, and the ritual is less and less inspiring. Having lost the power to inspire and thus to regenerate a social energy as well as to mobilize masses, rituals become excessively spectacle-oriented, stressing artistic performances and theatrical enactments. In other words, the artistic and aesthetic elements have developed from being auxiliary props to becoming the focus of the ritual. This, in a sense, is coherent with the increase in veneration of the individual and its self-expressions.

The prevalent sense of a vulnerable social order could be at least partly attributed to what Baudrillard (1983a) termed "the crisis of social reference"; and that, in its turn, can be traced both to changes in the relationship between the individual and the group (as has been already argued), and to historical exhaustion of ideologies and social utopias.

It is not difficult to comprehend this crisis of reference in light of the recent disillusionment with Western capitalism and Western socialism, not to mention Communism and Maoism. There is a disappointment in the welfare state and unions, in science and technology with their associated dangers to the environment as well as to the job market. In short, the disillusionment has brought about apathy among the majority; and among a few, particularly working-class European youth, it has created a readiness to embrace neofascism. The exhaustion of Western sociopolitical ideologies, while the welfare state's institutions seem to be on the brink of collapse, is taking place in a context characterized by relative economic affluence, especially among the middle class, that is geared toward high consumerism on the one hand, and social problems, such as drugs, alcohol, and stress, on the other hand. A perpetual search for leadership on both sides of the Atlantic has yielded an acute sense that the present malaise of Western society requires the remedy of altogether new and different kinds of leaders who have yet to make their appearance.

In summary, the social ideals that once defined and focused political energies, inspired new challenges for reform, paved the way to a more flexible stratification, and gave legitimization to a secular morality have reached a point of ineffectiveness, incapable of mobilizing and fulfilling expectations. In the meantime, no sweeping new ideology or set of visionary ideals has replaced the old ones in defining the present social reality.

Moreover, the inadequacy of the present collective references has given rise to a restless search for collective references centered around loose social movements, some of which have been around for some time, such as the environmentalists, the feministists with their derivates, or such alternative visions as New Age, self-actualization, and self-improvement. Common to all these is the unspoken assumption that there is an urgent need to reestablish a balance in the individual's life, to recreate the harmony destroyed by contemporary living conditions, thereby bringing people back to peace with nature, encouraging women's contribution to culture, liberating the irrational mystic, and freeing subconscious fears.

The individual's redemption as a social cause has brought about the ascent of social references that have naturally focused on the individual's contentment with the social environment. Consequently, this trend has also focused obsessively on "normality" as a reference that asserts the precedence of the individual over external detrimental forces. The American media, among others, reflects this context and dutifully supplies, apparently on the demand of its viewers and readers, a disproportional number of stories centering around borderline or problematic cases of normality that also force heated public debates. This is exemplified by such recent cases as the episode of Anita Hill, the case of the Menendez brothers, Michael Jackson's affair, the Bobbit affair, the execution of a serial killer, the O.J. Simpson trial, and others. This preoccupation with normality purports to set some normative social boundaries in a world increasingly dominated by private affairs.

The example of normality as a relatively new social construction is a good case in point of a public attempt to intervene in the world of individuals and their private lives by forcing a transformation of few individual uncommon cases into collective moral references. It does this by bringing private affairs into public debate and thus compelling individual references to obey normative rules. In short, the effort is not to stop an onslaught of individual references at the expense of collective ones (often by selecting the unusual ones) but to attempt to mediate between individual references and the public sphere, that meeting ground of all networks, with the purpose that some kind of order may be imposed. Individual references alone, without being tied to a higher order of generality, may become dangerously incestuous, likely to implode into an idiosyncratic reality defined by fantasy, among other things. The ubiquitous mass media in particular has become the most powerful intermediating system, but it is evidently not the only one.

The demand for mediation arises mainly from both the structure of group-networks and the nature of the relationships they incur. Because the network is the creation of an individual and there are theoretically as many networks as there are individuals, and because one knows what is taking place only in one's own network and marginally in a few others, one perennially senses an acute need for a broader scope of knowledge, information, and modes of interpretation beyond one's own network. Furthermore, an individual is forced to seek through his or her own limited and isolated relationships necessary information about other networks, as well as to be continuously alert to discover basic strategies for improving his or her own network. Such questions as "How did they get to know one another?" "Where did they meet?" "How does one find out about . . ?" have become common exchanges. Hence, the individual is compelled to seek constantly for "what is going on," to be constantly tuned to anywhere that might possess and provide information and interpretations about other networks and their subdivisions as well as strategies about networking.

Durkheim's observation that people do not think, but rather participate in thinking, could never have been more currently correct. The only difference is that in contemporary society, people participate in a common thinking process through intermediation. Thus a connection to mediating systems becomes a necessity, and mass media is the quintessential type among such systems.

It is the increasing intermediation of human relations in contemporary society that has eroded the collective sense of power and debilitated the potency of moral transcendency and eventually the possibility of emerging sacred symbols. The interposition of various intermediaries in the relationships between individuals interferes with their awareness of being part of an identifiable collectivity and therefore weakens the necessary strength to produce a vital sense of common morality and shared destiny that can be transcended into sacred entities.

A few specialized intermediary agencies stand out; they have become reified with a power that imposes dependency and, like everything socially invented, have superseded their original purpose. These agencies, which include many of what R. Barthes termed *myth makers* with a life of their own, become so autonomous that they tend to simulate the life of some kind of community and even simulate institutional practices such as politics. Such is the case with mass media, but also advertising offices, the commercial world, computer networks, leisure clubs, adult education classes, therapy support groups, volunteer political organizations, international exchange programs, manpower offices, travel agencies, and others. In total, the intermediary agencies have become a simulacrum apparatus that provides a false sense of fermenting social energy.

The group-network that is built upon, and in its turn generates, excessive individual representations harmonizes with the intermediary simulacrum because the latter bestows the sense that it is capable of filling the unbearable anomic gap between the strong individual representations and the feeble collective ones. In a society displaying excess in individual representations, an anomic disbelief also looms large; and in the restive quest to put an end to such a state, any display of intensive signs of social activity is credited with the quality of a center. The "noise" simulation of many specialized intermediary agencies seems sometimes deceptively to convey the character of a social center, though most of these are no more than ephemeral subcultures or temporary consumer groups.

The multiplicity of intermediary agencies that operate through self-promotion, ostentatiousness, and the high profile of publicity strive openly to succeed in the market place—be it political, economic, or cultural—while indirectly and often unconsciously participating in a latent struggle to define the newly emerging public sphere. In times when the anomie becomes incorporated into daily practices, when social relations are mostly intermediated and thus only scattered and relatively weak social centers that produce low social energy emerge, culture, rather than the social factor, has become the dominant and vital force in defining the public sphere.

Analyzing the postmodern era, Gergen (1991) argues, "In the postmodern view social outcry is not a matter of internal belief, basic morality or deep-seated feelings; it is simply another form of performance" (p. 186). In a time of relatively reduced social effervescence—avoiding Baudrillard's (1983b) use of the extreme "social demise"—cultural performances, especially spectacles, various ceremonies, and much of what is subsumed under the term *secular rituals,* are often confusingly regarded as social. The marginal social effervescence elicited from the contemporary cultural mechanisms does not contribute much to group solidarity and revitalization of social action. This brings us back to the position that contemporary rituals have become autonomous cultural mechanisms and thus strongly oriented toward performances, coherent in general with the stress on spectacle as a major feature of the network culture.

In summary, this chapter has attempted to analyze the crisis of the ritual by putting forward an interpretation of the state of anomie characteristic of contemporary society. On a further level of inquiry, it has been suggested that the group-network structural arrangement that increasingly defines the individual-group relationship also holds the key to the current type of anomie, and that it may provide an insight into the relationship between individual versus collective references and the intermediating efforts to transform the former into the latter. The mediation of social relations and the emergence of the simulacrum apparatus is seen as one of the major factors in the crisis of the ritual and the triumph of the spectacle.

References

Bar-Haim, G. (1996). Media charisma and the artificial global culture. In S. Bramen & A. Sreberny-Muhammadi (Eds.), *Globalization, communication, and transnational civil society*. Paramus, NJ: Hampton.

Baudrillard, J. (1983a). *In the shadow of the silent majorities or the end of the social*. New York: Semiotext(e).

Baudrillard, J. (1983b). *Simultations*. New York: Semiotext(e).

Bauman, Z. (1992). *Intimations of postmodernity*. London: Routledge & Kegan Paul.

Durkheim, E. (1964). *The division of labor in society*. New York: Free Press. (Originally published in 1893)

Durkheim, E. (1965). *The elementary forms of the religious life*. New York: Free Press. (Originally published in 1912)

Gergen, J. K. (1991). *The saturated self*. New York: Basic Books.

Hilbert, R. (1986). Anomie and the moral regulation of society. *Sociological Theory, 4*, 1-19.

Kis, D. (1990). *The encyclopedia of the dead*. London: Faber and Faber.

Lefebvre, H. (1968). *Everyday life in the modern world*. New York: Harper Torchbooks.

Martin, B. (1983). *A sociology of contemporary cultural change*. Oxford, UK: Basil Blackwell.

Merton, R. (1968). *Social theory and social structure*. New York: Free Press.

Mestrovic, S. G. (1985). Anomie and sin in Durkheim's thought. *Journal for the Scientific Study of Religion, 24*(2), 119-236.

Chapter 9

The Web of
Collective Representations

Knut Lundby

In a society of extended individual reflexivity, media, religion, and culture still are linked through an interrelated web of collective representations. Through his concept of collective representations, Emile Durkheim is credited for "the fundamental discovery of culture as an element analytically independent of social system" (Bellah, 1959). He offered a viable sociological contribution to the understanding of religion with *The Elementary Forms of the Religious Life* (1912/1968). Durkheim died before the advent of broadcasting and never experienced the modern media as such. However, because the media play with competing symbols and images, they play a crucial role in establishing, maintaining, and changing collective representations—concepts, categories, myths, beliefs, symbols—and language (Pickering, 1984, pp. 279-281; Rothenbuhler, 1993, p. 159).

▓ The Collective Interplay

Contemporary sociologists such as Giddens, Habermas, and Bourdieu (all drawing on Durkheim) have worked out more nuanced understandings of the dual relationship between the individual and society through some kind of intermediate agency. Linked to theories of social semiotics, we now have much more powerful tools to explain and understand the signifying and mediating processes than Durkheim was able to offer, as demonstrated by Robert White in the present volume.

Collective representations must be conceived as mediated. They are shaped in the ongoing signification processes, in the interplay between actors and structure. When modern media are involved in these processes, texts constructed by producers within specific cultural and structural settings may be experienced by users in totally different contexts. The representations will be collective only to the extent that the audiences subscribe to the symbolic constructions in the production process, and to the extent that the producers are able to listen in and adjust to the interpretations of the audiences. The four moments laid out in White's chapter in this volume presuppose some kind of community or collectivity between producers and audiences, sharing the collective representations that both parties simultaneously adjust through their signifying practices in production and reception.

This chapter contemplates the case of "global" mediations. It asks whether there can be world-encompassing collective representations, or whether they retreat into much more limited collectivities where their symbols are shared.

Durkheim did not really understand *how* the signification or meaning constructions by various actors (which he would subsume under the concept of individual representations) are turned into collective representations. However, he is responsible for the basic insight that collective representations make up society as more than the sum of individuals and their practices. It is necessary to grasp this idea of collective surplus in analyses of media, religion, and culture in contemporary society because it is in this surplus that we may find the sacred hidden.

The basic idea in Durkheim's (1898/1974) theory on representations is that when produced, they continue to exist in themselves for some time—like media products. Collective representations "become something else" besides the simple sum of private sentiments or individual representations. "No doubt each individual contains a part," he states, but collective representations transform and "surpass the individual as the whole the part." Collective representations "form the network of social life," establish mutual meanings in social structure, and thus, through communication and social interaction, create and recreate collectivity (pp. 23-26).[1]

The individual meets this collectivity as integrated into a seemingly objective world, learns from it through socialization and internalization, and uses this as capital in his or her own participation or externalization ("individual representations") in society. Berger and Luckmann's (1966/1971) account of this ongoing dynamic refers back to Durkheim. Collective representations make up a "symbolic universe" that could be a "sacred universe" (Berger, 1967). This, then, introduces "the sacred." According to Durkheim, "Every society is based on collective *reprèsenta-tions* and the sacred is not just *a* collective *reprèsentation*, the sacred is the symbol of the collective entity . . . the collective *reprèsentation par excellence*" (Pickering, 1984, p. 132).

This all-encompassing understanding of the sacred might appear on its surface not to apply to today's pluralistic signifying struggle. However, when White in this volume stresses that the "sacred" as the ultimate good has to be understood in relation to the "secular" everyday life and its imperfections, he is close to Durkheim's conception of the sacred in relation to the profane, while recognizing a more diversified pattern of cultures. Durkheim did analyze the sacred in society as a collective whole. However, as Pickering (1984) points out, the "most serious difficulty in dealing with Durkheim's notion of society is the fact that nowhere does he categorically define it" (pp. 248-249). His theory of collective representations might also be applied to subcultures and transnational societies.

Olympic Representations

Today, partly due to the existence of transnational electronic media, our notions of society stretch beyond the national. The televised Olympic Games pay tribute to global society as well as to nations as participating units. The opening and closing ceremonies of the Olympic Games are peak performances of collective representation with global pretentions. As cases, they are well-suited to exploration of the kind of macrolevel arguments put forward by Durkheim. As an example, I will relate my discussion of media, religion, and culture to the Opening Ceremony of the 1994 Winter Olympics at Lillehammer, Norway.[2]

Some point out a specific Durkheimian strand in cultural studies (Alexander, 1988). Durkheim's continuous influence on sociology of religion is beyond doubt; however, his theoretical impact on communication studies has been mostly implicit (Rothenbuhler, 1993), although there are media scholars, like Dayan and Katz (1988), who acknowledge the influence of Durkheim in their studies of media events. In his chapter elsewhere in this volume, Bar-Haim applies Durkheimian theory to an analysis of the complete web of media, religion, and culture.

The ceremonies of the Olympic Games are premier examples of the "megaspectacles" Bar-Haim discusses, with their "large-scale technical wizardry" in an attempt to "compensate for the loss of mythology and the absence of a metaphysical presence." At the same time, they are media events electrifying very large audiences into "a collective heartbeat." They are not, however, among the history-changing "transformative media events" described by Dayan and Katz (1992, pp. 5-9, 147). The Lillehammer Opening Ceremony was in many ways just a media spectacle, but still it was a case of the contemporary relations between society, religion, and collective representation.[3]

Bar-Haim and Dayan both define "the sacred" according to the Durkheimian principle that it is what people in a society "set apart" to worship or hold in awe (Durkheim, 1912/1968, p. 47). Behind megaspectacles, Bar-Haim discerns a weak and vulnerable social situation, an anomic society without sacred centers. According to his argument, a widely televised Olympic Opening would not be able to fill the gap and function as a real ritual celebration of the sacred. Dayan (1995), on the other hand, holds that in media events like this, television seems to be "invested with a liturgic role," which means that television "provides a frame that signals the sacred character of an event in progress."

Those responsible for the production of the Lillehammer Opening Ceremony apparently wanted to create a spectacular media event for the huge audience in 134 countries by playing with several religious and mythical elements in various cultural layers. It seems they succeded. The Opening Ceremony gave the 1994 Winter Games a remarkable start by inviting the global public into a fairy-tale world[4] of collective representations.

▦ Collective Representations: Complicated Constructs

The televised Opening Ceremony demonstrated that collective representations in modern media are constructed by individuals within certain structural frameworks, revealing "the constructedness of reality and the reality of construction" (Peters & Rothenbuhler, 1989, p. 11). Actually, as a media production, the opening of the Lillehammer Games was a quite complicated symbolic construct. As a collective representation, it did not quite become "something else" independent of the actors and the symbolic transformations they were able to invoke.

In the construction process, this broadcast had to undergo symbolic transformation following the requirements of a prescribed Olympic ceremony to be transferred into the format of transnational television for a worldwide public. The directors of the production had to work within the constraints of detailed instructions for this ceremony laid out in the Olympic Charter (International Olympic Committee [IOC], 1993). They then created their Artistic Concept within this formal framework (Baardson & Kvamme, 1993). On this dual basis, the artistic director, the executive producer, the television director, and their staffs worked out the Program Description (NRK ORTO, 1994), which was the script offered by the host broadcaster to the commentators of all the television companies to transmit the actual performed ceremony that had, all the way through, been planned as a televised ceremony—a media spectacle.[5]

The relationship between the performed and the televised ceremonies was intricate, worked out from the layers of texts in the Olympic Charter, the Artistic Concept, and the Program Description, each with their various advocates. The artistic director instructed all of the 35,000 spectators present in the arena to dress in white robes to prepare them for the ritual and to set the white, snow-like contrast for the cameras (B. Baardson, personal communication, July 3, 1994), thus practicing what the creator of the modern Olympics, Pierre de Coubertin, prescribed, "the crowd has a part to play, a part of consecration" (MacAloon, 1984, pp. 245-246).

What could be watched by the viewers all over the world was, at the end, the outcome of all the decisions taken by the television director, responsible "for turning [the ceremony] into superior television" (NRK ORTO, 1994) as a construct based on the input from 26 cameras and television photographers all over the arena. The host broadcaster presented a 2-hour television program consisting of three parts: first, the welcoming section, introducing the context of these games by animated flying figures transforming into real parachutists landing in the arena, where a presentation of host culture exploded, showing children, fiddle-players, dancers, national costumes, ski-jumpers, horses, and reindeer in a playing festival; second, the ritual elements laid out in the Olympic Charter; and third, the artistic program, with mythological beings taking over the arena.

The Televised Ceremony: Sacred Elements

The Lillehammer Opening Ceremony made visible that there are sacred representations defined into the Olympic ritual and furthered in the media spectacle encapsulating it. The Olympic Charter (IOC, 1993) laid out ritual elements in the Olympic religion intended by Coubertin, which could be "seen as an answer in action" to the call by Durkheim (his contemporary) "for 'new feasts and ceremonies' to guide mankind" (MacAloon, 1981, pp. 268-270; 1984, pp. 250-251; Rothenbuhler, 1989, pp. 142-143). At Lillehammer, however, there were some departures from the prescribed ritual, including a risky ski jump with the Olympic torch, which replaced the simple prescribed procedure of "runners relaying each other" into the stadium with a more television-friendly peak moment.

The ceremony began in the afternoon during daylight. When the time came for the artistic part of the program, darkness had fallen, inviting mystery as planned (B. Baardson, personal communication, July 3, 1994). The authors of the Artistic Concept decided to introduce the world to underworld beings: the *vetter* of old Norse mythology. Some of the *vetter* literally entered the arena from the underground. The idea was to let dancers, acrobats, and skiers visualize the *vetter* performing their own opening rituals, as an echo of the Opening of the Winter Games. In costumes made in the five Olympic colors, they presented themselves as five clans representing each of the continents.

The *vetter* were introduced as in a fairy tale, thus preparing for transformations between fiction and reality: "Once upon a time, in the endless forests and the high mountains, there lived some peaceful small beings—called *vetter*," the announcer read, drawing on the capacity of symbolic transformations of storytelling. The potential of the television medium for visual transformation was added when a camera focused on the "fairy-tale" book and a drawing therein showing an imagined *vette* shifting into a television image of a "real" costume-dressed *vette* looking exactly like the one in the book. While the announcer read that the *vetter* "were invisible to humans," but that "if you are quiet, you may hear them," the "real" figure began moving into the arena to summon more *vetter*.

The climax of the Opening Ceremony was reached when the *vetter* lifted an immense egg up from the ground. The *vetter* began to transform this egg into the terrestrial globe, and to further transform the globe into a flower opening into a huge dove of peace. Shifts in music were used to support the transformation of the moving images.

The music was integral to the overall media spectacle, offering another kind of symbolic transformation throughout the whole ceremony. The artistic director was deliberate in choosing music that would help mix elements from various religious traditions into his own blend. Fiddle players and dancers performed *Fanitullen* (*Devil's Dance*). While the *vetter* held the arena, there were sacred lamentations based on the Gregorian Catholic liturgical tradition. As they gathered to form a living, protective nest, a modern tune was used, *Stoneway* (also called *Rite for the Expulsion of Evil Spirits*). Written with the assistance of a computer "following the fractal theories of so-called chaos research," the music represented trying to "exorcise the evil spirits of our modern world," according to the Program Description. At the very climax of the closing, the ceremony featured a tune on modern organ and guitar. This was based on the hymn *Mercy*, well-known within the Norwegian Lutheran pietistic tradition.

▨ Rallies

When drafts of the Opening Ceremony became publicly known in Norway, several critical comments surfaced in the public debate. This created conflict with certain religious groups around several issues. These groups lined up to rally for their causes.

The main public controversy was focused on the Olympic Hymn. The translation of the hymn into Norwegian made the more pietistic or fundamentalist groups within the Norwegian Lutheran landscape aware of the fact that it calls upon Zeus as the Spirit of antiquity. "Why should we celebrate Zeus?" they argued. Why not portray the Norwegian Christian heritage for the world? Even one of the bishops of the Church of Norway joined in this public criticism. The critics, however, represented subcultures within the generally more pluralistic Norwegian society (Lundby, 1988).

This incident was quite instructive on how particular religious groups rally with regard to a major media event aimed at communicating with people in various religious and nonreligious traditions under a universalistic, symbolic umbrella. The Norwegian pietist groups acted out of a *substantive* understanding of religion, whereas the directors worked on the premise that the Opening Ceremony should *function* for viewers in various cultural contexts. The rallying pietists operated on a corresponding narrow and specific understanding of the functions of religion in society, whereas those responsible for the telecast based this part of their production on a substantively mixed and general understanding of sacred symbols operating on a level of global humanism.

The directors of the Opening Ceremony resisted the rallying efforts, even as they came under pressure to use only the tune of the Olympic Anthem (B. Baardson, personal communication, July 3, 1994). More than an attempt to *solve* the conflict over this symbolic representation, this was a maneuver to *resolve* it, for music opens to a wider range of interpretations due to various contexts than do explicit texts. This mechanism did, in fact, operate to address the rallying pietists during the crescendo at the end of ceremony. The use of the tune *Mercy* came to offer the criticizing religious groups, who were on the verge of becoming alienated from the Olympic Opening, a strong point of identification. One of "their" hymns was used as the underlying tune, thus Christianizing the closing part of the ritual for this specific religious public in the host culture. Importantly, it did so without demanding this interpretation from viewers in other cultures. No text was applied with the hymn. This facilitated the transcultural communication. Wordless religious tunes have this capacity for different interpretations according to various cultural positions. A consensual "truth" was made by the use of nonrational symbolism. However, seen from the point of view of the rallying religious groups, this was substantially a false solution, even if it did function partly to integrate them through affective identification.

▥ Rituals

After the rallying fights, the winning or dominant representations could be celebrated through ritual and spectacle—thus to that extent becoming collective, inviting even the opposing factions to join in.

Certainly, the Olympic Charter defines parts of the Opening Ceremony as a ritual. As a mediated spectacle, the Opening Ceremony of the Lillehammer Games came out with sacred elements from the Olympic ritual intact, even if the liminal potential of rituals was transformed into a mediated "liminoid" play with genres.[6] But other elements playing with the sacred were added through the artistic program: The *vetter* at Lillehammer brought liminal problematic into the liminoid spectacle. They offered interesting cross-overs: Stories of the *vetter* are taken from liminal experiences; however, in the Lillehammer Opening, they were put into a liminoid television spectacle, where in spectacular form they kept the liminal aspect alive.

The *vette* is mediating between "the underworld" and this world. A *vette*, according to folklore, is not a *he* or a *she* but an *it*—a sign mediating through the *vette* as object or intermediary. To get a proper understanding, however, we should not focus on the *vetter* as vehicles or intermediaries, but as articulations or mediations within a sociocultural context (Martín-Barbero, 1993, p. 187). When applied to people's lives and popular beliefs in former days, observing a *vette* was an articulation of a situation on the edge of the social system and the culture—a liminal situation (Honko, 1962, 1971; Solheim, 1952; Stattin, 1984). A *vette* made it possible to mediate across the borderline between the world here and now and the world out there, and thus to communicate out of the visible and immediate situation.[7]

The directors of the Opening Ceremony at the 1994 Olympic Games employed the *vetter* in a similar way, to mediate between the im-mediate (!) situation of the performance in the ski jump arena in Lillehammer, Norway, and the world of television viewers out there. The *vetter* also had the function of mediating between certain traditions in the host culture and the global variety of cultures taking part in the Olympic Games.

▓ Resistance

Collective representations in a mediated megaspectacle involve cross-cultural communication by searching for common denominators in the production process in relation to the variety of cultures in which people are watching. These contexts of reception at the outset represent resistance, based in their own cultural perceptions and values.

The symbolic construct put together by the host broadcaster at Lille-hammer was adjusted to minimize such resistance. The American network CBS even made its own abbreviated version, transmitted to the North American public with a few hours' delay. All broadcasting companies interfered in the final mediated product by making their own commentaries in their own languages, thus making their own versions of the televised representations.

The Winter Olympics in Norway 1994 caught the attention of a large, worldwide audience. For example, the viewing figures for the CBS transmissions to the United States were all-time highs.[8] But we do not know anything about how viewers in different contexts around the world actually interpreted the ceremony. How did they resist or reformulate the representations offered? Did this program correspond with substantive sacred meanings in these audiences? Did the media spectacle function in any religious way for those watching? We simply do not know. However, pilot studies in one U.S. city during the 1992 Winter Olympics showed that these viewers to a great extent approached the games as media events with a "potential to stimulate feelings of world-mindedness" (Emerson & Perse, 1995, p. 95). For the 1994 Opening Ceremony, no specific reception analyses were done. Thus we are not able to draw final conclusions on the extent to which there were collective representations at play. However, some helpful speculation is possible.

The directors of the Lillehammer Opening Ceremony faced the challenge of resistance in this intercultural piece of communication. The Artistic Concept was built on the presupposition that the public in front of the television screens "consist[s] of people from many nations and many cultures. Norwegian culture and Norwegian values therefore must be presented within a visual frame linking up with a meaningful 'television language'" (Baardson & Kvamme, 1993). The directors had to bridge among the elements of the Olympic tradition, the cultures or collective representations of the host country with its variety of secular and religious composites, the multiplicity of cultures represented by the athletes from 66 nations, and all the other countries that were to receive the event through their broadcasting systems. How, then, were they to construct one single television program that could be understood and interpreted across such a worldwide variety of settings?

The directors had to resist all *substantive* definitions of tradition and religion. The symbolic representations made had to be built into a higher unity, expressing a *functional* sacredness. Instead of "resistance through rituals," as in subcultures (Hall & Jefferson, 1976), they had to resist *all* rallying groups to make their over-bridging spectacle. The directors were faced with the necessity of constructing the televised opening in accordance with the demands (or inferred demands) of all-encompassing symbols to be interpreted and communicated within the various cultural and religious realms of their worldwide public. They contextualized the Opening Ceremony through locally based folklore and through the portrayal of children, folk participation, and flags as in the Norwegian Constitution Day and national sport events. However, they had to trust that this could be understood within root paradigms of various cultures around the world.

Root paradigms are "consciously recognized (though not consciously grasped) cultural models" held by individuals or groups; fundamental assumptions providing patterns for action (Biernatzki, 1991, p. 23; Turner, 1974, p. 64), similar to the structuring dispositions of practices and representations that Pierre Bourdieu termed "habitus" (Biernatzki, 1991, p. 25). Still, "divergencies of interpretation built on common attention to a common text are precisely what the religious element in modernity is all about" (Rothenbuhler, 1989, p. 142).

The representations applied in the Opening Ceremony were to a large extent reconstructed for this media event. The Olympic Rings and their colors might to a certain extent have become global symbols throughout the years and people's exposure to former Olympic Games through the mass media. This symbol was recreated by a choir of 400 children forming the Olympic Rings. The presentation of the symbolism in the giant "Tellus Egg" is even more telling. The Program Description explaining this is straight from the symbolic dictionary (Biedermann, 1992):

> Generally speaking, the egg became the symbol of the first ever vital germ, out of which the entire world has since developed. A symbol also of unity and wholeness, perfect within its shell, it represents the carefully planned creation. The white colour represents purity and flawlessness. (NRK ORTO, 1994)

The specific religious references or interpretations were, however, left out. Thus, in the presentation of the symbolism of the egg, the specific Christian meanings—linked to the resurrection of Christ—were removed. Also left out were specific Buddhist, Hindu, or other defined religious understandings (cf. Biedermann, 1992, pp. 86-87; Cooper, 1993, pp. 43-44). Believers within these religious traditions may have read the sequence with the Tellus Egg according to their specific religious understandings. The directors of the Olympic Opening, however, wished to emphasize what is unifying across religions: "The egg becomes the terrestrial globe. All the 'vetter' cooperate to protect their common symbol, the egg/globe, the safeguard of their lives and their future" (NRK ORTO, 1994).

In the closing peak of the Opening Ceremony, the different symbolic elements came together, combined into a new and higher unity: The *vetter*, coming out of the host country's mythological traditions, turn out to be defenders of the whole Planet Earth, dressed in the Olympic colors of the five continents. The egg as the general symbol of life, the opening for the dove of peace, followed by the tune of *Mercy*, all served to integrate. "The atmosphere exhales justice, reconciliation and peace" (NRK ORTO, 1994).

It should be possible to read the symbols in such a global media event in various settings all over the world, but hardly with the same meaning. The American soap opera *Dallas* traveled well over the globe on some universal root paradigms. Biernatzki (1991) has shown how this global success was at the price of the conceptual content it communicated. The symbols applied and their corresponding root paradigms became too open and general. This is probably the case with televised Olympic ceremonies, too. Collective representations have to be actively shared to become common. However, the interpretation and understanding of a symbol refers to a convention that may not at all be possible to establish globally.

Representations that aspire to universality, like those applied in the Opening Ceremony, may be read and interpreted within the innumerable local contexts of the viewers. The importance of the commentators from the various national broadcasting corporations emphasize this point. They brought the event closer to their audiences through the use of local languages. Even the Norwegian commentators had to explain the meaning of some of the symbols. When symbols have to be explicated, it is necessary to ask how universal they are. Collective representations are common, not by nature, but by use in shared culture.

A Cultural Reconstruction

The creators of the Artistic Concept for the Lillehammer Opening wanted to convey "the Olympic spirit as well as the Norwegian vision of the Olympic Games" based in the message of peace and international solidarity and in the multitude of Norwegian cultures and values anchored in folk traditions. According to the Program Description, the *vetter*, these "mysterious beings, often called 'the underworld people' have continued to exist in popular beliefs" in Norway (NRK ORTO, 1994). However, most Norwegians might have been surprised to meet this liminoid representation of figures from the fairy tales of their childhood in the Opening Ceremony.

At the same time that the 1994 Winter Olympics in the small town of Lillehammer revitalized traditional representations for Norwegians, the Olympic Games furthered Norway into modernity (Klausen, 1995a, 1995b). The Opening Ceremony ironically signalled this modernizing effect through the reintroduction of the *vetter* from old Norse mythology—barely active in root paradigms of today's Norwegians. Through this media spectacle, the *vetter* reentered as collective representations in Norwegian culture. In the liminoid play of genres, they had the capacity to link premodern traditions into late modernity. This might have worked for Norwegians, but what about other audiences?

Root paradigms are existential and fundamental for those adhering to them. Root paradigms are sacred in the Durkheimian sense, as basic collective representations. Representations of root paradigms are sacred representations. They need not be substantively religious; root paradigms can function in a religion-like way in their societies.

The Artistic Concept of the Lillehammer ceremonies is obviously based on old, partly outdated folkloristic presentations.[9] The directors of the Olympic Opening Ceremony built a new liminoid media production on the basis of old folklorist mediations. The directors of the Lillehammer production exhibited a very lax attitude and practice vis-à-vis the original folklore. They constructed their own Artistic Concept of the *vetter* for use in the 1994 Olympic Games.

The representation of the *vetter* in the Opening Ceremony at Lillehammer may well have activated some sleeping root paradigms in the Norwegian population. However, the intention of the liminoid televised ritual and the postmodern stories of the *vetter* was not to cater to any hidden Norwegian sacredness, but to create and support a global identification—just as Coubertin intended when he constructed the story of the modern Olympics with its "rites of intensification" for the spectactors, as part of the "festival of human unity." Coubertin "insisted repeatedly on the religious character of the Games." The sacred root paradigm or "transcendental ground" he sought for the Olympic ritual is just "the idea of humankind-ness" (MacAloon, 1984, pp. 248-253).

▨ Sacred, or a Site of Symbolism?

Should the ritualistic and folkloristic representations in a mediated spectacle like the Opening Ceremony of the Lillehammer Olympics really be regarded as "sacred," or is this televised ceremony simply to be conceived as a site of symbolism? On the one hand, there are definitions of religion built around the sacred-profane dichotomy, as in the work of Durkheim. On the other hand, there is a definition such as the one proposed by Clark and Hoover in this volume, in which religion is regarded as "the site of the synthesis and symbolism of culturally meaningful belief systems." According to this last option, religion is no longer "limited to what happens in a 'sacred' realm, traditionally conceived, but is that part of culture that persuasively presents a plausible myth of the ordering of existence."

The Clark-Hoover definition conceives of religion in terms of those collective representations "ordering existence" within the actual society. These collective representations might be *sacred*. The Clark-Hoover definition fits the web of collective representations in media, religion, and culture. However, it might be difficult to single out the more specific sacred elements within culture. We are left with degrees of sacredness as part of the symbolism in "the culturally meaningful belief systems." But because all symbols are cultural constructions, they end up in an ultimate reference that might be termed *sacred* or *religious* (Schütz, 1970, pp. 247-248). As such, all collective representations ultimately end up in a sacred reference. Religion is a *system* of such symbols, which means these representations have to be *collective* representations.

What is then rejected is the idea, rooted in Durkheim's works, that individual representations are profane, whereas collective representations must be sacred. The strict dichotomy of sacred/profane is itself problematic (Pickering, 1984, pp. 115-299), likewise the idea of one coherent society as the one sacred entity inherent in the Durkheimian sociology (especially when *society* is misread as *nation*). Society is not limited to one single collectivity. In the (post)modern condition, people move in and out of various groups and belong to shifting and overlapping collectivities, each developing their sacred references. Bar-Haim might be too pessimistic in his vision of weak networks without sacred centers. Dayan, on the other hand, might be too optimistic on behalf of the sacred. Liminoid media events like the Lillehammer Opening Ceremony do not have a specific sacred character. What is needed is a theory capturing the "fugitive communities" (Gitlin, 1995) of contemporary urban societies. Maybe most collective representations in (post)modern media culture are to be regarded as fugitive. However, even fugitive communities are communities based in, and supported by, collective representations of that community or collectivity. As such, they make up potential sacred centers, even if they might be weak and changing.

This keeps a basic insight from Durkheim's (1912/1968) definition: Religion unites in a "moral community" all those who adhere to what is there held sacred (p. 47). Religion has to be expressed in community. Thus we are reminded that religion is not only a system of collective representations or beliefs, but also of practices keeping this community alive.

Religiosity could never be reduced to ontology or meaning alone, for religiosity has "something to do with belonging and community," as Kohn (1995) reports out of a postmodern experience of the 1992 Winter Olympics (p. 108).

Religion always has a "site," to cite the Clark-Hoover definition, though not necessarily a place in traditional geographical-institutional sense.

This invites an understanding of the sacred as a *variable* ranging from the substantive to the functional. Religion usually is defined either by its substance or according to the functions it performs (Berger, 1974). The interplay among rallies, rituals, and resistance related to the sacred in an intercultural media spectacle such as the Olympic Opening demonstrates that there are substantive sacred elements and sacred functions simultaneously operating in relation to secularized ordinary everyday life. Some communities, like traditional religious groups, stress substantive elements of religion. Other, more fugitive communities might be more functionally based.

A Sacralized Moment

Even on a global arena, as in an Olympic Opening Ceremony shared worldwide, there is some sacredness, as in the case of the all-encompassing symbols of Lillehammer. However, as collective representations, these symbols are weak, temporary, and general. Global representations served by transnational television, as in the Olympic celebrations, can at best create feeble feelings of something sacred for that moment, corresponding to the liminoid character of the mediated spectacle.

The producers of the Lillehammer Opening Ceremony did their best to sacralize this media event in order to legitimize the Games and share the Olympic mystery to the world. However, due to the symbolic transformations inherent in the mediation process, the sacred functions of the Opening Ceremony were possibly based as much in the working of the television medium itself as in the cultural and ritual elements employed. Symbols were put together and reconstructed for the purpose of the media event and brought to the world by the magic of television. This megaspectacle did offer some sacred locus for the worldwide public, but such occasional sacred representations cannot last.

Notes

1. It is not correct to say that Durkheim simply equates society with these collective representations, or that he separates the individual from society in his analysis (Pickering, 1984, pp. 249-250). Cf. also Lukes (1981).

2. Roel Puijk and Arne Martin Klausen provided me with material and references to their ongoing research on the cultural dimension of the Olympics '94 (Klausen, 1995a, 1995b; Puijk, 1993). I would also like to thank Arvid Esperí and Bentein Baardson.

3. Discussions with Gabriel Bar-Haim and Daniel Dayan have improved this chapter, for which I thank them. The shortcomings are my responsibility.

4. Cf. comments by Chief Sports Correspondent David Miller of *The Times* in the main Norwegian daily *Aftenposten*, March 1, 1994.

5. MacAloon (1984) makes precise distinctions between the concepts of *spectacle, festival,* and *ritual*, which I try to take into account.

6. The televised Opening Ceremony of the Lillehammer Games was a ritual in the *liminoid* sense (MacAloon, 1984, p. 266). Here we are drawing on Durkheim through the work of Victor Turner (Rothenbuhler, 1988). Liminoid phenomena under modernity tend to be characterized by play and experiment in a leisure setting. (Post)modern television offers plenty of examples. The liminoid phenomena provide, like tribal rituals, a "transitional framework within which everyday social and cultural experience is transformed, i.e., liminality" (Alexander, 1991, pp. 20-22; Biernatzki, 1991, pp. 127-130; Turner, 1992, pp. 55-58).

7. Anne Eriksen introduced me to a folkloristic understanding of the *vetter* and gave valuable comments and suggestions for the work with this chapter.

8. Of Americans, 204 million watched more or less of the 16 days of the Winter Olympics, constituting 83.7% of the U.S. population or 92.5% of the households. An average of 27.5% of the U.S. population watched the reports from Lillehammer at any time of the transmissions. The 1994 Winter Games drew the most TV viewers ever in the United States according to the Norwegian *Aftenposten* March 1, 1994, and the *Washington Post* referred to in *Aftenposten*, March 5, 1994.

9. The Artistic Concept refers to a "Lower Mythology," a concept from folklorists in the middle of the last century, completely outdated by contemporary science. Even the distinction between "good" and "evil" *vetter* is highly controversial and not easily accepted by contemporary folklorists.

References

Alexander, B. (1991). *Victor Turner revisited: Ritual as social change.* Atlanta: Scholars Press.

Alexander, J. (Ed.). (1988). *Durkheimian sociology: Cultural studies.* Cambridge, UK: Cambridge University Press.

Baardson, B., & Kvamme, B. (1993). *Artistic concept for the opening and closing ceremonies at the 1994 winter games.* Unpublished manuscript (in Norwegian).

Bellah, R. N. (1959). Durkheim and history. *American Sociological Review, 24,* 447-461.

Berger, P. L. (1967). *The sacred canopy: Elements of a sociological theory of religion.* Garden City, NY: Doubleday.

Berger, P. L. (1974). Some second thoughts on substantive versus functional definitions of religion. *Journal for the Scientific Study of Religion, 13,* 125-134.

Berger, P. L., & Luckmann, T. (1971). *The social construction of reality: A treatise in the sociology of knowledge*. Harmondsworth, UK: Penguin. (Originally published 1966)

Biedermann, H. (1992). *Symbolleksikon*. Oslo: Cappelen. (Originally published as *Knaus Lexikon der Symbole*. München: Droemersche Verlagsanstalt, 1989).

Biernatzki, W. (1991). *Roots of acceptance: The intercultural communication of religious meanings*. Roma: Editrice Pontificia Universita Gregoriana.

Cooper, J. C. (1993). *Symbol-lex*. Oslo: Hilt & Hansteen. (In English, *An illustrated encyclopaedia of traditional symbols*. London: Thames and Hudson, 1990).

Dayan, D. (1995, January). *Television rituals: Redesigning collective identities*. Paper presented at the conference on Media and the Transition of Collective Identities, Department of Media and Communication, University of Oslo, Norway.

Dayan, D., & Katz, E. (1988). Articulating consensus: The ritual and rhetoric of media events. In J. Alexander (Ed.), *Durkheimian sociology: Cultural studies* (pp. 161-186). Cambridge, UK: Cambridge University Press.

Dayan, D., & Katz, E. (1992). *Media events: The live broadcasting of history*. Cambridge, MA: Harvard University Press.

Durkheim, E. (1968). *The elementary forms of the religious life* (6th ed., J. W. Swain, Trans.). London: Allen & Unwin. (Originally published 1912)

Durkheim, E. (1974). Individual and collective representations. In *Sociology and philosophy* (pp. 1-34). (D. F. Pocock, Trans.). New York: Free Press. (Originally published in 1898)

Emerson, M. B., & Perse, E. M. (1995). Media events and sports orientations to the 1992 Winter Olympics. *Journal of International Communication, 2*, 80-99.

Gitlin, T. (1995, January). *Illusions of transparency, ambiguities of information: Notes on the globalization of fugitive communities*. Paper presented at the conference on Media and the Transition of Collective Identities, Department of Media and Communication, University of Oslo, Norway.

Hall, S., & Jefferson, T. (Eds.). (1976). *Resistance through rituals: Youth subcultures in post-war Britain*. London: HarperCollins.

Honko, L. (1962). *Geisterglaube in ingermanland*. FF Communications No: 185, Suomalainen Tiedeakatemia. Helsinki: Academia Scientiarum Fennica.

Honko, L. (1971). Memorat och folktroforskning. In A. B. Rooth (Ed.), *Folkdikt och folktro*. Lund, Sweden: Gleerups.

International Olympic Committee. (1993). Rule 69 with bye-law. In *Olympic Charter*. Lausanne: International Olympic Committee.

Klausen, A. M. (1995a). *Olympic design and national identity—Between tradition and modernity*. Oslo: Norsk Form.

Klausen, A. M. (1995b). *Traditional and modern elements in Norwegian culture: Did the winter games change anything?* Lecture for IOC-members, Lillehammer.

Kohn, N. (1995). Exposed and basking: Community, spectacle and the winter olympics. *Journal of International Communication, 2*, 100-119.

Lillehamer Olympic Organizing Committee. (1994). *Program for the opening ceremony*. The XVII Olympic Winter Games. Lillehammer: Author.

Lukes, S. (1981). *Emile Durkheim. His life and work: A historical and critical study*. Harmondsworth, UK: Penguin.

Lundby, K. (1988). Closed circles: An essay on culture and pietism in Norway. *Social Compass, 35*, 57-66.

MacAloon, J. J. (1981). *This great symbol: Pierre de Coubertin and the origins of the modern Olympic Games*. Chicago: University of Chicago Press.

MacAloon, J. J. (1984). Olympic Games and the theory of spectacle in modern societies. In J.
J. MacAloon (Ed.), *Rite, drama, festival, spectacle: Rehearsals toward a theory of cultural
performance* (pp. 241-280). Philadelphia: Institute for the Study of Human Issues.

Martín-Barbero, J. (1993). *Communication, culture and hegemony: From the media to the mediations.* London: Sage.

NRK ORTO. (1994). *Opening ceremony, host broadcaster.* The XVII Olympic Winter Games,
Lillehammer (unpublished).

Peters, J. D., & Rothenbuhler, E. W. (1989). The reality of construction. In H. W. Simons (Ed.),
Rhetoric in the human sciences (pp. 11-27). London: Sage.

Pickering, W. S. F. (1984). *Durkheim's sociology of religion: Themes and theories.* London:
Routledge & Kegan Paul.

Puijk, R. (1993). Introduction. In R. Puijk (Ed.), *OL-94 og forskningen III* (pp. 1-11). Lillehammer: Östlandsforskning.

Rothenbuhler, E. W. (1988). The liminal fight: Mass strikes as ritual and interpretation. In J.
Alexander (Ed.), *Durkheimian sociology: Cultural studies* (pp. 66-90). Cambridge, UK:
Cambridge University Press.

Rothenbuhler, E. W. (1989). Values and symbols in orientations to the Olympics. *Critical
Studies in Mass Communication, 6,* 138-157.

Rothenbuhler, E. W. (1993). Argument for a Durkheimian theory of the communicative.
Journal of Communication, 43, 158-163.

Schütz, A. (1970). *On phenomenology and social relations.* Chicago: University of Chicago Press.

Solheim, S. (1952). *Norsk sætertradisjon.* Oslo: Aschehoug.

Stattin, J. (1984). *Näcken: Spelman eller gränsvakt?* Malmö, Sweden: Liber.

Turner, V. (1992). *Blazing the trail. Way marks in the explorations of symbols.* Tucson: University
of Arizona Press.

Turner, V. (1974). *Dramas, fields, and metaphors: Symbolic action in human society.* Ithaca, NY:
Cornell University Press.

Part III

Media, Religion, and Culture:
Changing Institutions

Chapter **10**

Changes in Religion in
Periods of Media Convergence

Peter G. Horsfield

The present period is widely recognized within the Christian community as one of significant change. The period is being characterized and addressed variously in theological circles and debate: as post-modernism (Bellah & Burnham, 1989; Griffin, Beardslee, & Holland, 1989); as post-liberalism (Lindbeck, 1984); as post-Christian (Hauerwas, 1991); as a crisis in modern or Enlightenment thought (Davaney, 1991; Oden, 1990; Toulmin, 1990); as pluralism (Burnham, 1989; Newbigin, 1989; Tracy, 1987); or as a new contextualism (Bevans, 1992).

Hans Küng and David Tracy (1989) suggest that the changes being faced by religious institutions are of such a nature that the very practice or discipline of thought that we know as theology could be affected, such that we could be looking at "the emergence of a new, different pattern of theology—a new paradigm" (p. xv). However, the impact of the changes on religion is felt beyond just the disciplines of theology. The formal institutions of religion in Western culture are all facing major organizational, economic, and authority changes, which are described at best as restructuring and at worst as decline (Wuthnow, 1988, 1993). What have been the central and binding functions and activities of these religious institutions—worship, nurture and religious education, pastoral care, and mission—can all be seen to be in a process of reexamination and transition in an effort either to find a new direction within the present challenges or to refind an old source of useful certainty (e.g., Bosch, 1991; Browning, 1983, 1987; Oden, 1984; Pattinson, 1993).

When one explores various dimensions of this theological and ecclesial debate, what is significantly absent is a recognition of the significant role that changes in media have had on this influential cultural ferment. But it goes deeper than lack of recognition. Reading through the major works of contemporary theological thought, one struggles to find even a mention to indicate that the thinkers and leaders of religious communities have any understanding of the foundational effect of changes in the patterns of social communication in the cultural transformation now being experienced. Specific texts on media and religion certainly can be found, but serious analysis of modern media within major theological analysis and debate is significantly absent.[1]

In relation to other social institutions, such as education, health, and welfare, religious institutions in most Western cultures have not only been actively involved as practitioners, but have played an influential role in shaping social philosophy and practice in those areas. Religious institutions' commitment and influence in the social institution and practice of electronic media, however, has been only marginal.

In an earlier essay, I proposed that much of this failure occurs at the stage where the frame of thought of religious leaders is set—that is, in centers of theological education—and I suggested a number of factors that have shaped this particular perspective (Horsfield, 1989). A more recent study by a U.S. National Council of Churches Media Education Committee supports this by illuminating the extent to which media understanding is seen as irrelevant or at best marginal to theological education and religious leadership (Bedell, 1993).

What can explain this failure of leaders of major religious institutions and seminaries to recognize the foundational place of media in cultural formation and change and to invest in and develop a sustained theological tradition of strategic reflection and engagement with it? I propose that what is being reflected may be understood within the framework of a major paradigm shift from largely nation-based cultures in which print was the dominant medium, to world-linked cultures in which electronic-based means of communication have become dominant.

In this shift, the major Christian institutions in Western culture have been closely identified with print-based culture and ethos, and their leaderships have also closely identified themselves with this culture and ethos. As the communication paradigm has shifted, these institutions find themselves losing many of their social privileges and having to participate competitively in a situation in which their status, recognition, and ability to fulfill a range of social and cultural functions competitively is being significantly diminished. The marginality of media studies within seminaries can be partly understood as a function of the decontextualization of ideas common to Western rationalism, partly as a result of the tradition of disciplinary segmentation common to Western theological education, and partly as a defensive stance by academic theologians whose social power and status, based in book culture, is threatened by the shift brought by electronic media.

▒ A Framework of Understanding

That religion and culture are closely interrelated has long been recognized and has been the subject of sustained theological reflection. To sustain the perspective that religious thought is also significantly influenced by shifts in media, it is necessary to establish a framework that lifts media out of the common religious frame of instrumentality and reestablishes it as a central and indispensable hermeneutic dimension of culture. In some cases, this means reaffirming some tenets that have long been elemental in media and cultural studies but have never seriously been considered in theological thought.

Communication and culture are symbiotic in relationship and inseparable in practice. "Every cultural practice is a communicative event. Every act of communication is a cultural event" (Kress, 1988, p. 10). How a society communicates with itself is a fundamental constitutive component of culture and will be reflected in the ways in which that society organizes, perceives, and thinks about itself.

Communication activities within any particular culture are complex and multiform. For a long time, communication analysis from both a U.S. and a European perspective stressed the directional, effectual, or dominative influence of media agents and institutions. In recent years, research and theoretical work has affirmed the personal and cultural interactiveness by which individuals and cultures appropriate and use media representations, rather than simply being subject to them. Martín-Barbero (1993) notes this in his proposal of reconceptualization from media to mediations:

> [C]ommunication began to be seen more as a process of mediations than of media, a question of culture and, therefore, not just a matter of cognitions but of re-cognition. The processes of recognition were at the heart of a new methodological approach which enabled us to perceive communication from a quite different perspective, from its "other" side, namely, reception. This revealed to us the resistances and the varied ways people appropriate media content according to manner of use. . . . This enabled us to break out of the circle of false logic which made it appear that capitalistic homogenisation is the only meaning of our contemporary modernity. For, in Latin America, cultural differences . . . [imply] a dense variety of strong, living popular cultures which provide a space for profound conflict and unstoppable cultural dynamism. (p. 2)

Despite affirmation of this cultural dynamism, the organization, interactions, and thought of any particular culture will be distinctively conditioned by the technological, social, ideological, and power characteristics of the media of communication that are socially, economically, or politically dominant or that hold superior status. Correlatively, changes in the dominant media of communication will also have a profound effect on the culture's self-perception, organization, meaning, and value systems. These changes may occur through influences that may be internal or external to the culture, and may be evolutionary or cataclysmic in nature. Changes in communication patterns will also be mediated in each culture through the complex and dynamic structures of existing cultural order and processes.

Substantial work has now been done on the relationship between communication and cultural form. Ong's (1982) anthropological work on the psychodynamics of primary oral and literate cultures is well known. A number of aspects of Ong's analysis have particular relevance for understanding impacts on religious thought and practice. One is his emphasis on the place of memory in culture and the impact of changes in knowledge storage and retrieval devices. A second is his discussion of the relationship between textual space and meaning, their impact on the development of knowledge, and the shaping effect that textual space and meaning have had on the "mentality" of the Western world (pp. 123-135).

Boomershine (1987) provides a similar correlation from the framework of New Testament hermeneutics. Drawing on Ong's framework, Boomershine proposes "a demonstrable correlation between media change and the emergence of paradigm shifts in the history of biblical interpretation" (p. 156). Boomershine identifies five major periods in biblical hermeneutics according to the dominant form of communication—oral, manuscript, print, silent print, and electronic—and provides a schema for identifying the characteristics of the biblical paradigm in each era according to elements of the hermeneutical system (p. 157).

Martín-Barbero's affirmation of the strength of popular culture in mediating mass messages serves as a useful reminder that media changes and their impact on culture cannot be seen without recognizing that new media and media changes are themselves cultural creations. How then can we affirm a causal relationship between media changes and cultural changes, while at the same time acknowledging the cultural genesis of new media and the symbiotic relationship that exists between media and culture?

Several images present themselves. One is that of culture as a multiform organism. It is precisely because it is multiform that changes may be generated within a particular segment of the culture that expand beyond that segment to effect changes and give new shape to existing relationships within the whole or beyond the whole. Such was the case with the development of printing, which originated within the culture of craft groups, extending beyond those craft groups to give a new shape to a range of other cultural practices and exchanges (Eisenstein, 1979, p. xv).

A second image sees communication functioning as the web of the culture—the complex, multiform, and multilevel pattern of personal, structural, and object connections that enables the dynamism of coherence and incoherent creativity to coexist. When a particular medium of communication becomes dominant, it does not obviate all other forms or patterns of communication, but it changes the complex character and functioning of the web, variously displacing some connections, changing the direction and importance of others, refiguring others by disconnection and reconnection, and changing the valency of recognized legitimacies and illegitimacies.

A third image sees the emergence and influence of a new medium within a culture in catalytic terms. A new medium arises from within a culture, but having arisen, begins to act as a catalyst for cultural refocus and more extensive cultural change. One could speculate that the ferment of cultural factors that gave rise to the new medium in the first place is the very cultural ferment that allows the new medium to have such a catalytic effect.

The case can be put, therefore, that there is a close connection between changes in dominant media and major changes in cultural perceptions and functions such as time, space, institutional life, authority structures, community formation, and so forth—arguing at the same time that it is too simplistic simply to propose a singular correspondence between the emergence of each major new medium of communication and the transformation of a prior cultural period into a major new one.

Major new media that have emerged do so, not out of the blue, but from within a process of cultural ferment or transformation. The emergence and influence of changes in media, therefore, are better understood if seen not in isolation, but in association with a convergence of cultural developments that both serve and are served by the emerging media. Change produced by changes in media, however, is greater than change in other single cultural factors because media changes alter the web that mediates the culture to itself.

A central element of culture that is affected by changes in means of communication is the aspect of power. Communication underlies and shapes the recognition and exercise of sociocultural power. Access to information, the status and resources to construct meaning; and the ability to identify, muster, and construct resources—all essential characteristics of communication—locate and sustain one within social power structures. The various media of social communication function competitively, in terms both of their association with recognized exercisers of power and of their ability to fulfill desired social functions. They coexist through a competitive process of ordering and by carving out a competitive place and function within a social or economic sphere.

When a new medium of communication enters a social or economic marketplace, a power struggle occurs, and a process of reordering and readjustment of power relations takes place. Uncompetitive means of communication—those that are unable to maintain a competitive place in fulfilling social functions—tend to be displaced and to atrophy.

▨ Religious Issues in the Shift to Electronic Culture

Within this framework, it was proposed above that we are in the middle of another major cultural paradigm shift, midwifed by the emergence of electronic media, which is provoking a convergence of cultural change and ferment.

The impact of the technologies and institutions of electronic communication need to be understood in relation to their intertwinement with two other major cultural movements, each of which is dependent on, and integral to, the other. One is the vast expanse of technological and scientific development spurred by the Enlightenment ideology of progress, reason, and control and resulting in the production of amazing machinery for controlling, changing, and creating physical processes and products. Although the optimism of the boundless frontiers of time and space that have sustained this momentum of progress has been significantly diminished in this century, this has not necessarily diminished its productions.

The second broader cultural movement is that of consumer capitalism, the intricate socioeconomic system that taps the human drives of individual gain and greed, selectively rewarding incentive and encouraging participation in the capitalist system by the prospect of increased consumption of pleasurable goods or services and access to otherwise restricted promises of satisfaction. The development of each of these would not have been possible without the infrastructure, supporting philosophy, and processes of the other.

Analyses of similar periods of communication-cultural convergence indicate that in each period existing religious institutions, along with other social institutions, have found that this convergence of factors, mediated by the new communication, presents challenges on a range of fronts—ideological, institutional, and practical.

The movement of the early Christian church out of its parent Jewish culture into Greek culture, for example, was not just a simple process of organizational expansion, but was a movement from a largely oral context into a manuscript context. The dynamic process of adjustment that followed took centuries, resulting in the redefinition of faith from a particular into a universal context, the shift of authority from an apostolic to a hierarchical episcopal base, the establishment of a written canon, and the stabilizing of orthodoxy through ecumenical creeds. A central functionary in this process was the apostle Paul. Scholarship that considers the role of Paul in both embodying and enabling the transition between Jewish and Greek culture can easily be expanded to elucidate the impact made by different uses of writing in those cultures (e.g., Boomershine, 1991; Gerhardsson, 1977; Watson, 1994).

Adjustments to the technology of writing and the integration of writing into the communication practices of the Christian communities was complex. One of the significant Christian apologists of the second century, Clement of Alexandria, found the prejudice against writing in the second century church such a barrier to effective cultural transition into the hellenistic context that he specifically addressed it at the beginning of one of his writings, the *Stromateis*. Osborn (1959) notes the specific nature of the resistance to writing challenged by Clement:

> The living voice was the best medium for the communication of Christian truth. Writings were public and it was wrong to cast pearls before swine. To write implied that one was inspired by the Holy Spirit and this was a presumptuous claim. If one must write, it were better that one should write badly. The heretics had shown that a clever style could mislead and corrupt. (p. 335)

Likewise, the major adaptation of religious thought to print during the period of the Reformation did more than provide an instrumental means for the sharing of different ideas. It redefined privileges of information and debate, authority, faith, and order in religious practice, as Edwards (1994) points out:

> [T]he printing press played far more than just an assisting role in this many-sided contest over authority. It broadcast the subversive messages with a rapidity that had been impossible before its invention. More than that, it allowed the central ideological leader, Martin Luther, to reach the "opinion leaders" of the movement quickly, kept them all in touch with each other and with each others' experience and ideas, and allowed them to "broadcast" their (relatively coordinated) program to a much larger and more geographically diverse audience than has ever been possible before. Yet, paradoxically, printing also undermined central authority because it encouraged the recipients of the printed message to think for themselves about the issues in dispute, and it provided the means— printed Bibles especially—by which each person could become his or her own theologian. (p. 7)

When one adds to that Toulmin's (1990) argument that Western rationalism arose in the 17th century as a necessary attempt to find a nonsectarian basis for social stability in response to the religious wars sparked by the European Reformation, it makes the impact of printing a significant cultural one indeed.

The nature and direction of the cultural convergence being mediated by developments in electronic media are still extremely fluid. The challenge it is posing to established religious institutions and the restructuring it is causing within religious institutions—both between different religious institutions and between religious institutions and their cultural location—is profound. I mention a few of those profound challenges to illustrate the thesis that the religious issues being dealt with are not adequately understood without taking seriously the changes that are occurring in the media of social communication.

The Expansion and Commercialization of Mediated Communication

Within the broader framework of consumer capitalism and technologies that allows for the instant dissemination of information and entertainment products worldwide, the potential of information and entertainment to be gathered, produced, protected, and distributed for commercial profit has lead to a shift in understanding of the nature and function of social communication.

This does not mean that social communication and the development of social and religious thought in previous eras was free of commercial influence. Edwards (1994), in particular, is informative on the extent to which the religious ideas of Martin Luther, in contrast to most of his Catholic opponents, were actively encouraged and promoted by commercial printers throughout Europe because they were so profitable as publications.

Rather, developments in electronic media, linked with increasing worldwide affluence and the breaking down of national boundaries in trading arrangements and cultural product dissemination has tended to move social communications away from an overarching concept of community good toward a relative concept of community good mediated through the broader desirability of commercial instrumentality.

Furthermore, the commercial process, again facilitated and necessitated by shifts in the character and implementation of communication technologies and integration, has lead to the increased subdivision of people into identifiable "markets" within which they are then cultivated, affirmed, and carefully solicited. These markets are identified or constructed by processes of market research and are subsequently legitimized by promotion through the media and reinforced by serving as loci in the provision and distribution of products. The broad cultural effect is that people are sociologically relocated, as it were, away from membership and identity within an integrated and general nurturing community and toward identification with, and membership in, a variety of different and specific markets.

This shift has dramatically affected the structure of the social base on which religious institutions have framed their organization, leading to the restructuring of religious organizations (as identified by Wuthnow, 1988). This shift has favored particular types of religious organizations, while disadvantaging others. Brasher (1994) postulates that those religious organizations that address themselves to particular fragments—or markets—of the society and have developed expertise in doing so, such as fundamentalist or parachurch specialist organizations, are doing well. Those most disdvantaged by this process of cultural segmentation are those moderate religious groups who

> preferred institutional forms and habitual practices that connect them with a diverse cross section of people whose values vary. In a time of cultural cohesion, sufficient shared values exist to congeal these groups in spite of the presence of significant differences; but, in the modern/post-modern rupture, it is this center of shared values that disappears. Moderate institutions, with ties to diverse constituencies due to their modernist commitments to unity, have discovered that during today's cultural rupture their lauded transvalue connections anchor them to constituencies so conflicted that they tear the groups apart. (pp. 4-5)

This view is supported by research on Australian churches (Hughes, 1993). Hoover's study on televangelism suggests that one of the major achievements of the evangelical broadcasters in the 1970s and 1980s was in providing a powerful public rallying point and face of coherence to these diverse and otherwise scattered religious market groups (Hoover, 1988).

One could speculate that the print-enculturated ethos of unity, coherence, and universalism that has characterized the theological thought and quest of mainstream ecumenically oriented religious groups has diminished their capacity to conceptualize the convergence now taking place and to formulate a response that requires a competitive approach in a redefined communication marketplace.

▓ The Changing Nature of Media as Institution

The dominant theory until recently has been one in which the media have been seen primarily as one social institution among others. In this view, it has been assumed that there is a separate and coherent social norm or reality, with the media serving primarily as tools for communicating this reality. The dominant approach has therefore been to study the "effects" the media have on people. In this view, institutions such as the church have tended to look at the media instrumentally; that is, how they can use the media best to convey "our reality." In recent years, as discussed above, there have been several crucial shifts in thinking about media.

One change has been away from seeing the media as just one aspect of culture. Rather, the media form, as it were, the "web" of the culture, the matrix where most people now get most of their insight, influence, values, and meaning. In the power shift that has taken place, other social institutions tend not to use the media to communicate their reality, but rather are placed by the media on the web of culture in different positions and for different purposes.

The second major change has been in shifting the center of focus and attention in thinking about media away from the intended effects of media messages and toward the active role audiences play in selection and use of their own media-mix for meaning-seeking and meaning-satisfying purposes. On a broad scale, people increasingly tend not to see the media through lenses developed through their enculturation in other social collectives. Media, individually and as an institution, are now so pervasive and such an inextricable part of people's lives and culture that we now see all other social collectives (including religious faith) through the lens of our enculturation in media.

The change in thinking about people's and culture's relationship to media is in this crucial dimension as Hoover (1993b) points out:

> This relationship between people and media is entirely a volitional one. . . . People live on the media "map" because they want to, and more importantly, because that map is an authentic one for them. (p. 89)

That is, people are not passive recipients of media messages generated by commercial media organizations. People now participate in the media-web of culture, not because they are coerced or duped into doing so, but because they choose to do so. They get enjoyment out of it, and it is meaningful and authentic for them.

The same applies to religious institutions. The media as the agents of convergence present a significant alternative source of religious information, sentiment, ethical guidance, ritual, and community, not only for the broader population, but also for those who are members of religious institutions. Religious organizations may no longer be the main source of religious information, truth, or practice, even for their own members.

▨ Changes in Churches' Visibility in the Public Realm

As a result of the competitiveness in communication fostered within the electronic era, churches have been significantly displaced from the public realm. Previously the church, along with the state, was a major, direct participant and influence in the public arena, with substantial control over how it was represented. Today, however, "an independent institution of publicity and publication—the media—predominates, and the Church and the State must submit themselves to this 'media sphere'" (Hoover, 1993a, p. 186).

Retaining the desire to be players in the public arena, but losing their power to control how their symbols are used and how they are represented publicly, has created confusion in most churches about how to participate publicly without privilege. Confusion about their public role has further diminished church institutions' relevance and visibility in public debate and issues. Because both people in society and people in churches live in the public realm, and because existence in the public realm validates authority and relevance, the absence of church presence in the public realm of the media diminishes people's perception of the relevance of faith to their everyday existence—their "real" life.

A challenge being faced by churches, therefore, is to rethink the public relevance and applicability of their ideology in a situation in which almost every function that the church used to serve is now alternatively available as an often more attractive consumer commodity, in which they can no longer control how they are represented or how their symbols are used. In short, how are they going to exercise influence as a diminishing minority in a utilitarian culture?

The Impact of Commoditization

This competitive nature of the marketplace applies particularly in the dynamic of consumer commoditization, that commercial process whereby noncommercial human activities and services are appropriated, re-formed, packaged, and then sold as commercial products or services. Religious institutions, whose ideology was previously promoted and sustained within a package of other functions and services, their monopoly in some cases often protected by their privileged social position or even by legislation, now find that many of these functions and services have been appropriated, repackaged, and sold by commercial interests, often in a much more attractive way than the churches were doing. This century, for example, has seen the pastoral and community functions of religious institutions in previous centuries commercialized as a major industry in the form of the secular therapies. In recent decades, the personal motivation and esteem dimensions of the Christian faith, which previously brought many people to church, have been repackaged (without the Christian ideology) as motivational seminars and sold to people for anything from $50 to $1,000 a seminar.

This competitiveness in the marketplace, even in the marketplace of social communications, means that to survive, communication institutions must become aggressive, imperialist organizations. It is instructive to note how significant has been the influence of consumerism as a philosophy, even as a hermeneutical lens through which Christian faith is understood and interpreted. One can note, for example, the influence of commoditization on the advertising and promotion of faith "products" and religious "services," the significant appeal of the marketing approach of the church growth movement, and the widespread debate about the reconfiguring of faith to give consideration to "what's in it" for the participant. Adapting to this new situation appears to be easier for those religious organizations whose ideology equips them for competitiveness than for those whose ideology seeks to foster cooperation and consensus.

▒ The Reformation of Moral Structures

A further major consequence of the new web of electronic communication has been the reformation of moral structures. Whether it is a break-up of moral structures toward a condition of social amorality or relativism, a reformation into a network of interrelated centers of moral discourse, or a process of reformation of cohering common values remains to be seen.

Several reasons are given for this reformation: (a) a logical extension of the Enlightenment separation of morality from an unconditioned imperative; (b) an emphasis on, desire for, and consumption of information for information's sake; (c) the lack of practical differentiation between different types and values of different information; (d) the lack of practical opportunity and incentive to live out a commitment to one body of moral information over another; (e) the constant influx and renewal of information that makes the development of durability and relevance in moral structure problematic; (f) lack of skill in the implementation of space and silence, which makes discernment of moral order and value difficult.

Babin (1991) links this ferment in moral structure directly to media change:

> The process of de-structuring takes place irresistibly, just as water dripping on a rock . . . we hear, read, and see countless things that mean nothing to us, either at the level of usefulness or at the spiritual level. . . . What counts is not the rational structure of a good basic training, but being in the flow of information. (p. 41)

Religious institutions, because of the joint membership of their constituency in both the institution and the broader society, must of necessity define their own moral frameworks within the broader framework of social morality, whether the definition be one of congruence, incongruence, or various intermediate positions. When the moral structures of the broader culture change, this has ramifications for the defined positions of religious institutions within that culture.

The dominant social structures of morality in most Western cultures have been traditionally strongly linked to, and supportive of, Christian faith to such an extent, in many cases, that churches have been seen as the moral educators and guides for the society. The shift in moral structure that is part of the social convergence of electronic media has important implications for both how religious institutions conceive their relationships to their host cultures and how they nurture ethical behavior within their adherents who also participate fully as members of the culture.

Note

1. Two exceptions may be noted. Martin Marty (1989), in his contribution to *Paradigm Change in Theology,* notes the close link between theologians, theology, and books and the changes being brought in theology because of the changing nature of the book (p. 186-187). In setting up a framework for analysis of postmodern visions, Joe Holland (1989) in *Varieties of Post-Modern Theology* proposes a theory of the journey of human culture through four stages. At each transition, Holland identifies the place of media change as a midwife for the subsequent cultural changes (pp. 98-111). These examples, however, are notable because of their exceptionality.

References

Babin, P. (1991). *The new era in religious communication.* Minneapolis, MN: Fortress.

Bedell, K. (1993). *Seminary study conducted for the National Council of Churches Media Education Committee—Summary of findings.* Unpublished document.

Bellah, R. N., & Burnham, F. M. (1989). *Postmodern theology.* San Francisco: Harper and Row.

Bevans, S. B. (1992). *Models of contextual theology.* Maryknoll, NY: Orbis.

Boomershine, T. E. (1987). Biblical megatrends: Toward a paradigm for the interpretation of the Bible in electronic media. In K. H. Richards (Ed.), *Society of biblical literature seminar papers* (pp. 144-157). Atlanta, GA: Scholars Press.

Boomershine, T. E. (1991). Doing theology in the electronic age: The meeting of orality and electricity. *Journal of Theology, 95,* 4-14.

Bosch, D. (1991). *Transforming mission: Paradigm shifts in theology of mission.* Maryknoll, NY: Orbis.

Brasher, B. (1994). *Life in multiple worlds: An archaeology of a UCC congregation alive and well in the modern/postmodern rupture.* Paper presented to the annual meeting of the Society for the Scientific Study of Religion, Albuquerque, NM.

Browning, D. (1983). *Religious ethics and pastoral care.* Philadelphia: Fortress.

Browning, D. (1987). *Religious thought and the modern psychologies: A critical conversation in the theology of culture.* Philadelphia: Fortress.

Burnham, F. B. (Ed.). (1989). *Postmodern theology: Christian faith in a pluralist world.* San Francisco: Harper and Row.

Davaney, S. (Ed.). (1991). *Theology at the end of modernity.* Philadelphia: Trinity.

Edwards, M. (1994). *Printing, propaganda, and Martin Luther.* Berkeley: University of California Press.

Eisenstein, E. (1979). *The printing press as an agent of change: Communications and cultural transformations in early modern Europe* (Vols. 1 & 2). Cambridge, UK: Cambridge University Press.

Gerhardsson, B. (1977). *The origins of the gospel traditions.* London: SCM Press.

Griffin, D., Beardslee, W., & Holland, J. (1989). *Varieties of postmodern theology.* Albany: State University of New York Press.

Hauerwas, S. (1991). *After Christendom?* Sydney: Lancer.

Holland, J. (1989) The postmodern paradigm and contemporary Catholicism. In D. Griffin, W. Beardslee, & J. Holland (Eds.), *Varieties of postmodern theology* (pp. 9-27). Albany: State University of New York Press.

Hoover, S. (1993a). Mass media and religious pluralism. In P. Lee (Ed.), *The democratisation of communication.* Cardiff: University of Wales Press.

Hoover, S. (1993b, Spring). What do we do about the media? *Conrad Grebel Review,* pp. 97-107.

Hoover, S. (1988). *Mass media religion: The social sources of the electronic church.* Newbury Park, CA: Sage.

Horsfield, P. (1989, October). Teaching theology in a new cultural environment. *Media Development,* pp. 6-9.

Hughes, P. (1993). *Faith alive: An Australian picture.* Melbourne: Christian Research Association.

Kress, G. (Ed.). (1988). *Communication and culture.* Kensington: University of New South Wales Press.

Küng, H., & Tracy, D. (Eds.). (1989). *Paradigm change in theology: A symposium for the future.* New York: Crossroad.

Lindbeck, G. A. (1984). *The nature of doctrine: Religion and theology in a postliberal age.* London: SPCK.

Martín-Barbero, J. (1993). *Communication, culture and hegemony: From the media to mediations.* London: Sage.

Marty, M. (1989). The social context of the modern paradigm in theology: A church historian's view. In H. Küng & D. Tracy (Eds.), *Paradigm change in theology: A symposium for the future* (pp. 174-201). New York: Crossroad.

Newbigin, L. (1989). *The gospel in a pluralist society.* London: SPCK.

Oden, T. (1984). *Care of souls in the classic tradition.* Philadelphia: Fortress.

Oden, T. (1990). *Agenda for theology: After modernity . . . what?* Grand Rapids, MI: Academie.

Ong, W. (1967). *The presence of the word: Some prologemena for cultural and religious history.* New Haven, CT: Yale University Press.

Ong, W. (1982). *Orality and literacy: The technologising of the word.* London: Methuen.

Osborn, E. (1959). Teaching and writing in the first chapter of the Stromateis of Clement of Alexandria. *Journal of Theological Studies, 10,* 335-343.

Pattinson, S. (1993). *A critique of pastoral care* (2nd ed.). London: SCM Press.

Regan, H., & Torrance, A. (Eds.). (1993). *Christ and context: The confrontation between gospel and culture.* Edinburgh: T & T Clark.

Toulmin, S. (1990). *Cosmopolis: The hidden agenda of modernity.* New York: Free Press.

Tracy, D. (1987). *Plurality and ambiguity.* San Francisco: Harper and Row.

Watson, N. (1994). "The philosopher should bathe and brush his teeth"—Congruence between word and deed in Graeco-Roman philosophy and Paul's letter to the Corinthians. *Australian Biblical Review, 42,* 1-16.

Wuthnow, R. (1988). *The restructuring of American religion: Society and faith since World War II.* Princeton, NJ: Princeton University Press.

Wuthnow, R. (1993). *Christianity in the 21st century: Reflections on the challenges ahead.* New York: Oxford University Press.

Chapter 11

Media, Meaning, and Method
in Religious Studies

Chris Arthur

In his study of the Ituri Pygmies, Colin Turnbull (1961) describes the key role played in their religious life by the *molimo*, or sacred trumpet. It is used by the tribe's elders to "waken the forest" on whose complex webs of life the Pygmies are utterly dependent. Eventually, having gained their trust, Turnbull is shown the *molimo*, which is treated with great reverence and secrecy. To his surprise, the Pygmies' most sacred object turns out to be a length of metal drainpipe (pp. 72-73). A similar example of how an unlikely object may be invested with religious meaning was reported recently from San Francisco. A traffic bollard, dumped some years ago in that city's Golden Gate Park, has come to be regarded by many as a sacred object. Hundreds of worshippers, some from as far away as India, have traveled to San Francisco to pray, meditate, and make offerings of flowers and incense in front of this latter-day lingam (Reeves, 1993). Such instances powerfully underline Mircea Eliade's (1958) thesis that "we cannot be sure that there is anything that has not at some time in human history been transformed into a hierophany" (p. 11). Eliade gives this generic name to the diverse ways in which religion finds expression (rituals, myths, cosmogonies, symbols, sacred places, scriptures, ceremonial costumes, shamanic dances, etc.). Hierophanies are the raw material of religious studies.

Given that human religiousness expresses itself over such a staggering range of forms—everything from traffic bollards to the *Summa Theologiae*—it is important for religious studies to try to cultivate a sensitivity to the variety of media through which its subject matter finds voice; otherwise we may end up uncritically assuming that religion admits of neater definition and more clear-cut boundaries than is in fact the case. Yet there is a tendency in the discipline toward media-blindness. Such blindness ignores what Len Masterman (1985) sees as the first principle of media studies, namely that "media are symbolic systems which need to be actively read, and not unproblematic, self-explanatory reflections of reality" (p. 20). Masterman offers a simple illustration of the way in which this principle tends to be ignored. An art teacher holds up a painting of a horse in front of a class and asks what it is. The invariable reply is: "it's a horse." The teacher shakes his head and asks again. Eventually the distinction between a horse and its representation on canvas is established. The same point is made in René Magritte's famous painting of a pipe across which is written, *"ceci n'est pas une pipe."* Perhaps books about religion should bear similar disclaimers on their covers to remind us of the way in which our worlds of meaning are constructed from media representations.

▨ Significant Breakthroughs?

A turning point, according to Ursula King, editor of *Turning Points in Religious Studies* (1990), "implies a significant breakthrough" (p. 15). Whether or not the contributors to this volume have been successful in identifying such breakthroughs is debatable. The final section, with chapters by John Hinnells, King herself, and Kim Knott, does seem to pinpoint—in the arts, gender, and information technology—three very significant currents that have the potential to alter in quite fundamental ways the course the discipline follows. That two of these newly emergent turning points (or paradigm shifts) are principally concerned with media issues, is indicative of the way in which the relationship between religion and media is likely to be increasingly seen as a crucially important area of study.[1]

In his essay on religion and the arts, John Hinnells (1990) begins by noting that mass literacy is "a relatively recent and still mainly 'western' phenomenon," a claim borne out by comparative surveys of national adult literacy rates. It follows, therefore, that "over the millennia the majority of the world's religious people have been illiterate." As such, when the study of religion focuses on textual sources, it risks "plugging in to a level of religion which most of the practitioners are not, or have not been engaged in." To counteract the risk of such a partial view, Hinnells argues that in addition to looking at written sources, the subject must recognize in the arts a second significant form of religious expression. The arts, he says, do not just constitute the earliest means of religious communication, "but represent a major form of religious expression in modern times as well" (p. 257). Marginalizing the arts—and Hinnells sees this as a common failing in religious studies—means "excluding the possibility of an adequate appreciation of what it is that makes religion a living experience for the practitioner" (p. 271).

Given the enormous diversity of hierophanies that constitute the raw material of our study, sampling those that manifest themselves in writing is, naturally, important. But it ought to be only part of a much more wide-ranging investigation.

Gregory Schopen's methodologically important paper, "Archaeology and Protestant Presuppositions in the Study of Indian Buddhism" (1991), substantiates Hinnells' warnings by pointing to specific examples in which media-bias leads to the misrepresentation of religion. Schopen is concerned with exposing a double peculiarity. The way in which the history of Indian Buddhism has been studied by modern scholars is, he says, "decidedly peculiar." But what is even more peculiar "is that it has rarely been seen to be so." The roots of these twin peculiarities lie in precisely the kind of media-blindness that Masterman (1985) identifies, and the lesson Schopen offers is analogous to the art teacher's efforts to get his class to recognize the difference between a horse and its representation in a painting. His paper reminds us that there are a variety of modes of religious expression to be considered, that different images of Buddhism can be constructed from different media sources.

Why is the study of Indian Buddhism "peculiar"? Because, says Schopen (1991), it operates a "curious and unargued preference for a certain kind of source material" (p. 1). There are two basic strands of media that cast light on this area. On the one hand, there is archaeological material; on the other, there are textual sources. Schopen identifies a clear scholarly preference for literary rather than archaeological material. Indeed, such is the strength of this preference that "textuality overrides actuality" (p. 11). Real Buddhism comes to be equated with textual Buddhism. And yet the literary material consists of heavily edited texts that are intended "to inculcate an ideal," that record "what a small atypical part of the Buddhist community wanted that community to believe or practice" (p. 3), whereas the archaeological material "records or reflects at least a part of what Buddhists actually practiced and believed" (p. 2).

Having noted the peculiarity of simply allowing literary sources to assume primacy, a media-bias that he also detects in the study of early Christianity, Schopen attempts to account for it. The idea that religion is located in written sources is, he suggests, "a decidedly non-neutral and narrowly limited Protestant assumption" (p. 19). In other words, our picture of Indian Buddhism may reflect Western theological values as much as it reflects the history and values of Indian Buddhism. By focusing too much on written sources, we may end up with a picture of Buddhism that inadequately reflects the variety of phenomena that make up this complex and diverse tradition.

In *The Meaning of Religion*, W. Brede Kristensen (1960) argued that if we try to understand religious data from a different viewpoint from that of the believers, we "negate the religious reality" (p. 13). Both Hinnells and Schopen are concerned that precisely such a negation may routinely happen because of a blindness to the significance of media, which in turn leads to an uncritical preference for written sources.

An assumption about what religion is, whether expressed explicitly in a definition, or implicitly as a media-bias that leads us only to consider one type of material, can have the effect of directing our inquiries away from the actual religiousness of those who constitute the living reality of a faith and toward abstract formulations whose claim to be representative of such faiths is open to question, thus Cantwell Smith's (1978) objection to the very concepts "religion" and "the religions" (p. 153). As Margaret Miles (1985) has shown, what until recently was regarded as being universal human history is, in fact, largely the history of an atypical, privileged minority, namely of those who read and write. If we want to democratize religious studies and ensure that our understanding of religions is fairly representative of the actual phenomena that make up the different faiths, then it is important not to adopt a single medium approach. There are, for example, many "whose sense of self and relationship was informed by images rather than words" (p. 152).

▨ Media and the Understanding of Religious Expression

The work of scholars like Hinnells and Schopen alerts us to the existence of different media of religious expression and shows how our understanding of religion may be skewed if we over-emphasize one type. Walter Ong and Jack Goody are more concerned with the extent to which different media can actually shape our religiousness in the first place. To try to summarize the work of such prolific scholars here would be misplaced; I want simply to touch on some of their ideas that serve to further strengthen the case for saying that the field of religious studies needs to adopt a more media-conscious methodology.

It is perilously easy to suppose that "after a theology is thought out or put together, media simply circulate it" (Ong, 1969, p. 462). Walter Ong's work challenges this kind of (still pervasive) naïveté by highlighting the cognitive consequences of introducing a new medium. According to Ong (1982), "more than any other invention writing has transformed human consciousness" (p. 78). Without writing, the literate mind "simply could not think as it does." Not only does a medium like writing influence the individual, it also affects societies. "Oral communication unites people in groups. Writing and reading are solitary activities that throw the psyche back on itself" (p. 69). Looking at differences between oral and literate cultures, Ong highlights the extent to which a medium facilitates and molds thinking, rather than just neutrally carrying its ideas. For instance, oral societies must invest much time and energy in repetition, saying things over and over again to avoid forgetting. "This need establishes a highly traditionalist or conservative set of mind that inhibits intellectual experimentation" (p. 41).

In contrast, the text frees us from such conservative memory tasks, thus enabling the mind "to turn itself to new speculation." Indeed for Ong, writing "separates the knower from the known and thus sets up conditions for 'objectivity' in the sense of personal disengagement or distancing" (p. 46). That this will have profound religious implications is clear.

Some of these implications are spelled out by Jack Goody. He suggests that in oral cultures a word like *God* "may hardly be conceived of as a separate entity, divorced from both the rest of the sentence and its social context. But, once given the physical reality of writing it can take on a life of its own" (Goody & Watt, 1968, p. 53).

By objectifying words and by "making their meaning available for much more prolonged and intensive scrutiny than is possible orally," writing "encourages private thought" (p. 62). Goody sees religion as being profoundly influenced by writing. Literacy facilitates the development of world, rather than more local, religions. It also gives rise to some of the characteristics of such world religions—universality, low tolerance of change, and so on—just as the absence of literacy helps to shape less encompassing traditions (Goody, 1986, pp. 3-5, 9-10, 20, 22).

The Media Dimension of Religion

In a review article in *Numen,* the journal of the International Association for the History of Religion, Hans Kippenberg (1992) identified what he terms "a new area for development in the study of religions," in which "the literary forms used by the great religions" would be examined (p. 107). Although it is good to see an article appearing in which the significance of Jack Goody's work is acknowledged, it would be a shame to confine this new area of development to literary forms alone. We need, rather, to attend to all the varieties of media used to express religiousness. Indeed, in much the same way that dentists use disclosing fluid to reveal the extent of placque, so some methodological equivalent is needed in religious studies so that the important media-dimension involved in this subject does not go unnoticed. Such disclosure is important, not so we can remove something unwanted, as in the dental model, but simply so we may be aware of its action and influence, both on the discipline and on its subject matter. In particular, we need to ensure that a multi- rather than a mono-media approach is adopted; that a range of media, appropriate to the range of hierophanies, are consulted. At least five arguments could be developed in favor of such a strategy.

First, as Hinnells, Schopen, and others have suggested, a media-bias in favor of writing can act to shift our focus from actual lived religiousness to abstract statements of ideals. But as Ninian Smart (1988) reminds us, "Ultimately the most important symbols communicating the essence of religion are the people involved" (p. 443). We risk losing sight of people as the most important medium of all, if we fail to take account of the full range of ways in which they express their religiousness—drain pipes, traffic bollards, cave paintings, dance, architecture, *and* writing.

Second, if, as Ong, Goody, and others have suggested, media are part and parcel of religious thinking, not simply inert means of conveying it, then if we want to access the full spectrum of such thought, we must not confine our attention to any single medium. If major religious developments are related to the evolution and availability of different media, then to understand the history of religion, we need a media-sensitive approach.

Third, if, as is often claimed, religious experience is in some sense beyond words, then it would be unwise to be over-reliant on verbal sources. Likewise, if we allow that inexpressibility in general tends to be an important feature of virtually all forms of religious expression, then in light of the apparent communicative failure underlying every hierophany, it would seem more appropriate to consider the full range of expressive attempts, rather than limiting ourselves to any one variety. I.T. Ramsey (1964) has suggested an elegant theory, based on the media-consequences of religion's ineffable, mysterious core, that helps to explain the seemingly endless diversity of expression found in this realm of human experience. Religious language, Ramsey argues, is peppered with "qualifiers," terms such as "infinite," "eternal," "perfect," "all powerful," and such like, that have a two-fold function: first, to remind us of the ineffable and mysterious generative aspect of religion that spawned them; and second, to indicate that no expression can fully describe, encompass, or exhaust that aspect. Qualifiers serve to "multiply models without end" (p. 60). As such, it would be inappropriate for religious studies to treat any one model or type of model as definitive.

Fourth, many of Ong's and Goody's insights have been stimulated by experiencing the move from literate to televisual culture. Such a change in the dominant social medium acts to sensitize us to the existence and impact of media in our lives. From a religious point of view, Thomas Boomershine (1987) has suggested that such changes are revolutionary in that they can transform the character of a community's experience of the sacred (p. 275). The way in which TV effects such a transformation, the recasting of religion that it demands, ought surely to be a matter of urgent, current, and substantial interest to religious studies.

Fifth, given the fact that television is viewed by some commentators as a religious or quasi-religious phenomenon itself (e.g., Babin, 1991; Fore, 1987; Goethals, 1990; Warren, 1992), aspects of modern mass media may be of quite direct interest to religious studies. If we locate religion in any one particular medium, we may prejudice our chances of seeing such novel manifestations of religiousness. Again, we need to avoid the blinkering of vision that can so easily result from the assumed definitions of uncritical media-bias.

This is to suggest, very briefly, some of the ways in which media influence religious meaning and some of the ways in which religious studies needs to reformulate its methodology to take account of this important fact. In expanding the argument, we might want to add to the work of Hinnells and Schopen a third example of a media-sensitive approach, in the form of William Graham's superb study of the oral dimension of scripture, *Beyond the Written Word* (1987). Attention might also be given to the way in which Rudolf Otto's (1923) picture of religion as a warp and woof of rational and non-rational elements, lends itself to supporting an approach that does not rely only on verbal sources.[2] And some attention might also be given to the way in which the discipline itself might inculcate an openness to new forms of media in expressing the results of its work.[3] However, the medium of a short chapter in a book imposes its own constraints, so the further exploration of these matters must be located elsewhere.

Notes

1. The present volume itself is, of course, expressive of this tendency. Further indication of the extent to which media-related issues have come to be regarded as highly significant for religion is voiced by many of the contributors to Arthur (1993). (See also my essay review of books in this area, in *Religious Studies Review*, 21(2), 98-104 [1995]). As the editors of *Concilium* 1993/6 put it, in an issue devoted to the mass media, media quite simply "shape

our perceptions of reality" and their significance ought to be assessed accordingly (Coleman & Tomka, 1993, p. vii).

2. For some interesting ideas about how Rudolf Otto's famous account of the relationship between rational and nonrational elements in religion can be linked to different media of religious expression, see Babin, 1991. (This aspect of Babin's work is highlighted in my review of his book in *Media Development, 38*(4), 44 [1991]).

3. For some ideas about possible new forms of media for academic communication, see the "calls for papers" section in the journal *Common Knowledge, 1*(1) (1992), pp. 4-11. The points made by Greil Marcus (p. 8) and Paul Feyerabend (pp. 8-10) are of particular interest.

References

Arthur, C. (Ed.). (1993). *Religion and the media, an introductory reader.* Cardiff: University of Wales Press.

Babin, P. (1991). *The new era in religious communication* (D. Smith, Trans.). Minneapolis, MN: Augsburg.

Boomershine, T. (1987). Religious education and media change. *Religious Education, 82*(2), 269-278.

Coleman, J., & Tomka, M. (Eds.). (1993). Mass media. *Concilium, 6.*

Eliade, M. (1958). *Patterns in comparative religion.* London: Sheed and Ward.

Fore, W. (1987). *Television and religion: The shaping of faith, values, and culture.* Minneapolis, MN: Augsburg.

Goethals, G. (1990). *The electronic golden calf: Images, religion, and the making of meaning.* Cambridge, MA: Cowley.

Goody, J. (1986). *The logic of writing and the organization of society.* Cambridge, UK: Cambridge University Press.

Goody, J., & Watt, I. (1968). The consequences of literacy. In J. Goody (Ed.), *Literacy in traditional societies* (pp. 27-68). Cambridge, UK: Cambridge University Press.

Graham, W. A. (1987). *Beyond the written word: Oral aspects of scripture in the history of religion.* Cambridge, UK: Cambridge University Press.

Hinnells, J. (1990). Religion and the arts. In U. King (Ed.), *Turning points in religious studies* (pp. 257-274). Edinburgh: T. and T. Clark.

King, U. (Ed.). (1990). *Turning points in religious studies.* Edinburgh: T. and T. Clark.

Kippenberg, H. G. (1992). The problem of literacy in the history of religions. [Review Article] *Numen, 39*(1), 102-107.

Kristensen, W. B. (1960). *The meaning of religion: Lectures in the phenomenology of religion.* (J. B. Carman, Trans.). The Hague, The Netherlands: Mouton.

Masterman, L. (1985). *Teaching the media.* London: Comedia.

Miles, M. (1985). *Image as insight: Visual understanding in western Christianity and secular culture.* Boston: Beacon.

Ong, W. (1969). Communications media and the state of theology. *Cross Currents, 19,* 462-480.

Ong, W. (1982). *Orality and literacy: The technologizing of the word.* London: Methuen.

Otto, R. (1923). *The idea of the holy: An inquiry into the non-rational factor in the idea of the divine and its relation to the rational* (J. W. Harvey, Trans.). Oxford, UK: Oxford University Press.

Ramsey, I. T. (1964). *Models and mystery.* London: Oxford University Press.

Reeves, P. (1993, October 31). Lo and behold, a bollard. *Independent on Sunday,* p. 1.

Schopen, G. (1991). Archaeology and Protestant presuppositions in the study of Indian Buddhism. *History of Religions, 31*(1), 1-23.

Smart, N. (1988). Communication. In E. Barnouw (Ed.) *International encyclopedia of communication* (vol. 3, pp. 443-446). New York: Oxford University Press.

Smith, W. C. (1978). *The meaning and end of religion.* London: SPCK.

Turnbull, C. (1961). *The forest people.* London: Jonathan Cape.

Warren, M. (1992). *Communication and cultural analysis: A religious view.* Westport, CT: Bergin and Garvey.

Chapter 12

Televangelism

Redressive Ritual
Within a Larger Social Drama

Bobby C. Alexander

This chapter calls attention to televangelism's role as redressive ritual within a larger social drama or social conflict in which televangelism's conservative Christian viewers are players. As we will see, as ritual, televangelism has the capacity and potential to contribute to the efforts of viewers to overturn their marginalized or peripheral social standing within American society. The analysis of televangelism as ritual presented here is offered as a reconsideration of the attraction televangelism holds for its viewers.

Broadly defined, *ritual* is a performance that makes a transition away from the everyday world to an alternative context within which the everyday is transformed. The transformations that ritual brings about are more than symbolic. They carry over into the everyday world, influencing people to view the world and to act in it in new ways. Ritual transforms the experiential base out of which people live their everyday lives (Geertz, 1973; Turner, 1974, 1985). Ritual is essentially "a *showing of a doing*"

(Schechner, 1977/1987). As demonstrative performance, ritual displays the fact that participants are engaged in actions by which they constitute themselves. By means of ritual, participants become their performing and perform their becoming (Driver, 1991).

We will see how viewers discover, in televangelism's capacity to serve as ritual legitimation, the potential to transform their status as a social group in American society from that of a marginalized group into a significant group, at least in their own eyes. We will also see how viewers discover, in televangelism's capacity as ritual to adapt them to some of the views and lifestyles of mainstream American society, the potential to transform their social status. Accommodation to the social mainstream has the potential to win for viewers greater acceptance by it, and hence greater inclusion and status within it. How the television medium and the public nature of its message lend themselves, at a more general level, to efforts of televangelism's marginalized constituency to construct a more mainstream identity is explored in the chapter by White in this volume.

The holy war waged by televangelism's viewers against contemporary American society is obvious, as is their battle to gain greater political power and influence within the wider society as religious conservatives. Viewers are also engaged in a battle that is less obvious: gaining greater recognition and inclusion within mainstream American society. Televangelism's viewers are a "marginalized" social group (Bruce, 1990; Wuthnow, 1989). Their commitment to their narrowly conservative religious belief and morality and their narrowly conservative position on social and political issues lead mainstream society to push televangelism viewers to its margins. The social mainstream is highly secularized, pluralistic in makeup, and committed to a democratic way of life in the broadest sense.

The American mainstream is itself religious (as shown by the recent study made by the Graduate Center of the City University of New York, 1991). Religion has long played a role in shaping American society, and Americans continue to look to religion to help shape public values. But mainstream society does not permit any single religion to be the sole supervisor, legitimizer, or arbiter of public values and public life (Bruce, 1988). Although American society and the Christian and Jewish religions are intermeshed, they are not synonymous.

Mainstream society considers the judgmental and exclusive religion of televangelism's conservative Christian viewers incompatible with the democratic way of life. Although viewers embrace democracy—freedom of religious expression makes airing the religious telecasts possible—they are not as tolerant of other views and would restrict the freedom of those not practicing conservative Christian morality. Mainstream society considers as outright hostile the political agenda of the Religious Right for which televangelism is a platform. Conservative Christian politics is viewed as an attempt to impose a narrow religious morality on others by redirecting legislation and court decisions. The American mainstream actively opposes these efforts, from denunciations by the news media, to punitive court decisions, restrictive legislation, challenges at the party precinct level, and the like.

To be sure, televangelism's conservative Christian viewers participate in secular society. They vote, engage in the entertainments, and so forth (Bruce, 1988, 1990; Hunter, 1983, 1987). But viewers are only partly secularized (Bruce, 1990). Their theological beliefs and morality have not changed significantly from the religion of viewers of televangelism in its infancy in the decade of the 1950s (Gerbner et al., 1984). Viewers believe the Bible is literally true, because, it is believed, it has been revealed by God himself. They hold fast to biblical morality, and they subscribe to the millenarian and antisecular view of scripture. These defining features of viewers' religion—most are fundamentalists and Pentecostals (Gerbner et al., 1984)—distinguish them from members of mainstream society. Although the social mainstream is religious in the main, their religion has long accommodated the secular worldview and lifestyle. The beliefs of televangelism's viewers lead them to oppose secular society.

Televangelism viewers believe secular society is allied with Satan in an effort to defeat God and God's purposes for the world. The militancy of viewers in promoting biblical morality is motivated by the view that the moral regeneration of the secular world is critical to the defeat of Satan and to God's redemption of creation. Viewers believe that they are God's agents in the world and that their efforts are vital to the defeat of Satan. Their militancy is also motivated by the belief that the cosmic battle between God and Satan for eternal dominion over the Earth is coming to a head, for Satan has stepped up his battle against God in these last days. Viewers believe they will have a share in God's perpetual rule as a reward for remaining faithful to God and to God's purposes.

Conservative Christian belief is not monolithic. There are significant theological and ecclesiastical differences among the viewers of the various programs. Fundamentalists, for example, reject speaking in tongues, the hallmark of Pentecostalism, and the belief that the spiritual gifts are necessary for full salvation. Pentecostals criticize fundamentalists' emphasis on church order. Most viewers, however, share a "fundamentalistic" belief (Gerbner et al., 1984).[1]

The relatively small number of viewers of televangelism accentuates their marginal status in American society. Only around 13.3 million people—5% of the American population—regularly watch some form of religious television, including conservative programming. Of these, only 55% report having had a "born-again" experience, the chief indicator of fundamentalistic Christianity. And those who watch religious telecasts are by and large already committed to their religion and are already churched (Gerbner et al., 1984). The small population of viewers is underscored by the relatively small number of conservative Christians. They make up only 16% of the American population (McKinney & Roof, 1987). The number of conservative Christians who watch televangelism is even smaller. The size of the Religious Right is also relatively small, as underscored by the failure of this group to effect the hoped-for sweeping political changes at the national level during the 1980s. Other indicators of the relatively small size of this group are the defeat suffered by Pat Robertson in his bid for the Republican party's presidential nomination and Jerry Falwell's closing down the Moral Majority due to inadequate financial support (Bruce, 1988, 1990).[2] The small number of viewers also calls attention to the marginal religious beliefs and morality of viewers.

Under threat and under fire by mainstream American society, viewers discover in the ritual base and features of televangelism opportunities to legitimate or establish in their own eyes the credibility and significance of their religion and morality as well as of their religious group. Self-legitimation is critical to the efforts of televangelism's viewers and promoters to mobilize politically and to promote their social agenda. At the same time, mobilization serves their interest in defending their religion and religious group, as well as their effort to promote themselves as a significant social group and to push for greater inclusion within mainstream society.

Viewers also discover in televangelism's ritual base and features means of adapting or accommodating themselves to the secularized outlook and lifestyle of the very society whose secularity and pluralistic makeup are opposed by their religion. Televangelism helps viewers learn more about social and political issues within the wider secular society. It gives them an opportunity to experiment with some of the sensibilities of secular society and with the secular lifestyle. Becoming more like those "out there" in the secular world makes viewers less suspect. Incentive for adapting grows out of the recognition that the social mainstream promises greater inclusion to those who become more secularized, who embrace a way of life that is in keeping with the broader democratic and pluralistic outlook of the social mainstream. Viewers are not just flirting with the secular lifestyle because they find it enticing. Experimentation with secular sensibilities is an adaptive strategy, undertaken to win the acceptance of mainstream society.

Self-legitimation of viewers' religion and adaptation or accommodation to some of the demands of secular society are contradictory ritual roles. The contradiction expresses the cross-pressures of competing religious and social interests pulling viewers in opposite directions. The conflict over televangelism's role as ritual also gives expression to viewers' ambivalence toward secular society—it challenges their religious beliefs—and toward their religion—it prevents them from gaining the acceptance of the social mainstream.

▨ Viewers' Ritual Participation in the Telecasts

Televangelism's effectiveness as ritual in legitimating and adapting viewers is enhanced by viewers' active participation in the television performances. (I am modifying the conventional understanding of ritual as face-to-face interaction to include home viewers as participants in the telecast performances.)

Viewers put themselves in a position to engage in the telecast performances by first ritualizing their viewing. They watch with regularity, and they also establish ritual routines that prepare them to participate actively in the telecasts. Of the viewers who watch Robertson, Falwell, and Swaggart, and who watched the Bakkers, 43% pray before they turn on the programs, and 77% pray after they turn off the program. Before they turn on the program, 40% read the Bible; and 29% do so after they turn off the program. (Of these, 23% purchased the Bible they use from the TV ministry airing the program they watch. In fact, 63% purchase study materials or mementos from the television ministry.)[3]

Viewers' ritualized preparation serves as a runway leading up to participating in the activities undertaken in the telecasts. Of the viewers who took part in my survey, 82% indicated that they participate in the worship format of the program (51% do so frequently); 82% pray along with the telecast; and 37% read the Bible along with the program.

Ritually engaging in the telecasts enables viewers to tap the transformative power of ritual and to participate fully in the reconstructions of the everyday world and of viewers' identity and status in it that are brought about by the telecast performances. These transformations are made possible as the telecast performances help viewers make a transition away from the everyday world to an alternative context within which the secular world is reconstructed along the lines of viewers' millenarian vision, or within which viewers experiment with mainstream views and styles of life.

The transition is begun as viewers ritually prepare to participate in the programs and is continued by the openings of the programs. The telecasts begin with a routine greeting extended by hosts or by an announcer. These are accompanied by the theme music for the various programs or by congregational singing. In the case of Falwell's *The Old-Time Gospel Hour*, the greeting segues into a worship service in progress. Logos identified with the various programs and other visual symbols also help viewers make a transition to the telecast performances. Frequent mention of the religious or moral theme for a particular program also helps viewers shift their attention away from the secular, everyday world and toward the world as reconstructed by the telecasts.

In addition to the religious interests viewers bring with them to the telecasts—they share the beliefs and morality expressed by the various programs and are therefore involved along with the telecasts in the production of religious meaning—they also bring their interest in redressing their marginalized social status, although they are not fully aware that they do so. Viewers consciously identify themselves as citizens of heaven first. But as creatures of flesh and blood, they also bring to their viewing their social needs and interests. Viewers find in the special, divine status generated by the telecasts in their role as ritual self-legitimation—that of a people who are special in the eyes of God—the added status of being a significant social group because they are significant to God. And viewers create for themselves the identity of citizens who are at home in the wider world and accepted by it as they experiment with a more secularized identity and lifestyle.[4]

▓ Ritual Legitimation

Televangelism provides an important venue within which to communicate the message of conservative Christianity and to present an intellectual argument that reinforces it. Televangelism makes the case that the conservative Christian religion, its morality, and its view of the world are true because they are based on God's own truths, which are found in the Bible viewers live by. Thus conservative Christianity is made congruent with a cosmic or divine order. Televangelism provides another important reinforcement. As ritual performance, it evokes certain emotional experiences that provide immediate, firsthand, experiential evidence of the authority of conservative Christianity's accounting of the world as well as the conservative Christian lifestyle as an effective means of negotiating a threatening world (Geertz, 1973, pp. 87-125).

Televangelism has played an obvious role in *communicating* the millenarian message of conservative Christianity. Not as obvious is televangelism's role in *legitimating* the message. In the millenarian religion that lies at the heart of the telecasts, viewers find support for their efforts toward self-validation. But it is the legitimation of viewers' beliefs by emotional experiences that ring true to their religious view of the world that makes their religion more convincing and compelling. The telecasts arouse anxiety and even fear as they dramatize Satan's presence in the world, especially in the "persecution" of, or opposition to, conservative Christians by the secular courts, legislative bodies, press, or civil liberties groups. The emotions reinforce the view that secular society is on the side of Satan, that persecution is masterminded by Satan himself as part of his effort to defeat God's purposes in the world by defeating God's people. Anxiety and fear also drive home the point that conservative Christians must not let down their guard, but must step up their moral battle against secular society during these last days.

These attacks on secular society were illustrated in a video clip aired on a program of Robertson's *700 Club*, which showed Atlanta police dragging to waiting police vans members of "Operation Rescue" who had blocked the entrance to an abortion clinic. It showed the "pro-life" demonstrators later incarcerated behind a high, chain-link fence. The clip was shown in conjunction with a report on the pro-abortion plank adopted by the 1988 Democratic National Convention, then meeting in Atlanta. The effect was to underscore the threat to pro-family, biblical morality and its conservative Christian supporters now represented by one of the nation's political parties.

Relief and exultation are aroused as the telecasts dramatize God's promise to protect and deliver the faithful, and as they dramatize the inevitable and imminent defeat of Satan and punishment of his secular allies, as well as the vindication of conservative Christians when God includes them in his rule over a transformed world. Exultation is also elicited by the reminder that conservative Christians stand in the long line of the nation's "Christian founders" and that they will be blessed by holding the nation to its "Christian heritage" and divinely appointed role as the vehicle through which God will accomplish his purposes in the world. The spiritual high often takes on a triumphalist, self-congratulatory tone. These emotions make God's presence equally real, reinforcing the belief that "God is who he says he is," and that God will protect and bless conservative Christians in return for their faithfulness and commitment to do moral battle against Satan and the secular world.

In the process of legitimating religious belief, the conservative religious lifestyle and morality are also authenticated. The telecast performances portray the conservative Christian lifestyle as intellectually defensible because it is in accord with the way their religious beliefs say the world is put together. The conservative lifestyle is presented as a reasonable strategy for negotiating the world as described by the religious worldview. The worldview is in turn reinforced when the world is shown to be arranged in such a way as to accommodate a particular style of life. Worldview and lifestyle are made to go hand in hand (Geertz, 1973).

Once worldview and lifestyle are legitimated or authenticated as ideal models *of* the world, they become models *for* viewing and living in the world. The ritual performances thus help viewers shape the everyday world, bringing it in line with their religious vision for it as viewers put into action conservative Christian religion and morality, whose credibility and authority have been reinforced (Geertz, 1973). Although the religious message of the television programs plays an important role in televangelism's power to move viewers, the ritual experiences created by the telecasts enhance the power of the religious message. The renewed experience of their religion as a powerful vision or explanation of the world and an effective strategy for living in it is critical to the mobilization of conservative Christians to do battle with the secular world on the political front, and thereby to enhance their power and standing in American society.

▓ Ritual Adaptation

Televangelism's ritual nature also gives it the capacity to broaden viewers' horizons. As ritual transition to an alternative context, the telecasts provide viewers an opportunity to relax their conservative beliefs and lifestyle and to experiment with a broader religious orientation as well as a more secular outlook and lifestyle.

As Stewart Hoover (1988) has observed, television programs like Robertson's *700 Club* have helped transform the consciousness of televangelism's viewers. The programs have moved viewers away from the "insularity" and "particulars" of traditional or sectarian roots of conservative Christianity. Coming from "outside their local frames of reference," the telecasts promote a "translocalism," transcending viewers' local beliefs, experiences, and culture. The programs introduce a range of perspectives on Christian doctrine, represented by hosts and guests, often presented on the same program. The programs move viewers toward a religion that is more open to the universe of the Christian religion, more aware and accepting of the diversity of religious belief and doctrine within Christianity, and more aware of the parochial character of traditional doctrine and its limited view of the world. And the programs make viewers more aware of and open to the wider world. "Religious broadcasting has been at the center of reformulation of the fundamentalist worldview" (Hoover, 1988, pp. 229-230).

Hoover's is the first study to recognize the ritual nature of televangelism and to recognize that its capacity to broaden viewers grows out of televangelism's ritual base. Drawing from Victor Turner, Hoover observes that as ritual, televangelism enables viewers to make a transition away from standard beliefs and commitments and to experiment with alternatives. Hoover has other interests, however, and does not pursue the discussion of televangelism as ritual or how the telecast performances work as ritual adaptation.

The conventional understanding of ritual is that it keeps things in place. The standard view holds that ritual assigns traditional roles and statuses on which the social-structural status quo depends. Turner (1974, 1969/1987, 1982/1993) argues that ritual's essential role is social. Its capacity to promote change grows out of its "liminal" nature. Ritual transition to an alternative context suspends the existing social structure as well as commitment to it. Putting the everyday social-structural world in limbo makes possible assigning or innovating new roles and identities. Ritual relaxes, if it never completely annihilates, the seemingly fixed identities, statuses, and duties that regulate routine, everyday life. In the process, ritual permits and invites participants to conceive of their identity and relations to one another in new ways, including ways that compete with the norms and routines in place within the everyday world, and to experiment with these.

As ritual, televangelism offers viewers a nonthreatening context within which to open themselves to the wider world and to explore ways of looking at the world and of living in it that are more in keeping with the secularized views and lifestyle of a changing American society. As ritual, televangelism provides viewers an opportunity to relax their grip on their conservative religion. Even as viewers turn to televangelism to legitimate their conservative religion, they discover in its liminal features the opportunity to let go with the other hand and to experiment—if tentatively—with certain features of the the secularized view and style of life. Televangelism has introduced viewers to, or has made them more familiar with, secular politics and has encouraged them to become more politically involved. It has introduced them to views on social and political issues that compete with their own. Televangelism has also introduced viewers to, or it has made them more familiar with, attitudes, dress, language, music, and other sensibilities of the secular world that fundamentalism and Pentecostalism have traditionally opposed.

Televangelism routinely reports on and discusses news events and social issues within the wider world. Although analysis is offered from the conservative Christian perspective, the commentary and news segments nonetheless expose viewers to the wider world, or further acquaint viewers who are more aware with the secular world. Televangelism acquaints viewers with points of view on social and political issues that compete with the conservative Christian view. It acquaints viewers with the reasoning behind the opposing views and with the various parties involved.

Additional exposure to the wider world comes with reports and discussions of challenges from the secular world to conservative Christian belief and lifestyle. There is discussion of challenges to marriage, rearing children who face the pressure to experiment with drugs and alcohol, and so forth. Robertson's program takes the lead, offering more straightforward opportunities to learn about the wider world through discussions on how to invest or how to run a business.

Through music and visuals, these television programs also expose viewers to some of the aesthetic sensibilities of the secular world—especially programs such as the *700 Club* and the Bakkers' *PTL Club* that have mimicked commercial television. These sensibilities loosen up the staid attitudes of more conservative viewers. The programs also adjust the attitudes of more conservative viewers toward entertainment, enjoyment, leisure, pleasure, and creature comfort. And the telecasts introduce more conservative viewers to the dress, hairstyles, makeup, current lingo, and attitudes of the secular world. These are introduced by hosts and guests, many of whom are personalities in the entertainment world, sports heroes, and successful business entrepreneurs (as well as the occasional politician) or Christian authors, musicians, and entertainers. Seeing hosts and guests display these secular sensibilities gives viewers the impression that they can do the same and encourages them to emulate the television personalities. The new identity of citizen of the wider world stands in tension with that of conservative Christian, however.

Conclusion

Televangelism is also attractive to viewers because it has the potential as ritual to create among themselves the community they seek but do not find in their relations with mainstream American society.

Turner (1974) argues that ritual's essential role is to create a more communitarian society. He observes that the relaxation of normative social roles and statuses and obligation to them in ritual liminality allows participants to encounter one another in more direct and egalitarian ways. Ritual permits and creates the experience of *communitas*, or human community. Ritual liminality invites participants to experiment with communitarian relations as alternatives to their everyday exchanges, which are principally mediated by the narrow roles and statuses they currently hold within society. The experience of community invites participants to create alternative, communitarian arrangements, or to infuse the traditional roles about to be assigned with communitarian purpose. Ritual's fundamental role is to put social structure into the service of community.

Turner argues that although social structure is necessary to organize society in the interest of more effectively meeting its material needs, it also works against human community. By nature, social structure is divisive, alienating, and exploititive; and thus it cannot meet the need for community, an equal social need. Turner's theory of ritual "anti-structure" goes against the view best articulated by Clifford Geertz, that ritual's essential role is to legitimate the existing social order. Instead, Turner (1993) argues that when ritual serves the existing order, its anti-structural core has been "circumscribed, . . . pressed into the service of" the status quo (p. 85).

The potential of televangelism to promote community among viewers is also explored in the chapter in this volume by Keyan Tomaselli and Arnold Shepperson. They show how communicating the cosmology or religious worldview of viewers, particularly with reference to the life crises and rapid social changes confronting them, encourages community.

The efforts of televangelism's viewers to create community among themselves are undercut, however, by the television medium itself, which does not permit direct interaction among them. Here community is not direct or immediate and spontaneous, as in the case of the usual, face-to-face forms of ritual that embody community.

The authoritarian, center-outward structure and interests of the television ministers and ministries and the manipulation of audiences to meet these interests (which promote political and economic interests) also limit the possibilities of community. The contradiction between community and televangelism's hierarchical arrangement of authority, which is invested in the televangelists, is also observed and emphasized by Tomaselli and Shepperson. They also note the restrictions placed on community by a certain lack of accountability of televangelists and television ministries to viewers. This has been corrected somewhat by new requirements of the National Religious Broadcasters. They also observe that the one-way message of televangelism contradicts community.

The emphasis in televangelism's role as ritual has shifted away from legitimation and adaptation toward encouraging community among viewers. Although televangelism continues to serve as legitimation and adaptation, the programs have increasingly focused on the need to build a nurturing community among viewers following the defeat and humiliation, even ridicule, suffered by televangelism: the defeat of Robertson's presidential candidacy and Falwell's Moral Majority, the exposure of Bakker and Swaggart for sexual indiscretion, and the exposure of Bakker's questionable business practices. Robertson returned from the campaign trail, and Falwell from leading his political lobby, to pastoring, counseling, and guiding their faithful followers, which each announced to be his new priority. Swaggart and Bakker received forgiveness from their flocks (or for Bakker, from a small remnant of the faithful). They were then rehabilitated and set about to restore harmony and support among followers.

Ritual legitimation and ritual adaptation are both strategies for gaining a more significant place and role within mainstream society—the first by force, and the other by accommodation, in an attempt to win the approval of mainstream society along with greater inclusion within it. Legitimation and adaptation are thus flip sides of the same coin.

Televangelism's roles as legitimation and adaptation are at cross-purposes, however. The contradiction cross-wires televangelism, crippling the conservative Christians' efforts to gain greater inclusion in mainstream American society as religious conservatives. In its role as adaptation, televangelism is a secularizing force on conservative Christianity. Ritual adaptation undercuts viewers' effort to legitimate their conservative religion as well as their effort to mobilize themselves as conservative Christians and push for their religious interests. The ongoing effort to legitimate viewers' conservative religion is a countervailing force that works against full accommodation to mainstream society and greater inclusion in it. Legitimation for viewers of a religion that is suspicious and condemning of the wider society, and legitimation in the eyes of viewers of their conservative Christian community as a community of the saved, puts in place "we-versus-they" distinctions that close off viewers from the social mainstream rather than encourage more open encounters. Reinvigoration of conservative Christianity only encourages the social mainstream to keep viewers at a distance and even to oppose them. In addition, the new focus on community among viewers turns their attention inward, rather than toward creating greater community with mainstream society.

As ritual, televangelism nonetheless affords viewers an opportunity to respond to their social marginalization rather than to remain entirely subject to the forces of secularization and social change or completely at the mercy of the mainstream society. As ritual, televangelism puts viewers in the position to become active agents who can adjust to their social circumstances rather than be allowed to be determined by them. It offers viewers vehicles by which to address and attempt to work out the larger social struggle in which they are caught up.

Televangelism's ritual capacities and roles help viewers concretize their struggle. To be sure, televangelism gives viewers a platform from which to protest against their exclusion from mainstream society. Ritual legitimation of viewers as a significant religious and social group concretizes their protest. And ritual legitimation mobilizes viewers to go on the offensive. Ritual adaptation is an inverted form of protest. Ritual accommodation concretizes viewers' interest in being included in mainstream society by actually moving them closer to acceptance. Ritual adaptation transforms them into citizens of the wider world, if only by inches, and if only as ambivalent citizens. Televangelism's attractive power includes the opportunity it presents conservative Christian viewers to become active subjects of their own lives as they embody their struggle for empowerment within the wider American society.

Notes

1. For discussion of similarities and differences among fundamentalists and Pentacostals see Bruce (1990) and Wuthnow (1989).

2. On televangelism's role in promoting the interests of the Religious Right, see Bruce (1988, 1990) and Hadden and Swann (1981).

3. See Alexander (1994) for additional findings of a national survey of these viewers, along with an elaboration of the analysis of televangelism as ritual offered here.

4. On the production of meaning relevant to the wider social context by television viewers, see Fiske (1987); for discussion of the production of meaning relevant to the wider social context by participants in ritual, see Geertz (1973) and Turner (1974).

References

Alexander, B. C. (1994). *Televangelism reconsidered: Ritual in the search for human community.* Atlanta, GA: Scholars Press.

Bruce, S. (1988). *The rise and fall of the new Christian right: Conservative Protestant politics in America 1978-1988*. New York: Clarendon/Oxford University Press.

Bruce, S. (1990). *Pray TV: Televangelism in America*. London: Routledge & Kegan Paul.

Driver, T. F. (1991). *The magic of ritual: Our need for liberating rites that transform ourselves and our communities*. San Francisco: Harper SanFrancisco.

Fiske, J. (1987). *Television culture*. London: Methuen.

Geertz, C. (1973). *The interpretation of cultures*. New York: Basic Books.

Gerbner, G., Gross, L., Hoover, S., Morgan, M., Signorielli, N., Cotugno, H., & Wuthnow, R. (1984). *Religion and television*. Philadelphia: Annenberg School of Communications, University of Pennsylvania, and the Gallup Organization, Inc.

Graduate Center, City University of New York. (1991). *Survey of religion in America 1990*. New York: Author.

Hadden, J., & Swann, C. E. (1981). *Prime-time preachers: The rising power of televangelism*. Reading, MA: Addison-Wesley.

Hoover, S. M. (1988). *Mass media religion: The social sources of the electronic church*. Newbury Park, CA: Sage.

Hunter, J. D. (1983). *American evangelicalism: Conservative religion and the quandary of modernity*. New Brunswick, NJ: Rutgers University Press.

Hunter, J. D. (1987). *Evangelicalism: The coming generation*. Chicago: University of Chicago Press.

McKinney, W., & Roof, W. C. (1987). *American mainline religion: Its changing shape and future*. New Brunswick, NJ: Rutgers University Press.

Schechner, R. (1987). *Essays in performance theory: 1970-1976*. New York: Drama Book Specialists. (Originally published 1977)

Turner, V. (1974). *Dramas, fields, and metaphors: Symbolic action in human society*. Ithaca, NY: Cornell University Press.

Turner, V. (1985). *On the edge of the bush: Anthropology as experience* (E. L. B. Turner, Ed.). Tucson: University of Arizona Press.

Turner, V. (1987). *The ritual process: Structure and antistructure*. Ithaca, NY: Cornell University Press. (Originally published 1969)

Turner, V. (1993). *From ritual to theater: The human seriousness of play*. New York: Performance Art Journal Publications. (Originally published 1982)

Wuthnow, R. (1989). *The struggle for America's soul: Evangelicals, liberals, and secularism*. Grand Rapids, MI: Eerdmans.

Chapter 13

Resistance Through Mediated Orality

Keyan G. Tomaselli
Arnold Shepperson

Televangelism is defined here as the broadcast of a theology of expressive Calvinism. Televangelists are part of an evangelical-fundamentalist movement organized through local church infrastructures. They use highly personalized communication within geographically homogeneous congregations to finance their multimedia networks by appeals to their viewers. *Teleministries* refers to the institutional business operations and administrative structures run by televangelists. These two terms—televangelism and teleministries—are often referred to in the research literature as *the electronic church*. The electronic church is located at the confluence of a variety of processes, each of which influences its operations and appeal in quite unique ways.

This chapter examines (a) the political economy of the electronic church in the era of information capitalism; (b) the electronic church's assumptions about what constitutes communication; and (c) the electronic church's primary use, in a visual medium, of oral codes that revive the rituals and language structures of preliterate forms of expression. We will analyze the relationship between televangelistic oratory (which uses primary orality) and secondary electronic orality (codes of radio and TV) with a view to understanding teleministries in industrial and postindustrial societies. This relates to issues of community, cosmology, and the recovery of the religious imagination in the modern secular world.

▓ Political Economy of Media Technologies: *Homo Mechanicus*

Historically, discussion of how media affect audiences has been grounded in two opposing political economies, one nomothetic (*homo mechanicus*) and the other teleonomic (*homo sapiens-volens*). The mechanical metaphor emphasizes humankind's "natural" propensity for manipulation. The teleonomic conception models humans in terms of rational democracy in the Information Age. In this chapter, we propose a new approach, that of *homo sapiens communicare*. This condition locates people as active agents within discursive contexts. It permits individual agency in the context of inherited, but rapidly shifting, broader social, economic, and historical structures.

One of the more plausible theoretical outcomes of Descartes' epistemology has been the philosophical anthropology that proceeds from the assumption that the human organism is some kind of machine. In short, the model places a mechanical organism at the center of human beings. Following theories of early mechanics, this organism is essentially passive; it will exhibit an effect (in the form of movement, for example) if and only if it has been caused to do so by some external stimulus. Schematically, this is the basis for what we will label the Stimulus-Organism-Effect (S-O-E) paradigm, the status of *paradigm* indicating that there is a family of theories that can be identified with the model.

In following this stimulus-response type of logic, the *homo mechanicus* paradigm affirms a certain kind of instrumental rationality. By doing this, it has become a favorite bogeyman of the conservative tradition. For them, the direct-effects metaphor justifies the idea that audiences, like machines, will misbehave when confronted with error (or evil) or socially dysfunctional messages. Classes or social strata that wish to preserve the status quo ante will therefore follow this paradigm in framing messages that deflect broader concerns about the reasons why conditions should change.

To the extent that evangelists constitute a wealthy bloc, it lies in their capacity to mobilize a sizable body of the electorate. As Jeffrey Hadden (1980) asserts, "They don't have to expend the great amounts of energy that other movements have had to do, over a long period of time, to gain media attention. All they have to do is to turn on their cameras and transmitters and they have access to very substantial and sympathetic audiences" (p. 16). We now try to make sense of one of the ways in which this "very substantial and sympathetic audience" might be understood.

▨ Orality and *Homo Mechanicus:* The Televangelistic Signifier

The inventions of writing and printing have contributed to thinking of words as objects—objectifying speech—rather than as happenings and as parts of processes (Ong in Bartz, 1988, p. 25; Goody, 1968, p. 1). This shift has fundamentally influenced how industrialized societies make sense of their worlds in comparison to those governed by orality, and it explains why conflicts have arisen between oral and literary ways of understanding. Part of the industrial world's construction of the Other is thus due to differences in oral and literate language environments (Ong, 1982). Each context generates quite different cosmologies: ideas of what the world is, how it works, and how individuals and groups relate to it. People working within signifying grids of industrial positivism, secular humanism, and their successors have become victims of their literacy. Their object-centered Cartesian consciousness is unable to really comprehend the depth, fundamentalism, and apparent irrationality and superstition of oral cultures.

Because literacy tends to separate individuals from their cosmological contexts, evangelism and televangelism as primary and secondary oral codes are able to penetrate the Cartesian consciousness of individuals in industrial societies. By recovering oral residues embedded in their collective memory, the word (of God) is not objectified by these readers/listeners. Their encounter with "the word" occurs in terms of an emotional bond with fields of spiritual forces concretely linked to the materiality of everyday life.

Televangelists use the expressive techniques of orality to recuperate the suppressed or compartmentalized religious sense of meaning and life into an all-embracing cosmology that reconnects Subject and Object—even within a Cartesian consciousness. The socially atomized individual as participant in the electronic church is thus organically reconnected into a spiritual center of authority that stands above the alienation of everyday life—but not necessarily material life.

This "reconnection" primarily occurs at the level of the local. Oral culture can only be conceived in local terms. In the world of established modernity, however, individuals are generally not expected to remain in one locality all their lives. Certainly in the United States and in Europe, institutions and communications are structured for mobile individuals.

However, in more settled sections of modern society, communities consisting of more than one generation develop. The irruption of events or conditions that threaten the encountered stability of the generations present in such a community challenge the accepted local "cosmos" within which those present have lived together. Such crises of experience cannot readily be explained as part of some intellectually coherent social process, like the economy, post-industrial production, the forces of supply and demand, and so on. These are forces beyond local experience, and the community or individual crises of experience (joblessness, a collapse in commodity prices, and so on) are usually described as insignificant in relation to these forces and processes.

Televangelism, with its oral presence on the screens of TV watchers experiencing these crises, provides answers to these questions in a familiar voice and style. The oral mannerisms, or codes, of the studio preacher are those of village green rhetoric, with messages related both to the causes of the crisis of experience and to its solutions. Both the content and style of the message draw on a comprehensible source, the word of God, to offer explanations for people's feelings and frustrations.

For televangelists, governance is defined through their interpretation of God's will alone, mediated by communications technologies (e.g., Fore, 1987; Frankl, 1987). They fight fire (the mass media) with fire (teleministries), attempting to protect their cultural/religious spaces (cosmologies). The appeal of televangelism, therefore, also works through the reconnection of experience and intelligibility to those whose worlds have not been forged on a need for expert intellectual literacy. Accommodating this disconnection of reality and common sense, and clarifying the contradictions of televangelism, then, require an understanding of the ways in which people in a local, predominantly oral context find significance in their worlds.

Local Knowledge, Orality, and Significance

The individual subject begins to encounter the world in an oral environment, and one's consciousness retains residues of this primary orality. The nature of the encounters between different thought systems, marked by literacy on the one hand and orality on the other, requires an explanation and periodization of the *homo* that is different from those offered above.

A starting point for this explanation lies in the nondualistic cosmos of Charles Sanders Peirce. Although the whole body of his work is too vast and full of changes of direction to summarize here, there is an aspect of his theory of signification that makes the appeal of televangelism concrete in terms of nonacademic people's experience.

Peirce's philosophy was developed in conscious opposition to Descartes' mental-material cosmological dualism. Peirce's cosmos is triadic and both contains and is the condition for signifying organisms. His philosophy's three cosmological categories are (a) Firstness, which we call the Encounter: the concrete being-there in the cosmos of a signifying organism; (b) Secondness, which we call Experience: the signifying organism's active or conscious directedness toward the local and particular; and (c) Thirdness, or Intelligibility: the realm in which organism and cosmos are fed back, so to speak, into the other categories so that new significant encounters and experiences become possible.

Peirce maintained this triple categorization throughout his theory of signification (semiotics). His elucidation of the relation between signs and the signifying organism is relevant here. Signs act in the signifying subject as interpretants. There are many different kinds of interpretants (Fitzgerald, 1966), but the triad of dynamical interpretants is important here. These are:

1. The emotional interpretant. This has as its effect the feeling of recognition that accompanies a sign. Because they are so general, emotional interpretants "can range from the first feeling of comprehension of

linguistic signs to the feeling that is generated by listening to a musical composition" (Fitzgerald, 1966, p. 79).

2. The energetic interpretant, which is present when more complex signification is intended. The energetic interpretant develops out of the emotional and involves some form of mental labor; there is always some kind of work done at this level of interpretation (Peirce, 1965, vol. 5, p. 475). Consequently, it involves the time-bound activity of recognizing this sign as opposed to all others.

3. The logical or ultimate interpretant. Peirce recognized that any given sign can become rationally applicable across different situations because the activity of signification leads to a logical interpretant that is in itself a sign. These interpretants relate to the sign as law, intelligibility, or potentiality and contain the possibility of future interpretations of the sign (Peirce, 1966, vol. 8, p. 184). At the local level, signs attain meaning as they are realized in the form of habits and habit change (Peirce, 1965, vol. 5, p. 476).

There are two key ways in which televangelism acts through interpretants so that communities make sense of their conditions:

1. Emotional and energetic interpretants are experienced under conditions brought about by the Cartesian collapse of the bodily into the material universe. Emotions and habits, being essentially bodily in nature, are made subject to explanation in terms of the natural or life sciences.

2. Voluntary aspects of action and other mental or logical-discursive spheres of human existence have been idealized. As such, they became subject to other (psychological) kinds of explanation.

These conditions are not necessarily obvious for those not privy to the arcane analysis and convoluted jargon of intellectual professions. Everyday people get on with life as they encounter it, draw on their experience as a basis for getting along, and make it all intelligible by virtue of the fact that what they do works for them (Shepperson, 1995, p. 70).

In situations brought on by influences beyond ordinary people's control, familiar things can begin to work differently. To use Peircean terms, conditions elicit a different kind of emotional interpretant for habitual energetic and logical interpretants. Things become unfamiliar; consequences follow differently from the way they did before. In cultural terms, traditional activity and responses fail. The lure of televangelism, then, can be seen in the way its practitioners offer to reconnect a community with its vision of what has always worked.

▓ Teleministries and Communication

Televangelists connect with their audiences by offering some kind of intelligibility to people for whom the familiar ways of going-on have begun to break down. The form and content of these offerings are, as we will expand below, contradictory; however, the oral style and local organization of the electronic churches assist in making people's habitual activities consonant with experience once more. This restoration by televangelists is characterized by their steady colonization of country stations and use of local communications (telephones, faxes) both to elicit and to follow up on responses to their broadcasts.

At the national level, intelligibility is reproduced by the figureheads of the evangelical-fundamentalist movement such as Pat Robertson, Jimmy Swaggert, Oral Roberts, and Jerry Falwell. These people offer hope for those sectors of society feeling threatened by the results of modernization, secularization, and rationalist culture. Their messages focus on ways in which the secular state and multinational economics have disconnected people from both their inherited everyday going-on and the most powerful authority that had previously underpinned that life: God's Law. They confirm that people's local habits ("family values") were always just fine; their problem lies in the habits of others who ignore God's Laws (the president's wife, the candidate for surgeon-general, and so on).

The contradiction, however, is that although resistance to instrumentalist rationality is one of the principles driving televangelism, their methods of communication often derive from the *homo mechanicus* paradigm. Televangelists offer through S-O-E the populist promise of a restoration of a "center of authority" vested in God. They tend to follow the *homo mechanicus* paradigm by treating broader popular concerns (such as women's rights) as being socially dysfunctional.

Whereas *popular* describes "bottom-up" relationships, *populist* describes "top-down" leadership. Populist teleministries use the electronic media's S-O-E discourse to identify and connect disparate individuals and groups who have become disaffected with the conventional church into a meaningful, mediated, two-way relationships with charismatic televangelists (Hoover, 1988). The electronic church's discursive networks and context thus partially recover the individual's place in the (tele)community.

Unlike Vatican II theology and similar approaches that facilitate dialogical communication methods, national televangelists appear disinterested in their audience's local ambience or *Sitz im Leben*. Rather than debating concepts with their congregations, televangelists go ahead as if people simply believe them anyway. Theirs is an authoritarian emphasis on the mechanics and technicalities of the medium and the codes of orality, intended to elicit specific responses from receivers/participants. For this reason, televangelists tend to be intolerant of other perspectives. Dialogue, where it is encouraged, takes place on the message maker's terms; recipients are simultaneously discouraged from questioning the message's perspective.

Neither is the accountability and structure of the teleministries a point of discussion (Fore, 1987; Frankl, 1987; Hoover, 1988). Televangelistic messages empasize:

1. Experiential/emotional theologies. The commonsense collapse of emotional and energetic interpretants in congregations' lives is reproduced.
2. Charismatic personality cults of the broadcasters. Emotional and logical interpretants are collapsed into a media simulacrum of community that reproduces previously unquestioned relations of authority.
3. Business values in broadcasting control. The energetic interpretant of what the televangelist is doing there reproduces associations with conditions that previously signaled the successful achievement of "traditional" activities.
4. Faith in mass media ordained by God. The final interpretant, as a form of habit change, is deferred to an ultimate authority, the power of which is unquestionably greater than those who ordained the conditions leading to the local crisis of experience.
5. Conventional, high-budget, and slick media formats and programming. The congregation's encounter and experience with televangelism takes place in a context of familiar and assured forms of authoritative presence.
6. Spin-off ministries and fund-raising during broadcasts (Frankl, 1987; Schultz, 1990, p. 113). Personal contact is obtained through telephones and computers (Fore, 1987, p. 85). The community that is initially established through scheduled viewing slots is extended by personal

contacts outside the media, reinforcing emotional and energetic interpretants through the intelligibility of concrete community situations.

▦ Bottom-Up Dialogical Communication: *Homo Sapiens Communicare*

Sections of the established churches have successfully harnessed the
new media toward recovering the community of persons. A variety of
channels ranging from "group media" to "community-based print media" have been established. Reception of Vatican II theology opened an
extraordinary development in popular communication theory and practice in Latin America and Africa (Lowe, 1983, pp. 73-84; see also the work
published in the journals *Media Development* and *Group Media Journal*).

Conventional churches found that making and transmitting magazine programs and documentaries elicited greater community and dialogical communication than did the "tub-thumping mass approach of the
electronic church" (Lowe, 1983, p. 44). Viewers will tune in to programs
about their own communities, especially if they have participated in their
production. This is an empowering and communal experience that en-
hances communicative potential. "Communication," "access," "participation," and "community" are parts of a unified development process,
connecting the concerns of local public spheres to questions of national
concern (Nair & White, 1987).

This institutionalization of "bottom-up" media forms the background
for the idea of *homo sapiens communicare*. In this model, humankind is
functionally "literate" in an electronic media environment that is not
controlled as an arm of governance. As indicated, this kind of literacy is
best understood in terms of orality. Here the order of knowledge begins
with a different vision of media organization and an associated shift in
theories of signification and meaning.

Media policies that incorporate grassroots sentiment raise questions
of theological significance (Traber, 1984; WACC, 1984, p. 18): The word
communication comes from the Latin *communis* "common" and *communicare* "to establish a community, to share." Theologically, communication
begins and ends with that dimension of dialogue. The opposite of communication, argues Michael Traber (1989), is not "silence but sinfulness—
the refusal to communicate and to be in communion" (p. 61). Traber's

conclusion can be seen to derive from an even deeper root to the *communicare* paradigm: the Old Latin word *munus* (public duty) is the root of *communicare* and its cognates. This places the Latin origins of the meaning in the realm of public duty, and the "sinfulness" of which Traber speaks can therefore be related to a connection between communication and the rules and norms under which community is constituted.

To the extent that communication involves both communities and individuals, we approach the idea of *homo sapiens communicare* from two interpretations of how such a person is possible. On the one hand, persons are contingent. This results from the historical constitution of the modern world as a consequence of modern institutions. Individuals encounter the world in a place and time not of their own choosing and come to act in and make sense of it in the ways they encounter there and then. Acting and making sense in accordance with traditional ways encountered from birth is not necessarily wrong; what is decisive is how people mobilize these acts and justifications in relation to others. In this modern world, tradition, invoked in support of actions that are imposed on others individually and collectively, reflects an instrumental and not a religious attitude.

On the other hand, people are necessarily bound by rules and norms. We have already noted that this condition is inherent in the ideas of community and communication. In other words, the human activity of communication has a kind of ethics. This nomothetic dimension of communication is, in line with our Peircean approach, a threefold one:

1. There are rules (or maxims) of moral action. These are encountered in the realm of nurture and generation (Williams, 1963, pp. 131-137) and are associated with people's emotional interpretants in relation to ideas like goodness and beauty. Moral significance can be contested in the light of life experience (Shepperson, 1995, pp. 47-50).

2. Ethical norms and rules govern social and political relations between communities and thus have a relationship with justice (Heller, 1987, pp. 14-17). They are part of experience and therefore relativized to the contexts within which interpretations of sociopolitical ideas need to be be negotiated.

3. Philosophical value ideas are the issues arising out of people's reflected experience in the plurality of their encounters with the world (Heller, 1985, p. 120; Shepperson, 1995, p. 54).

For us, the environment of *homo sapiens communicare* is essentially that of democratic action. The ethics of encounters between people and social groups are therefore chosen on the grounds of democratic social existence. In a pluralistic sociopolitical world, democratic social existence can be realized in two simple value ideas of justice: freedom and life. *Freedom* is not a transcendental state or condition, but a concrete demand of people in the here and now. *Life* relates to the right of people to develop their endowments into talents that express freedom but do not infringe on others. We follow Agnes Heller (1987) in positing the condition of freedom in the maxim that people must always be treated as ends-in-themselves and not as means (pp. 101, 248).

A further cultural consideration arises from the activity of developing people's endowments into talents. The Latin root of the word *culture* is *colere, cultum*, which means, among other things, "to tend, to nurture, and to inhabit." People can only become capable of choosing to be democratic communicators after they have gone through a greater or lesser cultural experience in the presence of other generations who have carried on the business of raising their successor generation (Shepperson, 1995, pp. 68-70).

We now come to the issue of an alternative to televangelism, which draws on the dialogical nature of democratic communication. Televangelists proceed from the position that individuals are subjected to the necessities of specific logics of punishment (eschatology) or salvation (soteriology), and that these necessities are realized in confessional organization. In this view, people are caused to be eternally saved or punished by virtue of rules and norms that are perhaps of their own choosing, but are not subject to interpretation or discussion; the rules and norms are given by authority. Such subjection to authority is indistinguishable from subjection to laws of nature; the *homo mechanicus* paradigm works as well in this context as it does with its applications in commercial communications practices.

In fitting media and information technologies to the idea of *homo sapiens communicare*, we turn to Michael Traber's principles for religious public broadcasting (1984, pp. 68-70). We suggest that his guidelines, along with alternative media strategies and the *communicare* model, have the potential to democratize religious communication on both the local and the national scale.

1. Investment in communication: Any failure to invest is a limitation on the life chances of people in general. Withholding access to communication both limits the ways in which people's endowments can be raised into talents and limits their ultimate ability to participate in value discussion.

2. Emphasis on equality and egality: An intersection between "top" and "bottom" demands that neither participant (individual or collective) be treated as a means to someone else's ends. In this way, communication policies must be designed to be equitable, enhancing the world of those least well-off in a situation, while not using others as means in so doing (Heller, 1987; Honderich, 1989).

3. Replacing communications hierarchies with a covenant relationship: This guideline speaks for itself because in a democratic environment, it translates into the right to recognition on the grounds of people's being human in the here and now. Hierarchically structured communication can also be recognized under these conditions, but the means-ends rule permits us to distinguish between relations of genuine dependence on the one hand, and of tutelage on the other.

4. Provision of affirmative access: Individuals cannot become skilled at democratic communication in the absence of democratically open media. To deny equitable and affirmative access in this case is contrary to both values of justice anyway.

5. Finally, Traber's suggestion that media language be overhauled accords with both our approach through the semiotic nature of communication and our focus on *homo sapiens communicare* as a person who has chosen the best possible democratic sociopolitical world as the means whereby people might become ends in themselves.

Homo sapiens communicare is a normative idea, but only one way among many in which people can realize the many choices they face as a result of their contingency. Under any set of conditions in the world of here and now, we recognize that some people, if not many, may seek to create some kind of *nomenklatura* with which to control communications infrastructures and thereby place others in relations of tutelage. The point is that if democratic values of justice, which we equate with the values held dear by persons with a religious attitude, are to become part of a global communications practice, then those who seek to use media to keep others in tutelage must do so openly so that they can be resisted.

▓ Conclusion

Communication is central to both democratic and religious experiences; however, the institutions of communication tend toward top-down organization of communication flows. They thus seek control not only of media channels, but also of the messages transmitted, and often of the behavior elicited. This is a fundamental betrayal of the relationship between communication and community, and it usually results in the elites who own and control communication technologies becoming distanced from the real needs of their constituencies. The resulting power relationship entrenches the elites and disempowers ordinary people, though resistance often results. Ecumenical media need to become part of the solutions of the future, not rooted and forgotten in the past.

Dialogical or popular communication facilitates a bottom-up empowering of the community. Ironically, during the 1970s and 1980s, because of management and production needs for rapid worldwide interactive communication, multinational capital produced electronic communications technologies able to facilitate global interaction (satellites, electronic mail and computer networking, teleconferencing, interactive telecommunications such as video-text, hypermedia, and so on).

The public service broadcasting system and the the idea of a public sphere are paradoxical in the Information Age. On the one hand, there are extraordinary electronic technological developments that not only permit, but also encourage interaction between communities of interest from the local to the international. This kind of communication eludes space and time, culture and location. On the other hand, these means of communication are both controlled and served by an unholy alliance of transnational corporations and governments (Garnham, 1986, p. 38). This situation simultaneously removes access from the public through price as well as through regulatory and licensing mechanisms. We argue that this tendency can be resisted by encouraging technology organization through which *homo sapiens communicare* can reconnect the religious aspects of signification with the fight for social justice.

We have also argued that televangelists seem to have a way of recovering compelling aspects of preliterate oral consciousness, thereby restoring the power of dynamic relations of cosmological force to names and labels that are lost to Cartesian literate consciousness through the objectification of meanings attached to words. Televangelists have been able to reconnect, in a very particular kind of way, the Subject and Object through integration of verbal, pictorial, and literate discourses that make sense to people otherwise located within Cartesian subjectivities.

This enormous power has been harnessed, as we have argued above, to the demands of the political economy of the electronic church. Our conclusion is that the recovery of oral consciousness in *homo sapiens communicare* can reconnect the democratic and religious attitudes in the public spheres made possible by interactive information and media technologies.

Note

1. This chapter is developed from K. G. Tomaselli and Fr. N. Nkosi, "Political Economy of Televangelism: Ecumenical Broadcasting Vs. Teleministries," *Communicare*, 1995. We are indebted to Robert White, Fr. Nhlanhla Nkosi, Stewart M. Hoover, Ruth Teer-Tomaselli, and Eric Louw for their helpful critiques and advice on aspects of this study. Travel funding facilitating the study was provided by the Department of Theology, University of Uppsala, Sweden, the World Association for Christian Communication, London, and the Natal University Research Fund.

References

Bartz, J. (1988). *The many words of Walter Ong*. St. Louis MO: Universitas: The Alumni Magazine of St. Louis University.

Fitzgerald, J. (1966). *Peirce's theory of signs as foundation of pragmatism*. The Hague: Mouton.

Fore, W. F. (1987). *Television and religion: The shaping of faith, values, and culture*. Minneapolis, MN: Augsburg.

Frankl, R. (1987). *Televangelism: The marketing of popular religion*. Carbondale, IL: Southern Illinois University.

Garnham, P. (1986). The media and the public sphere. In P. Golding, (Ed.), *Communicating politics: Mass communication and political process*. Bath: Leicester University Press.

Goody, J. (1968). *Literacy in traditional societies*. Cambridge, UK: Cambridge University Press.

Hadden, J. K. (1980, October). Evangelical influences on America's future. *Presbyterian Outlook*, p. 16.

Heller, A. (1985). *A radical philosophy*. Oxford, UK: Basil Blackwell.

Heller, A. (1987). *Beyond justice*. Oxford, UK: Basil Blackwell.

Honderich, T. (1989). *Violence for equality: Inquiries in political philosophy*. London: RKP.

Hoover, S. (1988). *Mass media religion: The social sources of the electronic church*. Newbury Park, CA: Sage.

Lowe, K. (1983). *Opening eyes and ears: New connections for Christian communication.* London: World Association for Christian Communication/World Council of Churches/Lutheran World Federation.

Nair, K. S., & White, A. (1987). Participation is the key to development of communication. *Media Development, 3,* 15-18.

Ong, W. (1982). *Orality and literacy: The technologizing of the word.* London: Methuen.

Peirce, C. S. (1965). *The collected papers of Charles Sanders Peirce. Vols. 1-6.* (C. Hartshorne & P. Weiss, Eds.). Cambridge, MA: Harvard University Press.

Peirce, C. S. (1966). *The collected papers of Charles Sanders Peirce. Vols. 7-8.* (A. W. Burks, Ed.). Cambridge, MA: Harvard University Press.

Schultze, Q. J. (1990). Defining the electronic church. In R. Abelman & S. M. Hoover (Eds.), *Religious television: Controversies and conclusions* (pp. 41-52). Norwood, NJ: Ablex.

Shepperson, A. (1995). *On the social interpretation of cultural experience: Reflections on Raymond Williams's early cultural writing (1958-63).* Unpublished master's thesis, University of Natal, Durban.

Traber, M. (1984). Communication for peace and justice. In J. Bluck (Ed.), *Beyond technology.* Geneva: World Council of Churches.

Traber, M. (1989, June). Theological reflections on communication, participation and transformation. *Group Media Journal,* pp. 12-14.

WACC (World Association for Christian Communication). (1984). Communication versus alienation: Latin American challenge of WACC. *Media Development, 31*(1), 18-19.

Williams, R. (1963). *Culture and society.* Harmondsworth, UK: Pelican.

Part IV

Media, Religion, and Culture:
Individual Practice

Psychologized Religion
in a Mediated World

Janice Peck

Television talk shows, now the most prominent genre in American day-time programming, have come under fierce criticism for pandering to, and promoting, viewers' most base sensibilities. Oprah Winfrey, host of one of the most popular of these programs, has attempted to distance herself from this critique by emphasizing more upbeat and uplifting topics.[1] Her commitment to more "positive" programming was launched in early 1994 in an episode featuring Marianne Williamson—a self-described "spiritual psychotherapist" who has greatly influenced Winfrey's own spirituality.[2]

Williamson is a "student" of *A Course in Miracles* (1992, first published in 1975), a set of three books, now in its third printing, claimed to have been "scribed by Jesus" and transmitted to two New York psychologists in the 1960s. The *Course* represents "an integration of psychology and spirituality" (Wapnick, 1989, p. 17). Williamson's book, *Return to Love: Reflections on the Principles of A Course in Miracles* (1992), has sold more than one million copies and was on the *New York Times* bestseller list for

9 months. Williamson lectures regularly in New York and California; tours the United States, Europe, and Australia; appears on cable television; and has been featured on Winfrey's program several times. She also met with U.S. First Lady Hillary Rodham Clinton in 1993 to talk about her vision for "healing America" ("More Meaning," 1994).

The episode analyzed here, titled "What Is Going on With the World?" opened with crime footage from television news. The day's topic, Winfrey told the studio and home audiences, was "how to end the violence around us." During the program, she and Williamson identified various social problems (crime, drug addiction, TV violence, war, child abuse, prejudice) as "the price we pay for ignoring our souls." Born of "denial," this neglect of soul produces a "diseased" and "dysfunctional" society. To counter such "soullessness," Williamson proposed a "shift in paradigm on the planet" to activate "an amazing healing force"—the "spirit of divine consciousness which is within our souls." She prescribed various steps toward planetary healing, from praying and attending church to joining support groups and seeing a therapist, united around the idea of replacing "negative thoughts" with positive ones because "our thoughts determine the experiences of our lives." Significantly, Williamson accused the mass media of fostering "negativity" by imposing "societal thought forms" on "individual thought forms." An antidote, she noted, was Winfrey's "position of power as someone who touches millions of people" through her talk show.

Winfrey closed the program vowing to organize a "weekend of prayer for the nation" and inviting the studio audience and "those of you who are watching around the world" to join hands and hearts while Williamson prayed to God to transform them into "vessels of light and healing and love." This was the second instance of prayer in the show's 10-year history; the first occurred in Williamson's 1992 appearance.[3] Winfrey prefaced the prayer with two qualifications: It was not directed to a specific God, but to "whoever you pray to," and it was a "universal" rather than a "religious" petition. These comments reflect Winfrey's awareness that her international television audience represents great diversity in religious (as well as nonreligious and antireligious) leanings. They also reveal the uneasy relationship between religion and American mediated popular culture.

How are we to understand this fusion of religion and psychology, its view of and relationship to the mass media, and its compatibility with

America's most popular daytime television talk show? What historical and contemporary conditions make this form of psychologized religiosity, and its "mediazation" (Thompson, 1990), not only possible, but a plausible, attractive explanation for "what is going on with the world"? Such questions demand an approach to cultural analysis that is historical in orientation and dialectical in practice, one that sees religion as both creative and determined—signified by historical, material conditions *and* signifying praxis that responds to and acts upon those conditions.

That method was proposed three decades ago by Sartre (1963/1968) in *Search for a Method*, in which he criticized a "frozen marxism" that had turned its "concepts into dictates" and could no longer "grasp the process which produces the person and his [sic] product within a class and within a given society at a given historical moment" (p. 56).[4] Sartre sought to overcome such reductionism by integrating Marx's theory of history and capitalism with existentialism's insights into subjective praxis. Hence, his call for a method that remained faithful to Marxian principles but was sensitive to

> the mediations between concrete men [sic] and the material conditions of their life, between human relations and the relations of production, between persons and classes. (p. 76)

In an earlier study of religious television, I argued that cultural forms, including religious belief and practice, reveal and respond to problems that history has posed (Peck, 1993). Here I continue that argument using Sartre's conception of signification and the "progressive-regressive" method of cultural analysis outlined in *Search for a Method*. The strengths of Sartre's approach are its insistence on the dialectical relation of the ontological and historical dimensions of signification (located at the site of practical mediations) and its focus on questions of being and meaning that are of central concern to students of religion, culture, and media.[5] Drawing on Williamson's appearance on *The Oprah Winfrey Show* and one of her public lectures,[6] I argue for the value of Sartre's method. This chapter introduces Sartre's view of signification, history, and method; considers the historical and ontological dimensions of religion; and examines Williamson's spiritual psychology in relation to the historical contexts and processes of modernization, mediazation, and globalization.

▩ The Ontological and Historical Dimensions of Signification

Lipsitz (1988) has argued that we are "historical beings who make meaning out of the present in dialogue with the past and in anticipation of the future" (p. 154). Sartre (1963/1968) grounds that dialogue ontologically. We are "signifying beings," he argues, because we are "always *outside of [our]selves toward*" in a state of "perpetual disequilibrium." The ceaseless "production of oneself by work and praxis"—what Sartre terms the "impulse toward objectification"—is our ontological structure. In objectifying ourselves through praxis, we act in the present on the basis of the future to "reveal and determine [our] situation by transcending it" (p. 151). To be a signifying being, then, is to be a "dialectical surpassing of all that is given" (p. 152). Any particular act of signification must be understood "both in relation to the real and present factors which condition it, and in relation to a certain object, still to come, which it is trying to bring into being" (p. 91).

Signification is also grounded materially in history, in "the structures of a society" created by past and present human praxis that establish for each of us an "objective situation as a starting point." These historically created structures determine the "field of possibles" available to individuals and social groups that are differently positioned in society, and become the condition and site of praxis. A field of possibles is "a strongly structured region" shaped by material conditions, and "the goal toward which the agent surpasses his [*sic*] objective situation" to "contribute to the making of History" (p. 93). The social present, therefore, always appears as "a perspective of the future," calling us to produce the world and ourselves (p. 96). Human beings are thus historical products and historical agents—signified objects and signifying subjects.

Sartre (1963/1968) argues that to understand the dynamic relationship of objective structures and subjective praxis, we must attend to the mediations that link them. This means that

> the milieu of our life, with its institutions, its movements, its instruments, its cultural "infinities" . . . its fetishes, its social temporality, and its "hodological space" . . . must also be made the object of our study. (p. 79)

Sartre thus conserves the concept of social reproduction central to Marxian theory with the aim of recovering its creative dialectical character. Because signification is a dynamic process, it can be grasped only with a method that recognizes that dynamism and reproduces it in practice. His "progressive-regressive" method "explains [an] act by its terminal signification in terms of its starting conditions" (p. 153). This method involves a "continuous cross-reference"—a "movement of comprehension"—that advances toward the signified object and the future it enacts and embodies, travels back to the originating conditions that motivated the particular signification, and attends to the complex mediations constituting that journey (p. 154).

Through this dialectical movement, which seeks the meaning of a historical period in concrete acts of signification and the meaning of those significations in the historical conditions they respond to and attempt to surpass, we arrive at what Sartre calls "the profundity of the lived" (p. 145). This conception of signification "affirm[s] the specificity of the human act, which cuts across the social milieu still holding onto its determinations, and which transforms the world on the basis of given conditions" (p. 91).

To approach Williamson's psychologized religion from a Sartrean perspective, we would ask not only where it came from, but where it is headed; how the future it imagines is signified and motivated by its past, yet goes beyond reproducing that past because it also acts on its determinations by signifying—to bring into being—a future.

▓ Religion as an Ontological and Historical Phenomenon

Beyer (1994) argues that religion is organized around a central dichotomy of "immanence/transcendence." The immanent world is the site of "the core problems in human life: failure, insecurity, disappointment" that perpetually remind us of "the seeming final indeterminability" of the world in human experience (p. 5). The transcendent is that which lies outside or beyond indeterminacy and explains these core problems: "religion posits the transcendent to give the immanent world meaning" (p. 6). This parallels Geertz's (1979) view that religion addresses the "problem of meaning" arising from human limitations (intellectual, physical, moral), which is experienced as bafflement, suffering/finitude, and injustice/evil.

Religious belief systems operate within concrete sociohistorical contexts and must be sensitive to changes in the cultural environment to retain their relevance and legitimacy for believers. Amin (1989) argues that the great world religions are historically flexible because of their "double nature": They both respond to enduring metaphysical concerns (the problem of being and meaning) and are "a means of legitimating social orders shaped by historical conditions" (p. 84). A particular belief system is thus a historically constituted, objective structure and a field of possibles for signifying praxis.

To understand the meaning of Williamson's psychologized religiosity, we must attend to the way its ontological mission (defining the immanent/transcendent relationship and responding to the problem of meaning) is shaped by particular historical mediations (the concrete field of possibles, available technical instruments—including media—structured social relations, etc.) that call it forth and that it acts upon based on a perspective of the future.

▨ Modernization as a Historical Problem for Religion

The "originating conditions" paving the way for the psychologized religion expressed in this TV talk show begin with the process of capitalist modernization, which destabilized traditional religion and gave birth to the modern science of psychology. Sociologists of religion generally hold that religion was profoundly reconfigured in the process of socioeconomic modernization. Hunter (1983) identifies three central tendencies of modernization that have had particular consequences for religion: rationalization, cultural pluralism, and structural differentiation of the public and private spheres. These mutually reinforcing structural tendencies of modernization contribute to the "*deinstitutionalization of religious reality* in the worldviews of modern people" (p. 14).

Religion did not wither away as a result of modernization; it exercised historical flexibility to remain isomorphic with the larger cultural environment and to respond to the ontological problem of being and meaning (Bushman, 1967; Hunter, 1983; Thomas, 1989; Wilentz, 1984). Hunter (1983) outlines various ways religion has responded to the "disaffirming" effects of modernization. A religious belief system may accommodate functional rationality by downplaying supernaturalistic elements; by providing rational explanations for beliefs; by adopting an inward-directed, utilitarian orientation; or by reinterpreting its cosmology into a "grammar of naturalism" (e.g., translating religion into ethics, psychology, or politics) (p. 16). It may respond to cultural pluralism by emphasizing common elements of various religions or recognizing the monopolistic claims of other beliefs. It may adapt to structural pluralism by downplaying the public significance of its beliefs and practices and by inflating its relevance to the private sphere. Finally, a religious belief system may resist deinstitutionalization by reasserting the universal relevance of its particular truth claims and adopting a strategy of "recharismatization" (a common route for various forms of fundamentalism) (p. 17).

The psychologized religiosity endorsed by Williamson and Winfrey is a combination of accommodation and recharismatization. It seeks legitimacy by borrowing the scientific grammar of psychology; recognizes the validity of, and commonalities among, all religious belief systems; defines its public significance as the cumulative result of private transformations; and attempts to recharismatize public and private domains of experience. These strategies are doubly inflected by modernization. Williamson's claim that modern society is "soulless" and that modern people have "forgotten who we are" is a response to the deinstitutionalization of a religious worldview. At the same time, her "new paradigm" is legitimized by reference to the modern science of psychology, itself institutionalized within the context of rationalization, cultural pluralism, and the structural division of the public and private spheres.

Psychology emerged in the 19th century as a means of rationalizing (e.g., folding into a positivist scientific paradigm) the domain of human experience, conduct, and social relationships. Dedicated to explaining human motives and behavior for purposes of prediction and management, psychology has, at different historical junctures, conceived of human beings as the product of natural instincts, behavioral laws, cognitive processes, genetic outcomes, or chemical reactions. Such conceptions are isomorphic with a "disenchanted" universe where no aspect of being escapes the purview of scientific rationality. Psychology is not threatened by cultural pluralism because its explanations of human experience are anchored to science, which is assumed to transcend the particularity of cultural contexts (Sampson, 1981); it thus legitimizes its worldview by reference to nature, rather than to culture. Psychology also enjoys extensive utility and plausibility in the modern public sphere because it is guided by functional rationality.

This concomitant deinstitutionalization of a religious worldview and institutionalization of a psychological worldview corresponds to the emergence of a "therapeutic ethos" that many critics say has come to characterize contemporary American culture (Bellah, Madsen, Sullivan, Swidler, & Tipton, 1985; Fairclough, 1989; Illouz, 1991; Lears, 1981; Peck, 1995; White, 1992).[7] Williamson's conflation of "redemption" with "healing" reflects that ethos—an equation that is neither unique to her spiritual psychotherapy, nor to "New Age" religion, but is also increasingly found in more traditional belief systems (Allen, 1994; Hunter, 1983).[8]

In Sartrean terms, Williamson's psychologized religiosity arises from the objective conditions of modernity through which traditional religion was displaced by science as the publicly privileged domain of signification and meaning. Through the disenchantment, relativization, and privatization of religion, in conjunction with the institutionalization of a psychological framework of interpretation, the premodern, metaphysical soul is subsumed by the modern, rationalized psyche as the source and site of being and meaning. The transcendent is thereby collapsed into the immanent, explained in terms of natural phenomena, and stripped of its ability to endow the immanent world with meaning. As Williamson argues, modern society has "marginalized the sacred experience." Her spiritualized psychology is both a product of these historical determinations and a quest to surpass the contradictions inherent in them. Its appeal resides in its attempt to resolve the loss of the transcendent and restore ontological meaning. It repairs the disenchantment of the soul by conflating psyche and soul, re-enchanting both terms, and reviving the immanent/transcendent relationship. By fusing healing with redemption, Williamson's cosmology strives to satisfy the ontological quest for meaning and being in a way that is isomorphic with a social environment inflected by a modern therapeutic ethos.

▓ Religion and the Mediazation of Modern Culture

Williamson's and Winfrey's ability to "touch" millions of people is predicated on the "mediazation of modern culture," defined by Thompson (1990) as "the rapid proliferation of institutions of mass communication and the growth of networks of transmission through which commodified symbolic forms [are] made available to an ever-expanding domain of recipients" (p. 11).[9] Mediazation is central to the historical process of modernization. In conjunction with the development and expansion of industrial capitalism and the rise of the modern nation-state system, mediazation is part of what "constitutes modern societies as 'modern'" (p. 15).

Mediazation has transformed the way symbolic goods are produced, transmitted, and received; the way we experience the actors and events encountered at a distance through the media; and our interactions with others via our relationship as receivers of mediated symbolic forms. The mass media provide access to events that are spatially and temporally remote, increase public scrutiny of distant actions, and provide information on which we might act individually or collectively. But because mediazation also diminishes our "capacity to contribute to the course and content of the communicative process" (p. 219), it makes us susceptible to manipulation and control by those with greater access to the production of symbols.

As the media have become primary sites for the global exchange of symbolic forms in modern society, the form and content of our knowledge increasingly depends on the institutions and mechanisms of mass communication. When Williamson points to the media's power to fuse "individual thought forms" with "societal thought forms"—because "we all read the same newspapers, watch the same TV programs"—she relies on listeners' ability to recognize this as a real effect of mediazation, and on their awareness of the signifying power of mass media in modern society. She also appeals to their fear that they are powerless to affect the course, content, and consequences of public meanings. Here Williamson homes in on a core contradiction of mediazation: The media give us a vast array of information and knowledge about the world beyond our immediate experience, but this knowledge can be a source of paralysis because it exceeds the practical scope of our praxis. We find ourselves unable to act on what we know because "the publicness (visibility) of events or individuals in the public and private domains is no longer linked directly with the sharing of a common locale" (Thompson, 1990, p. 241).

For Sartre (1976/1982), a primary effect of mass media is their constitution of the audience as an "indirect serial relation" united by an external object (e.g., the broadcast, newspaper, etc.). This "serial" relation among audience members is characterized by "absence" because outside of a limited circle of acquaintances, reciprocal dialogue and praxis with other receivers and with producers of the message are structurally precluded. As members of the "series," we can refuse to be part of the "indirect gathering" (p. 270) by turning off the set or canceling the subscription; we can also argue individually against a particular message. But neither action changes the "real work" of the mass media—that of maintaining the audience members' separation and ensuring "their communication through alterity"—in Sartre's view (p. 271). Both responses affirm absence as our "mode of connection" to others in the audience. The real work of mediazation is the creation and maintenance of the sociotechnological diaspora that preserves seriality and undermines the possibility of collective praxis. Mediazation therefore engenders a sense of "impotence" that

> does not only lie in the impossibility of silencing the [broadcast] voice; it also lies in the impossibility of convincing, *one by one,* the [other] listeners, all of whom it exhorts in the common isolation which it creates for all of them as their inert bond. (pp. 272-273)

This experience of impotence is not solely an effect of mediazation; all praxis is subject to and limited by the past and present action of others (e.g., we do not create our own field of possibles). Although we contribute to the making of history, we are not alone in that endeavor, and we control neither the conditions of our praxis nor its final outcome. As Sartre (1963/1968) argues, "[I]f History escapes me it is not because I do not make it; it is because the other is making it as well" (p. 88). A key consequence of the mediazation of modern culture is that it makes us aware, on a historically unprecedented scale, of the praxis of others. As Williamson argues, the mass media have made the world "such a small place."

Inundated daily with a mediated world that appears to be not of our own making, we confront the myriad forces that constrain our individual praxis.[10] It is the recognition of those constraints, and the sense of individual impotence it evokes, that Williamson's cosmology addresses and attempts to resolve. She blames the media's emphasis on "bad news" and "negative thinking" with spreading a "contagion of violent thoughts." In contrast to a world where the "negativity" prevalent in the media determines the content of our perceptions, she paints a future where the force of the collective "positive" thoughts of believers will determine the content of the media:

> If enough people in America at the end of the day joined in thought, joined in prayer about what happened today, it would affect the news that happens while we sleep and the news of tomorrow. It's the ultimate act of taking responsibility—taking personal empowerment for things—praying.

Here the re-enchanted psyche/soul intersects with mediazation: Through spiritual reflection, positive thinking, and prayer, believers can affect the content of the symbolic forms circulated by the media. In so doing, they can intervene in the "societal thought forms" that produce "individual thought forms"—hence Winfrey's vow in the episode to use her media-based influence to organize a weekend of prayer for the nation and to refocus her program from "talking about how bad things are" to "bring[ing] more peace to the world."[11] At the same time, this attempt to resolve the core contradiction of mediazation also conserves it: Williamson's and Winfrey's imagined future is predicated on maintaining the existing structure of the mass media that allows them to touch millions with their message. Their new paradigm challenges neither the seriality of the audience nor the "real work" of mediazation.

▓ Religion and Globalization

According to Beyer (1994), innovations in communication technologies and the emergence of transnational media conglomerates have played a crucial role in globalization, understood as "the spread of vital institutions of western modernization to the rest of the globe, especially the modern capitalist economy, the nation-state, and scientific rationality in the form of modern technology" (p. 8). The establishment of worldwide networks of communication and exchange, based on structures of political-economic power and interdependence, creates a global environment in which "people, cultures, societies, and civilizations previously more or less isolated from one another are now in regular and almost unavoidable contact" (p. 2). These developments have exacerbated the "relativization and marginalization of religion" (p. 4) by pushing it into the domain of mere cultural difference.

To maintain legitimacy in a globalizing world, modern religion must respond to the relativization of belief. One response is to assert the primacy of a particular belief system—the "conservative option" adopted by various forms of fundamentalism that have experienced resurgence across the globe. The "liberal option," in contrast, accommodates globalization by embracing religious pluralism. Denying the primacy of any particular religion while at the same time affirming a religious worldview, liberal religion acknowledges differences but downplays their divisive potential. The liberal option also reformulates traditional religious definitions of evil. No longer a substantive entity or force, evil in liberal religion "cannot be consistently or clearly localized or personified" and is instead defined "negatively" as a social or individual "lack" (p. 186). This latter view of evil is more culturally flexible, less tied to any particular religious doctrine. It also resonates with a therapeutic ethos that stresses subjective motives over objective deeds and individual self-realization over collective morality. Thus, as Beyer (1994) notes, liberal religion is increasingly directing its public practice toward "the helping services, including a celebration of life passages and . . . the 'cure of souls' for those who feel the need" (p. 87). This reorientation toward helping and healing makes the liberal option—like that of Williamson—isomorphic with a therapeutic cultural environment. Its embrace of religious pluralism and cultural diversity also make liberal religion compatible with a global political-economic order whose legitimacy depends on winning acceptance for cultural differences and the universal benefits of transnational capitalism. Indeed, the planetary paradigm shift Williamson envisions is imaginable only because we live in a globalizing world.

This accommodation to globalization creates a contradiction for the liberal option: Abandoning particularist claims to truth and connection to a specific cultural tradition and geographical space makes liberal religion especially vulnerable to relativization. Williamson's psychologized spirituality attempts to resolve that contradiction through recharismatization: It incorporates religious pluralism into a universal paradigm that includes all particular belief systems; identifies with the Judeo-Christian tradition, but stresses its commonality with other great world religions; weaves together sacred/spiritual language (God, soul, divine consciousness, redemption) with secular/scientific terminology (dysfunction, denial, disease, recovery, healing); and unites secular routes of healing with sacred paths to redemption.

▨ Global Capitalism, the Field of Possibles, and Religious Praxis

The eclipse of the transcendent that would grant meaning to the complexity of the modern world; the daily encounter with the mediazation of that complexity without a clear way to intervene in its course or content; and the encounter with a global political-economic order whose operations seem increasingly remote, inevitable, and beyond comprehension produce a pervasive sense of individual impotence. Williamson's cosmology is appealing because it addresses and promises to resolve its audience's feelings of powerlessness in the face of these contemporary historical circumstances. To comprehend this cosmology in its historical concreteness, we must examine the given it seeks to surpass and the other "possibles" it refuses (Sartre, 1963/1968, p. 93). That means returning to globalization, understood not as a quantitative increase in modernization, but as a qualitative change in how capitalism operates on a world scale.

Since the end of World War II, capitalism has been undergoing a transition from a monopoly to a transnational form (Amin, 1990; Harvey, 1989; Lipietz, 1992). Effectively accomplished in the 1970s, this transition has involved deep structural changes in the function of the nation-state; in relations among First World nations and between the First and Third Worlds; in technology, production processes, and patterns of consumption; in the world division of labor; and in international trade relations and global finance.

In a global capitalist economy, nation-states face diminished control over the operation of capital within their borders; no longer tied to individual nations, transnational corporations "now see themselves, even advertise themselves, as 'stateless'" (Barnet, 1994, p. 754). In response, nation-states increasingly look outward to the global economy with the goal of creating "a 'good business climate' to act as an inducement to transnational and global finance capital, and to deter . . . capital flight" (Harvey, 1989, p. 170). Transnational capital thus exerts significant influence over the conduct of national political-economic policies. In the United States, as Barnet (1994) notes, "transnational corporations now exercise more power over the political system than at any time since the early decades of this century" (p. 754).[12] This political-economic transformation has been accompanied by a withdrawal of support for the welfare state, a diminishing tax base, accelerated joblessness, shrinking real wages, fiscal retrenchment and economic austerity programs, deregulation in favor of "free market" capitalism, erosion of the social compromise between big labor and big government, and efforts to curb the power of organized labor and other social movements that might threaten transnational capitalist investment.

Innovations in communication technologies enable capital and information to move unimpeded around the world and give transnational corporations great flexibility in financial, market, resource, and labor decisions. In addition, global mediazation facilitates the worldwide marketing of goods, symbolic forms, and "lifestyles." Transnational capitalism is predicated on the unfettered flow of capital, information, and commodities and on the existence of an international pool of labor that does not enjoy the same fluidity. Advances in labor-saving technologies and the relative fixity of labor forces allows transnational corporations to shift production from the First World core to take advantage of nonunionized, cheap Third World labor; to win concessions from workers in core industrialized nations; and to bend national economic policies to their own priorities. In the United States, this transformation is manifested in a shift from an industrial to a service economy, corporate "downsizing," a striking decline in organized labor, mounting insecurity in the workplace, widespread disillusionment with government, a widening gap between rich and poor, growing anti-immigrant sentiment, and deepening anxiety about the attainment of the "American Dream."[13]

The emergence of transnational capitalism, according to Amin (1990), has produced a "crisis in the State and in politics" in the past two decades (p. 51). As transnational corporations shed their loyalty to particular nations, nation-states lose their ability to "control capitalist expansion or modulate it." As a result, national political discourse is increasingly characterized by "the constraint of competitiveness on a world scale," which is "presented as an inescapable and unavoidable fact" (p. 50). In the United States, where the Republican and Democratic parties have both embraced the mantra of global competition, their political-economic agendas have grown markedly similar. National politics has evolved into the mediated dissemination of candidate images, staged spectacles, and moralistic slogans, while political parties have declined as a practical site of clear political choice and citizen participation. So too have the other primary locations of liberal political activism—labor unions and progressive social movements—whose effectiveness has been drastically curbed under transnational capitalism. The eclipse of these avenues of political engagement has been accompanied by increased activism by the Religious-Political Right—an unattractive option for a religious liberal like Williamson. Indeed, she describes the rise of the Religious Right as a "dark force" arising from the suppression of "a genuine, authentic spiritual conversation" in contemporary American society.

This is the "field of possibles" within which Williamson forges a vision of the future. Faced with objective conditions that seem to deny the possibility of collective, public, political praxis, she signifies a future based on individual, private, psycho-spiritual transformation. Williamson's psychologized religiosity confronts the historical problem of an "objective situation" that seems to paralyze praxis, and the ontological problem of the loss of a transcendent "frame of orientation and devotion" (Fromm, 1947, p. 47) that would explain and overcome that paralysis. Her cosmology answers both problems by equating powerlessness with objective, material determinations, and "empowerment" with the transcendence—indeed, eradication—of those constraints. In so doing, she severs the dialectic of objective determination/subjective experience. Early in the episode, Winfrey announces that "our thoughts are the most powerful thing on earth." Given Williamson's insistence that "our thoughts determine the experiences of our lives," changing the world means simply changing one's ideas. Societal transformation follows from "healing inside us as individuals, which will then become collective healing." Social divisions of race, class, political affiliation, and so on, will be vanquished when enough individuals renounce "aggressive" thoughts. Thus, for Williamson, "the work of personal growth and personal recovery—spiritual work on ourselves—is the most important work of all."

This idealist, subjectivist solution dissolves the material determinants of praxis by making them a product of mind (via cognitivism) or a profane illusion (via a spiritual-vs.-material dichotomy). The future Williamson envisions thereby conserves the present even as it seeks to surpass it. Refusing the objective determinations that brought this form of religiosity into being leaves those structural determinants unexamined and untouched; it also validates a form of subjectivity that denies their reality (a subjectivity that refuses to see itself as signified). This psychologized religiosity is not simply a reproduction of its historical determinations.[14] In privileging changes in individuals' subjective experience over changes in their objective situation, it participates in the making of history by imagining a future that helps legitimize and reproduce a particular socioeconomic order.[15]

Williamson's spiritualized psychology reveals a deep dissatisfaction with the way the world is and a deep desire for what it might be. Her resolution is appealing because it speaks to our need to participate in the making of the world and to recognize the results of our praxis there. Williamson's promise that we can change the world by changing ourselves is seductive because the experience of present powerlessness, and the longing for future transformation, are genuine. At the same time, the idealism and subjectivism of her cosmology undermine recognition of the concrete historical sources of that discontent and the creation of forms of effective public praxis to transform them. The structural tendencies of modernization, the institutions and operation of mediazation, and the political-economic effects of transnational capitalism cannot be spirited away by a change of heart or mind. Rather, to transform this "objective situation" that is our "starting point," we must recognize how it has signified us and how it continues to signify our significations. As Sartre (1963/1968) reminds us, signifying beings cannot shed their determinations because these are the very ground on which praxis arises. The value of Sartre's method for the study of religion, culture, and media is that it maintains the dialectical tension of objective determinations and subjective praxis. It encourages us to grasp, theoretically and concretely, how praxis "hold[s] onto its determinations" *and* "transforms the world on the basis of given conditions" (p. 91).

Notes

1. *The Oprah Winfrey Show,* which premiered in 1986, is the top-rated American daytime talk program; it is also distributed in 55 other countries (Freeman, 1992; *Oprah Facts,* 1992).

2. Sales of Williamson's books have undoubtedly been boosted by her appearances on Winfrey's program.

3. Williamson's subsequent appearance on the show in December 1994 also concluded with a prayer.

4. *Search for a Method* is an introduction to the much longer *Critique of Dialectical Reason* (1976/1982), which supplies the "critical foundations" for the method Sartre proposes. Both works reject any notion that history is the product of mechanistic natural or economic laws.

5. This chapter proposes an ontological unity of being and meaning, following Geertz's (1957) view of human beings as "symbolizing, meaning-seeking animals" (p. 436), Burke's (1966) view that human beings are characterized by their capacity for "symbolicity," and Sartre's notion that to be human is to be a "signifying being" (1963/1968, p. 151). In keeping with the aim of this collection—that of furthering theoretical understanding of the intersection of religion, media, and culture—I propose that students of media and culture have chiefly focused on human beings as meaning *makers*, whereas students of religion have primarily been interested in human beings as meaning *seekers*. Both are concerned with signification—the former in terms of how people make meanings from their experiences through signifying practices and products, and the latter in terms of how people make their existence meaningful in relation to metaphysical frameworks of significance. The relationship of religion, media, and culture might therefore be conceptualized as the intersection of meaning-making and meaning-seeking within particular sociohistorical contexts and processes.

6. Public lecture given in Minneapolis, MN, December 1, 1994. All of the direct quotes from Williamson in this chapter come from the episode of the *Oprah Winfrey Show*, although many of the themes were reiterated in this public lecture.

7. Lears (1981) argues that the rise of this ethos is related to the emergence of a capitalist "culture of consumption" in the late 19th century. He proposes that traditional Protestantism's ethos of salvation and self-denial, which was isomorphic with mercantile capitalism's emphasis on the virtues of production, was replaced by a therapeutic ethos of self-realization more compatible with industrial capitalism's objective of advancing mass consumption.

8. This conceptual conflation flows both ways witness the fusion of psychological and religious terminology in the whole ensemble of 12-step "recovery" programs and the increasing penetration of spiritual concerns into more traditional psychotherapeutic paradigms.

9. Fornäs (1995) uses a different term—*mediatization*—but a similar conception: "the process whereby media increasingly come to saturate society, culture, identities and everyday life" (p. 1).

10. An exact correspondence between intentions and results in praxis is impossible because our actions are objectified in a social world: "[T]he consequences of our acts always end up by escaping us, since every concerted enterprise, as soon as it is realized, enters into relation with the entire universe, and since this infinite multiplicity of relations goes beyond our intentions" (Sartre, 1963/1968, p. 47).

11. Winfrey put this promise into action, and the content of her program has become noticeably more "positive" and less sensationalized. Interestingly, this shift has been accompanied by a decline in her ratings, which some critics believe are causally related. Despite this ratings slip, Winfrey has asserted her commitment to positive programming. She also brought Williamson back for a year-end visit in December 1994 (Lorando, 1994).

12. According to Barnet (1994), "more than a quarter of the world's economic activity now comes from the 200 largest corporations." As the power of transnational corporations

grows, their public accountability wanes, allowing them to "walk away from the enormous public problems their private decisions create for American society" (p. 754).

13. Barnet (1994) notes that the salary of an average CEO in the United States is now 149 times that of the average factory worker. It is estimated that nearly one in five American workers with full-time jobs earns poverty-level wages; fewer than 12% of the U.S. workforce in private industry is now unionized (pp. 754, 755).

14. Nor is it the only possible religious response to the "given" of transnational capitalism. Like the various fundamentalisms, liberation theology can also be understood as a response to the problems of capitalist globalization—one that points out inequities and injustices of such a system and points to solutions that are sociostructural rather individual in character. The challenge for liberation theologies is to retain their religious dimension to avoid charges that they are merely secular political movements (See Beyer, 1994. pp. 134-159).

15. Sampson (1981) makes a similar argument about the ahistorical character of cognitivism (the dominant paradigm in psychology), which "offers a portrait of people who are free to engage in internal mental activity . . . and yet who remain relatively impotent or apparently unconcerned (in psychology's worldview) about producing changes in their objective social world." By substituting "mental transformations for real world transformations," cognitive psychology helps legitimize "existing arrangements of power and domination" (p. 735).

References

Allen, M. (1994, September 19). Therapists bridge gap between spiritual, mental. *Minneapolis Star-Tribune*, p. 4A.

Amin, S. (1989). *Eurocentrism*. New York: Monthly Review Press.

Amin, S. (1990). *Delinking: Towards a polycentric world*. London: Zed Books.

Barnet, R. (1994, December 19). Lords of the global economy. *Nation*, 754-757.

Bellah, R., Madsen, R., Sullivan, W., Swidler, A., & Tipton, S. (1985). *Habits of the heart: Individualism and commitment in American life*. Berkeley: University of California Press.

Beyer, P. (1994). *Religion and globalization*. London: Sage.

Burke, K. (1966). *Language as symbolic action*. Berkeley: University of California Press.

Bushman, R. (1967). *From Puritan to Yankee: Character and the social in the twentieth century*. Cambridge, MA: Harvard University Press.

A course in miracles (1992). Glen Ellen, CA: Foundation for Inner Peace. (Originally published 1975)

Fairclough, N. (1989). *Language and power*. New York: Longman.

Fornäs, J. (1995). *Cultural theory and late modernity*. London: Sage.

Freeman, M. (1992, June). Talk shows flourish during May sweeps. *Broadcasting, 15,* 11.

Fromm, E. (1947). *Man for himself*. Greenwich, CT: Fawcett.

Geertz, C. (1957, December). Ethos, world-view and the analysis of sacred symbols. *Antioch Review,* 421-437.

Geertz, C. (1979). Religion as a cultural system. In W. A. Lessa & E. Z. Vogt (Eds.), *Reader in comparative religion* (pp. 78-89). New York: Harper and Row.

Harvey, D. (1989). *The condition of postmodernity*. Oxford, UK: Basil Blackwell.

Hunter, J. D. (1983). *American evangelicalism: Conservative religion and the quandary of modernity*. New Brunswick, NJ: Rutgers University Press.

Illouz, E. (1991). Reason within passion: Love in women's magazines. *Critical Studies in Mass Communication, 8,* 231-248.

Lears, T. J. J. (1981). *No place of grace*. New York: Pantheon.

Lipietz, A. (1992). *Towards a new economic order: Postfordism, ecology and democracy*. London: Oxford University Press.

Lipsitz, G. (1988, June). "This ain't no sideshow": Historians and media studies. *Critical Studies in Mass Communication, 5*, 147-61.

Lorando, M. (1994, November 8). Oprah focuses on the light side. *Minneapolis Star-Tribune*, pp. 1E, 3E.

More Meaning. (1994, January 4). *Minneapolis Star-Tribune*, p. 1E.

Oprah Facts. (1992). Chicago: Harpo Productions.

Peck, J. (1993). *The gods of televangelism: The crisis of meaning and the appeal of religious television*. Cresskill, NJ: Hampton.

Peck, J. (1995). TV talk shows as therapeutic discourse: The ideological labor of the televised talking cure. *Communication Theory, 5*(1), 58-81.

Sampson, E. (1981). Cognitive psychology as ideology. *American Psychologist, 36*, 730-43.

Sartre, J.-P. (1968). *Search for a method* (H. E. Barnes, Trans.). New York: Vintage. (Originally published 1968)

Sartre, J.-P. (1982). *Critique of dialectical reason*. London: Verso. (Originally published 1976)

Thomas, G. (1989). *Revivalism and social change: Christianity, nation-building, and the market in the nineteenth century United States*. Chicago: Chicago University Press.

Thompson, J. B. (1990). *Ideology and modern culture: Critical social theory in the era of mass communication*. Stanford, CA: Stanford University Press.

Wapnick, K. (1989). *A talk given on A Course in Miracles*. Roscoe, NY: Foundation for A Course in Miracles.

White, M. (1992). *Tele-advising: Therapeutic discourse in American television*. Chapel Hill: University of North Carolina Press.

Wilentz, S. (1984). *Chants democratic*. New York: Oxford University Press.

Williamson, M. (1992). *A return to love: Reflections on the principles of A Course in Miracles*. New York: HarperCollins.

A Utopian on Main Street

Claire Hoertz Badaracco

Women's resistances are defined by the alterations they forge in the systems of rules that create their scripture and limit their practice.
—Fulkerson, 1994

A "classic" feminist philosophy of resistance to patriarchal culture developed globally in the 20th century. The argument resists subjugation of women by any philosophy contrary to the utopian, liberationist principles that define feminism. This chapter addresses the congruent thought in contemporary feminist theology and philosophy as well as in women's critical reading of ancestral or sacred texts that constructs "neo-feminism" as a postmodern philosophy.

In North America, women first directed their energies toward achieving the vote, then control over domestic life, then access to jobs and better wages (Lerner, 1977, 1993). Women's concurrent resistance to their subordinate role in the world's religions has been less visible. The impression of feminism created by the media has historically been more about the body than about the economy, spirit, and mind (Bloom, 1992; Hoover, 1988; Lichter, Lichter, & Rothman, 1994; Marsden, 1990; Peck, 1993). Media have demonstrated little awareness that "classic" feminism was less modern than democratic: as concerned with freeing the human spirit from oppression as with establishing civil rights.

Classical feminism extended the liberationist spirit found in civil society to religion, philosophy, law, literature, science, and the material economy. Each wave of feminism claimed its part in a centuries-old evolutionary process that defined heroines from scripture, novels, poetry, art, or film as representing advances in self-determination. But the willingness to invest belief in fictional and historical models is heightened and intensified by the absence of recognizably "real" women in mediated culture.

A great deal of critical energy has been devoted to effectively reconstructing visual stereotypes about women over the past three decades. Equal fervor has been devoted to unpacking the pathology of the patriarchal structures of organized religion in the past two decades. Much of this cultural criticism has diverted attention from the central discussion, a fact recognized by "neo-feminist" writers, critics, and journalists. The critic Suzanne Walters (1995) observed that arguing about social stereotypes does not change the deep attitudes and habits that create symbols from superficial images.

Women currently find a basis for constructing feminist identity through the language of scripture. They also seek to overthrow the stereotypes embedded in the images of material or mediated culture by offering a text-based reconstruction of feminist identity using sacred language embedded in patriarchal religious texts. This chapter draws several distinctions between "neo" and "post" feminism and describes representative work by writers "reactivating" scripture (with the understanding that there are many more writers operating in a similar vein who are not included).

Among the silences in public discourse contributing to women's oppression, the absence of attention by media to the spirituality inherent in feminist philosophy is pervasive. The media disseminate images of women as commodities and portray feminism as a disestablished movement made up of individualists who are hostile to traditional values and whose anger has precipitated the current backlash among white males in a "politics of resentment" (Faludi, 1991). For the North American public, the association between women's rights and "sexual liberation" has been wedded in the public mind through the media. Clichés of sexual appeal, the slogans of advertising, epitomize the mediated discourse about gender (Schudson, 1986). Similarly, the rhetoric of the "culture wars" described by Hunter (1991) and Carter (1993) are framed in metaphors of the body, particularly over abortion. Academic feminists also connect their legal and aesthetic arguments to the body: Camille Paglia (1992) claims that by restricting pornography, bloodless women deprive the public of art. Assertions by Catherine MacKinnon (1987, 1989, 1993) that the U.S. Constitution should be amended to exclude pornography from the protections of free speech have received less attention.

So accustomed has the public become to the commodified female as victim that nonmaterialism is jarring. The mediated discussion about "women," and "women's experience," as though shared gender caused one monolithic response to life, is belied by the reality of race and class. Contemporary philosophers, theologians, and critical theorists who respect the integrity of, and necessity for, multiple interpretations of texts call for a "change of subject" (Benhabib, Butler, Cornell, & Fraser, 1995). The trend in contemporary analysis is to turn away from generalizations toward a greater philosophical particularity and the recognition that each woman must tell her own story, so that words counterbalance image.

The generational milestones that separate one wave of feminism from another include enduring literature as well as fashions in media stereotypes, and both play a role in public opinion formation. Those from the late Victorian era, for example, such as Elizabeth Cady Stanton's *Women's Bible* (1895), or Kate Chopin's *Awakening* (1899), are historically significant and are linked with a tradition of modern social tracts such as Betty Friedan's *The Feminine Mystique* (1963), Kate Millett's *Sexual Politics* (1970), and Germaine Greer's *The Female Eunuch* (1971), among others, which exhibited the militancy about gender identity typical of the "second wave" of white middle-class woman. Among novelists of the same period, Doris Lessing's *Four Gated City* and *Golden Notebook*, Margaret Atwood's *Surfacing*, Alice Walker's *The Color Purple*, Ntozake Shange's *for colored girls*—and among poets, Adrienne Rich's *Dream of a Common Language*—represented an attempt to challenge the literary canon that positioned feminism squarely within modernism.

As Carol Christ (1980) observed, these books have common themes: The experience of nothingness and mystical awakenings in the wilderness gave each woman an image of her own power that led to a "new name" for herself and her world, like the genre of wilderness journal or "spiritual journalism," that uses Nature as a mirror for both divine spirit and human identity. Works by Patricia Hampl, Kathleen Norris, Annie Dillard, and Gretel Ehrlich are representative of a larger conversation going on in American culture since Henry David Thoreau and the Transcendentalists. In this literature, there appears an insistence on reinventing women's religious culture as the literature of outsiders. What makes this "new" is the way in which feminists are integrating an alternative vision about religious orthodoxy and secular materialism (Badaracco, 1996).

Paradoxically, what earlier generations of feminists perceived as a weakness is now read as strength: Being countercultural, the resident alien in the public square, or an outsider in orthodox biblical culture enables women to reinterpret custom and language with fresh insight. Critical distance enables women to transform the experience of being a subject defined by scripture (or a sexual object in material culture) to reconstruct a transcendent identity.

"Neo" Versus "Post" Feminist Critical Theory

The term *neo-feminism* denotes a deliberate distancing from many of the earlier constructs associated with women's mediated image as consumers, from the popular idea of modernism, and from postmodern feminist theory. Neo-feminism is about building theory out of popular literature, public language, mediated scripts, and how cultural beliefs influence the contemporary practice of religion (Fiorenza, 1993; Hewitt, 1995). Postmodern feminism questions the authority of scripture in order to derive more authority over the academic disciplines that inform its theory. Neo-feminism uses the ephemeral authority that language and literature have over culture, whether rational or irrational, in searching for the earliest meaning of ancestral texts, or for the interpretive dimension to the transformative potential of language over the defininition of culture itself. As the Bible and Culture Collective concluded, postmodern feminist critical inquiry is more interested in the ideological effects of biblical texts than in their "redemptive" aspects (Castelli, Moore, Phillips, & Schwartz, 1995; Fiorenza, 1993; Hewitt, 1995; King, 1995).

Modernism and feminism have been on a collision course from the standpoint of intellectuals, whereas popular culture homogenized both "isms" into an image of women that reinforced the hegemony of a consumer economy. According to the philosopher Nancy Fraser (1995), hypotheses central to the definitions of postmodernism concerning the death of metanarratives from history and philosophy involving Marx, Freud, God—even feminism itself—constitute a "retreat from utopia" that is "disabling" for women. As her colleague Morny Joy (1994) points out, the feminist "reparation" that is a renaming of the "self" as central rather than peripheral occurred within an evolution in postmodernism that questions individual autonomy.

Three principles are central to definitions underlying neo-feminist identity: "selfhood," "agency," and "alterity" (Benhabib et al., 1995). The idea of self, the worth of humans over things or systems, the distinction between the social role of a person and an individual's spiritual reality are based on the concept of mutual selfhood: God is in each person, and each person is in God. The reconfiguration of the idea of self is the grounds for a "participatory consciousness" (Edwards, 1995). The indwelling of Spirit is the conceptual ground upon which neo-feminist writers, philosophers, and theologians base their ideas about transformation of a system embroiled in patterns of domination into a society that is comprehensive, communal, and interdependent.

A body of exegesis, biblical history, and theopolitical philosophy published between 1975 and 1995 placed women within androcentric culture. What Fiorenza (1983) termed the "hermeneutics of suspicion" belongs to the "discourse of resistance" that Fulkerson (1994) and others today assume is part of neo-feminist Christian identity. Chief among the landmark texts that contribute to that identity are Fiorenza, *In Memory of Her* (1983); Rosemary Radford Ruether, *Sexism and God-Talk* (1983); Elaine Pagels, *The Gnostic Gospels* (1989); and *Adam, Eve and the Serpent* (1988); Elizabeth Johnson, *She Who Is* (1992); and more than two dozen other texts identifying the school of thought that links feminism with the theological reconstruction of early bibilical history through original texts fundamental to Christian biblical interpretation.

Some theologians, such as Mary Daly, have "used God as a weapon" in trying to reach the public, according to Edwards (1995). The work of polemicists such as Daly paved the way for newcomers who "mix liberation philosophy, social justice critique, and religious images" to explain power relationships in art, literature, and in society (pp. 177-179). As Carol Christ (1980) observed, popular fiction identified as "women's" explores the nature of the feminine in sacred as well as secular culture, and belongs to "a new emerging sensibility"—an evolving awareness that "women's culture as a whole" is undergoing a "megashift," with implications for how society is structured (p. 20). This literature resists the lack of status embedded in the subordinated identity assigned to women by church and society.

Furthermore, this resistance is not "merely" a First World phenomenon. As the philosopher Ursula King (1995) explains, feminists rereading scripture can be regarded as part of global democratization (see also Eck, 1993). An Indian expatriate living in Australia, Ranjini Ribera (1994), reasserts the belief that through religion, women can change society: "You can judge the degree of civilization by the social and political position of women in the country. In Guatemala, Rigoberta Menchu (1994) reads the Bible as a "weapon" in a "just war." Elsa Tamez (1994) in Mexico marks change in progressive Protestant communities, where reading scripture is done from the perspective of the poor. Grace Eneme in Cameroon, writes of the African Protestant church among the Bakossi people who categorize stones as living (grinding, building) or dead (boulders). Eneme (1994) concludes that women, who make up 85% of the congregation, are "rejected" by the official church, but remain steadfast cornerstones: "Christ alone assures us that we are not subordinate." Jean Zaru (1994), a Christian Palestinian living in Israel, writes about seeking peace by causing strife: "Wherever injustice and wrong exist, we should be there to say, this is not the will of God, this should be changed." Chung Hyun Kyung (1994) in Korea observes that the key to Asian women's theology is anthropology, and the key to Asian religious cultures is the mix of Christian texts and myths of many male gods and female goddesses: "Asian women view God not as an individual but as a community," and "To know the self is to know God for Christian Asian women."

A 1987 report on Mariology from Singapore signed by 32 women from 16 Pacific Rim countries calls for a "rediscovery" of Mary and self-liberation from 2,000 years of "destructive effects" of the male interpretation of Mary: "In the Catholic Church, Mary's exaltation has been used to reinforce women's oppression, whereas in the Protestant Church, the rejection of Mary has oppressed women," the ecumenical, international convention concluded (King, 1994, p. 271). Among Cuban American women, theology has led to renaming their collective ethnic identity. The *mujeristas*, according to Ada Maria Isasi-Diaz (1995) is a self-attribution growing out the political protest songs of the 1960s and the liberation theology of women religious working in Central and Latin America (Castillo, 1994a, 1994b; King, 1995).

Black American women's theology, according to Dolores Williams (1994), is the work of "retrieving" the "hidden or diminished female tradition of catalytic action," an important task for "womanist" theologians and ethicists. *Womanist*, a concept rooted in black history, religion, and culture, is used by those who have criticized the feminist movement for being mostly about white, middle-class women (King, 1995).

▓ Reactivating Scripture

Resistance to androcentric reading of religious texts rescripts meaning within the context of history, politics, and society as part of a "throwing off" of sweeping generalities about gender committed by media, patriarchy, and previous generations of feminists. For neo-feminists, reconstructing scriptural texts—not solely by theologians or biblical scholars, but by popular writers whose target market is Main Street—is a search for female prototypes actively resistant to cultural stereotypes by dominant political systems and patriarchal religious cultures as equally subordinating. Unlike the spiritual journalists (Norris, Dillard, Ehrlich), neo-feminists connect contemporary social paradigms to reading the Old Testament, the Torah, and the Koran. It is a search for roots, an act of resistance to "new age" styles of modern piety, and especially to the televisual gloss on the most profound questions about women's religious identity (Hoover, 1988; Peck, 1993; Riaño, 1994).

The spirituality of women writers tends to be "intensified" rather than "dissipated by independence of dogma," and the spiritual freedom to imagine women at the center rather than on the periphery of the sacred drama drives a "syncretism" rather than a separatism from traditional textual interpretation and its inherent moral lessons (Briggs, 1990; Ostriker, 1993). A philosophy of reading as a political act emerges from the syncretic drive Ostriker (1993) describes:

> Instead of Image we possess Word. An alternative beauty bursts into existence, through the language of the stutterer Moses. It is a triumph of Language . . . for are we not commanded by the text itself to interrogate, to engage in dialogue with each other, with the text, with God? (p. 50)

The poets' resistance to textual interpretation as culturally determined is a simultaneous, three-way conversation—with the reader, God, and the "sacred" talents of the text itself.

All readers filter sacred texts through historical, political, and cultural analysis to derive meaning. According to the writer Allegra Goodman (1994), "The prophets do not speak in a vacuum: they raise their voices in a specific culture, and like all artistic expression, their language is grounded in particular social circumstances" (p. 302). Theologian Walter Breuggemann calls this "perspectivalist" rather than "fundamentalist" criticism (1978, 1993). The moral burden individual writers bear is proportionate to their perspectivalist approach to scripture. "We all live a version, not a story," Patricia Hampl (1994) writes. "Even a memory with a part missing or lost has as many readings as there are players in the action" (p. 300). Elizabeth Rosen (1994) concludes similarly that reading has instructed her in the "extent to which the era in which one lives determines what one sees in a biblical text and how that is further modified by who does the reading" (p. 23).

Assumptions about the audience as a passive recipient are rooted in archetype, myth, metaphor, and image. Both literal and historical principles drawn from the androcentric imagination imply that the Bible operates critically on an audience in a fashion similar to the daily news. The neo-feminist critic would say that all texts endure across cultures and over time and have a life of their own that transcends and transforms readers. When readers activate the meaning embedded in texts, they may aspire to change church and society so that they are congruent with the meaning of the texts.

The neo-feminist reader acts as an ethnographer, assuming that no text is complete but that each is a cultural shard or artifact to be examined for the parts that are lost, lacking, or chipped away by time. Ethnographies, according to the anthropologist John Van Maanen (1988), display the "ways individuals and groups establish the basis for new genres." Communities establish identities by exchanging interpretive products, as Theissen (1991) calls them, in the form of scripts. The public nature of religious scripts, or the genre in which those scripts are located, makes them as accessible to the common reader as popular songs. Public texts are literary narratives with the potential for being history. As objects of shared belief, they are made up of meanings exchanged between cultures or subcultures in a community, so that equilibrium is attained rather than dominance, silence, or control (Theissen, 1991). All texts introduced into the public square—news stories, spiritual journalism, novels—are attempts to negotiate the meaning of texts that govern, or are assumed to govern, public behavior and private belief.

Cultural bartering of public texts means that the liberationist challenges patriarchal culture by publicly debating inherited notions of community or historical identity by calling into question how critical theory determines historical exegesis. This challenges "traditions" that are the basis for historical assumptions about women's identity. The critical viewpoint expressed through the principle of "alterity," or the voice of the outsider, is the basis for a neo-feminist interpretative paradigm in which the outsider reads in order to interpret the values of the culture. Language is two-dimensional; it may be interpreted as artifact for its omissions as well as for its content. The elements of this paradigm are (a) the person observed: e.g., Yahweh, Allah; (b) the observer: an evangelist who shared historical time with the text; (c) the narrator: a character distant from the observer or author; (d) the audience: contemporary readers who determine whether the text is a chronicle or message; (e) mystery: ambiguity as a form of prototype or symbol (Van Maanen, 1988).

The Theopolitics of Reading

Neo-feminist critical principles can be applied to derive a global philosophy of resistance. Rebecca Goldstein (1994), for example, reads Lot's wife, Irit, as an allegory about obedience to God's will and "the demands of transcendence and the backward pull of love and accidental attachment" (p. 8). What motivated Lot's wife to look back? Goldstein speculates: Was it "voyeurism, or skepticism, nostalgia or bravado?" Her interpretive method elicits from the Old Testament heroic patterns of meaning and behavior that can teach women today about their identity. Traditional rabbinical teaching reads this story as one of retribution for disobedience, according to Goldstein, who reads the story differently. Irit desired to "be one with" her children out of womanly instinct, and she did not care to count the cost. She looked back because she wanted to see if her daughters were following her, and she was so overcome by her grief at what had happened to them that she desired to join them. God mercifully accommodated her desire by turning her into a pillar of salt.

The Old Testament figure of Hannah represents for writers Cynthia Ozick, Marcia Falk, and Margaret Ann Doody, a matrix for feminism rooted in Torah. The traditional reading of this story is that Hannah, the mother of Samuel, is counted as a heroine of Jewish civilization because she was a barren woman who prayed to have a child and was "rewarded" with one by God the Father who responded because she promised to give the boy back through service in the temple. Rather than a story about maternity, Ozick (1994) reads it as one about conformity, self-assertion, and personhood. At a time when the synagogue was the site of public prayer, Hannah moves civilization forward by "inventing" inward prayer, according to Ozick. Of course this public act in the temple gives rise to Eli's misinterpretation of her identity: He sees her moving her lips silently and assumes she is drunk. Though Hannah's prayer is consistent with the rules of patriarchy (she prays for a son), it is her husband Elkanah who asserts her "personhood" by questioning her grief with a challenge, "*lameh tivki?* Why weepest thou?" Ozick reads this interchange between husband and wife as a transcendent, metaphysical moment, "the earliest declaration" of the first principle of feminism: "let every human being be treated as an end in herself or himself" (p. 90). Ozick reads Hannah as a prototype for what she calls "classical" feminism; that is, the transcendence of biology, a defeat not only of the idea that anatomy is destiny, but of "separateness" itself.

Marcia Falk's (1994) reading of Hannah is consistent with Ozick's, though she sees the Old Testament figure as a story of "reversals" about mistaken identity and a lesson against judging another's behavior. Picking up where the rabbis left off, Falk reads Hannah as a prototype for changing inaudible, invisible prayer into a communal voice that included everyone, a "truly inclusive, spiritual community," a "community of equals." Hannah's triumph, according to Falk's reading, is not in bearing successfully the son she longs for, but in internalizing her prayer: "Hannah the petitioner becomes Hannah the benefactor, who approaches even her relationship to God with self-respect and the assumption of reciprocity" (pp. 100-101).

Margaret Anne Doody's (1994) reading of Hannah also explores the classic nature of the text and its connection to the "lost child recovered" theme used in the dramas of Euripedes. Because Hannah fulfills her pledge to give Samuel back to God through service to the temple, according to Doody, he is a man "cut off from the feminine" and must regard all other women as substitute mothers. As a child of the temple, he is burdened by becoming the ultimate insider who thinks holiness unremarkable; he has been raised to think it routine, his right. He exists, Doody imagines, in a "state of superb latency," having been raised "Peter-Pan-like, without parents" (p. 116). Samuel sits in the heart of the sacred shrine but lives without feelings of dread, awe, or excitement about his privilege. He never has experienced a state of "alterity," being on the perimeter, in exile, excluded.

Marina Warner's (1994) explication of the Queen of Sheba's story reads the Old Testament figure as a paradigm of "alterity." Anomalous, foreign, Ethiopian, dark, she neither commits a crime nor experiences a miracle, which sets her apart from many of her cohorts in the biblical landscape. She only "asks hard questions," according to Warner, a privilege afforded few others in the Old Testament, including Samson, Daniel, Nebuchadnezzar, and Solomon himself. In Christian exegesis, the Queen of Sheba is the church—a foreshadowing of all female prophetic figures (Muslim and Jewish traditions offer variants). The Queen of Sheba represents the experience of alterity as an asset, rather than as a disadvantage (p. 158).

The poet Kathleen Norris (1994) reads the book of Psalms as a celebration of alterity, of living on alien soil, because it leads to a deepening of spiritual life (p. 230). In an off-Broadway production, the dramatist Elizabeth Swados styled Job as a clown, the ultimate outsider, the quintessential loser who has a great deal to teach about what it means to be human (Buchmann & Speigel, 1994; Chittister, 1990). Patricia Hampl (1994) reads the story of Jonah as a lesson in the consequences of humans' separating themselves from others and from God. Jonah, according to Hampl, has told his fellow sailors that he worships Yahweh, but he "talks to God as if he were a rival author, part of the competition, ever a book ahead of him" (p. 299).

Rather like Eve, who was the quintessential outcast, the cause of all others being "cast out," the neo-feminist critic absorbs alterity as part of her critical method, asserting that being acted upon as a subject, or excluded by patriarchy, has instilled in women the value of compassion and unity, antidotes to custom, scripture, and culture:

> Compassion is the acknowledgment of connection, the refusal to see the world as divided into distinct units that can do without one another. . . .

For the truth is that all creation is connected, attached, together, inter-twined—compassionate. (Hampl, 1994, p. 298)

▓ Textual Framing of Classic Identity

The problem remains for neo-feminists to penetrate the public mind on Main Street with a postmodern redaction of religious texts so that their ideals will be unembarrassed. Neo-feminist writers are obliged to search for a vernacular unencumbered by animosities associated with earlier waves of feminism and free of the sexual freight of media images. The struggle to speak a language that is both "common" and "utopian," global and particular, relevant to secular society but employing sacred scripture as an "acceptable canon" breaks precedent on textual, critical, narrational, and generic levels. This line of inquiry places a particular emphasis on explaining power in relationships through the political life of the text.

The neo-feminist ontology acknowledges the "death" of Freud and Marx. The self is a spiritual construct rather than a psychological or revolutionary one. Neo-feminism advances the argument about women's identity toward the next level of consciousness, the global and communal, recognizing that "networks of intricate interdependencies" are being discovered in all disciplines (Fulkerson, 1994; Winter, Lummis, & Stokes, 1994). To employ the vernacular, neo-feminism is "holistic," posits the "complementarity" of male and female, and "coexistence" over polariza-tion or politicization.

The political life of the text constitutes its "agentry." Post-structuralist critical theory seeks to "locate" the political power of language. Neo-femi-nist theory seeks to identify texts as a source of spiritual power in order to transform society through those who read them. Theologian Fulkerson (1994) concludes that whether a text is "oppressive" or "liberating" is not a quality inherent in the text, but one that exists primarily in its reception. Similarly, communication scholar Martín-Barbero (1993) says he has "still" to explain women's resistance to messages, stories, and images imposed by clerical culture in favor of those that emanate from women's grassroots movements (see also Riaño, 1994). All public texts, whether scripture in ancient, sacred printed books, or scripts for the secular media, are socially activated (Wolff, 1995). Public texts are enacted—able to silence, corrupt, free, or transform—to the degree they are able to engage believers.

The principle of alterity offers the neo-feminist philosopher a language for the idea of text as performance. The values of religious scripture enacted in performance, worship, reading, or preaching give rise to subgenres, as Fulkerson demonstrated, including "testimony," "witness," "call," "homiletic," and "journey" (Wolff, 1995). To these subgenres, I would add "wilderness journal," in which the self becomes objectified in a transcendental landscape, with a sacramental language of its own enacted through the absence of things and through its proximity to the void (Badaracco, 1996). The neo-feminist resistance to genres long associated with the literary "canon" results in what philosopher Benhabib (1995) calls an "aesthetic proliferation of styles" that blur distinctions between history and literature, factual narrative and imaginary creation. Emerging from these blurred genres is a vernacular of resistance in "narratological strategies" (p. 112). It occurs between the silences; it is an "attempt to account for what is absent" in mediated discourse, in scripture, and in biblical history.

The activist reader, an outsider struggling to define a collective self based on gender, achieves a utopian or symbolic dimension in interpretation when texts belong to the culturally specific genres of religious scripture. In Fulkerson's (1994) study of the Pentacostal church, women's stories account for their "oppression within a capitalist economy and their freedom within a canonical order." Fulkerson calls the interrelationship of text and performance a "regime of resistance," that includes "rescripting" women's silences along with the world's disdain for those who are both poor and religious. She observes that resistance occurs not only in practice, performance, and belief, but especially through reading (p. 290). Readable texts that simply "mirror or distort" reality, identity, or history have evolved into interactive texts that derive meaning when met by an audience willing to experience the text or to read it actively. An ongoing pattern of resistance to assumptions about women's subordination requires that "dominating patterns" be "dismantled" through "nonsubmissive behavior" on the part of the oppressed (Castelli et al., 1995, p. 234; Edwards, 1995, p. 186). Patriarchal reading of scripture, but one means of subordination, accounts for women's absence from biblical history and their silence in the assembly.

Resistance to patriarchal readings of scripture leads women to an ideological "location" in which they are neither a problem nor an issue, but an agent for transforming the "other," the androcentric religious culture. In the process, they may expect to revolutionize secular and civil society (Benhabib, 1995, p. 114). Through their liberationist ideas about a nonviolent, just social order, women writers engage in the public square by challenging inherited definitions and cultural assumptions about who women are and who they aspire to be. In doing so, they are "changing the subject," as philosophers and theologians describe: "Feminists need both deconstruction and reconstruction, destabilization of meaning and projection of utopian hope" (Fraser, 1995, p. 71). As Drucilla Cornell (1995) pointed out, feminism is about the "reimagining" and "rearticulation" of philosophy, law, and history so that utopian "aspirations" are not undermined by "accommodating" preconceived terms of gender, race, and class to a system of domination (p. 78).

Terms evolve when reading can be considered a political performance. Reimagining identity, not as one individual story, but as part of a macrostory, breaks down the media rhetoric that universalizes women's experience. By asserting the particularity of women's individual stories embedded in one narrative or historical tradition, reading and writing become not only a single act of resistance to women's mistaken identity, but part of a social fabric of resistance that challenges genre, memory, and faith as they construct social identity (Fulkerson, 1994). The theopolitical definitions embedded in neo-feminist readings of scripture revitalize the "collective memory of failed forms" that Breuggemann (1993) established is the reason why new genres come into being, in an effort to reform what has identified women.

When reading fails to yield meaning, something relevant to either our identity or culture, we are apt to create a parallel discourse that establishes a separate universe of meaning and interpretative value. In this context, reading becomes a bartering process between the individual engaged with the text and the macroculture. In neo-feminist philosophy, evolution from the androcentric to the performed text implies a paradigm shift that involves the macrocultural imagination. As the paradigm shift from passive reception to actively resistant reading occurs, the moral power also shifts from the tale teller to the tale bearer, from the author as accurate to the reader as actor, instructor, evangelist, journalist. Reading that resists cultural assumptions constantly renegotiates identity through the audience, which in a sense performs the text. From the neo-feminist perspective, acceptance of being the subject, or of being subjugated, is a failure of the imagination to transcend stereotypes that subordinate women's spirit by placing it on the periphery of culture.

References

Badaracco, C. (1996). Animated outsiders: Echoes of Merton, Hampl, Norris, Dillard, and Ehrlich. *Thomas Merton Annual, 8* (pp. 150-161). Minneapolis, MN: Liturgical Press.

Benhabib, S., Butler, J., Cornell, D., & Fraser, N. (1995). *Feminist contentions: A philosophical exchange.* New York: Routledge & Kegan Paul.

Bloom, H. (1992). *The American religion.* New York: Simon & Schuster.

Breuggemann, W. (1978). *The prophetic imagination.* New York: Fortress.

Breuggemann, W. (1993). *Texts under negotiation: The Bible and postmodern imagination.* Minneapolis, MN: Fortress.

Briggs, S. (1990). "Buried with Christ": The politics of identity and the poverty of interpretation. In R. Schwartz, (Ed.), *The book and the text: The Bible and literary theory.* New York: Blackwell.

Buchmann, C., & Speigel, C. (Eds.) (1994). *Out of the garden: Women writers on the Bible.* New York: Fawcett.

Carter, S. (1993). *The culture of disbelief: How American law and politics trivializes religious devotion.* New York: Basic Books.

Castelli, E., Moore, S., Phillips, G., & Schwartz, R. (1995). *Postmodern Bible: The Bible and culture collective.* New Haven, CT: Yale University Press.

Castillo, A. (1994a). *Massacre of dreamers: Essays on Xicanisma.* Albuquerque: University of New Mexico Press.

Castillo, A. (1994b). *So far from God.* New York: Penguin-Plume.

Chittister, J. (1990). *Job's daughters: Women and power.* New York: Paulist.

Christ, C. (1980). *Diving deep and surfacing: Women writers on spiritual quest.* Boston: Beacon.

Christ, C., & Plaskow, J. (Eds.). (1992). *Womanspirit rising: A feminist reader in religion.* San Francisco: Harper.

Cornell, D. (1995a). Rethinking the time of feminism. In S. Behnhabib, J. Butler, D. Cornell, & N. Fraser, *Feminist contentions: A philosophical exchange* (pp. 145-156). New York: Routledge & Kegan Paul.

Cornell, D. (1995b). What is ethical feminism? In S. Behnhabib, J. Butler, D. Cornell, & N. Fraser (Eds.), *Feminist contentions: A philosophical exchange* (pp. 75-106). New York: Routledge & Kegan Paul.

Doody, M. A. (1994). Infant piety and the infant Samuel. In C. Buchmann & C. Speigel (Eds.), *Out of the garden: Women writers on the Bible* (pp. 103-122). New York: Fawcett.

Eck, D. L. (1993). *Encountering God: A spiritual journey from Bozeman to Banaras.* Boston: Beacon.

Edwards, F. (1995). Spirituality, consciousness and gender identification: A neo-feminist perspective. In U. King, (Ed.) *Religion and gender* (pp. 177-194). Oxford, UK: Blackwell.

Eneme, G. (1994). Women as living stones. In U. King (Ed.), *Feminist theology from the Third World* (pp. 214-219). London: SPCK/Orbis.

Falk, M. (1994). Reflections on Hannah's prayer. In C. Buchmann & C. Speigel (Eds.), *Out of the garden: Women writers on the Bible* (pp. 94-102). New York: Fawcett.

Faludi, S. (1991). *Backlash: The undeclared war against American women.* New York: Crown.

Fiorenza, E. (1983). *In memory of her: A feminist theological reconstruction of Christian origins.* New York: Crossroad.

Fiorenza, E. (1993). *Searching the scriptures.* New York: Crossroad.

Fraser, N. (1995). False antithesis. In S. Behnhabib, J. Butler, D. Cornell, & N. Fraser (Eds.), *Feminist contentions: A philosophical exchange* (pp. 59-74). New York: Routledge & Kegan Paul.

Fulkerson, M. (1994). *Changing the subject: Women's discourses and feminist theology.* Minneapolis, MN: Fortress.

Goldstein, R. (1994). Looking back at Lot's wife. In C. Buchmann & C. Speigel (Eds.), *Out of the garden: Women writers on the Bible* (pp. 3-12). New York: Fawcett.

Goodman, A. (1994). Prophecy and poetry. In C. Buchmann & C. Speigel (Eds.), *Out of the garden: Women writers on the Bible* (pp. 301-309). New York: Fawcett.

Hampl, P. (1994). In the belly of the whale. In C. Buchmann & C. Speigel (Eds.), *Out of the garden: Women writers on the Bible* (pp. 289-300). New York: Fawcett.

Hewitt, M. (1995). *Critical theory of religion: A feminist analysis.* Minneapolis, MN: Fortress.

Hoover, S. (1988). *Mass media religion: The social sources of the electronic church.* London: Sage.

Hunter, J. D. (1991). *Culture wars: The struggle to define America.* New York: Basic Books.

Isasi-Diaz, A. M. (1994). The task of hispanic women's liberation theology—mujeristas: Who we are and what we are about. In U. King (Ed.), *Feminist theology from the Third World* (pp. 88-104). London: SPCK/Orbis.

Joy, M. (1994). God and gender: Some reflections on women's invocations of the divine. In U. King (Ed.) *Feminist theology from the Third World* (pp. 121-144). London: SPCK/Orbis.

King, U. (1994). *Feminist theology from the Third World.* London: SPCK/Orbis.

King, U. (1995). *Religion and gender.* Oxford, UK: Blackwell.

Kyung, C. H. (1990). To be human is to be created in God's image. In U. King, (Ed.) *Feminist theology from the Third World.* New York: Orbis.

Lapide, P. (1986). *The sermon on the mount: Utopia or program for action?* New York: Maryknoll.

Lerner, G. (1977). *The female experience: An American documentary.* Indianapolis, IN: Bobbs-Merrill.

Lerner, G. (1986). *The creation of patriarchy.* New York: Oxford University Press.

Lerner, G. (1993). *The creation of feminist consciousness: From the middle ages to eighteen-seventy.* New York: Oxford University Press.

Lichter, R., Lichter, L., & Rothman, S. (1994). *Prime time: How TV portrays American culture.* Washington, DC: Regenery.

MacKinnon, C. (1987). *Feminism unmodified: Discourses on life and law.* Cambridge, MA: Harvard University Press.

MacKinnon, C. (1989). *Toward a feminist theory of the state.* Cambridge, MA: Harvard.

MacKinnon, C. (1993). *Only words.* Cambridge, MA: Harvard University Press.

Marsden, G. (1990). *Religion and the American culture.* New York: Harcourt.

Martín-Barbero, J. (1993). *Communication, culture and hegemony: From media to mediations.* London: Sage.

Menchu, R. (1994). The Bible and self-defense: The examples of Judith, Moses, and David. In U. King (Ed.), *Feminist theology from the Third World* (pp. 183-189). London: SPCK/Orbis.

Norris, K. (1994). The paradox of the psalms. In C. Buchmann & C. Speigel (Eds.), *Out of the garden: Women writers on the Bible* (pp. 221-233). New York: Fawcett.

Ostriker, A. (1993). *Feminist revision and the Bible.* London: Blackwell.

Ozick, C. (1994). Hannah and Elkanah: Torah and the matrix for feminism. In C. Buchmann & C. Speigel (Eds.), *Out of the garden: Women writers on the Bible* (pp. 88-93). New York: Fawcett.

Paglia, C. (1992). *Sex, art and American culture.* New York: Vintage.

Peck, J. (1993). *The gods of televangelism: The crisis of meaning and the appeal of religious television.* Cresskill, NJ: Hampton.

Riaño, P., (Ed.) (1994). *Women in grassroots communication: Furthering social change.* Thousand Oaks, CA: Sage.

Ribera, R. (1994). Challenging patriarchy. In U. King (Ed.), *Feminist theology from the Third World* (pp. 105-113). London: SPCK/Orbis.

Rosen, N. (1994). Rebekah and Isaac. In C. Buchmann & C. Speigel (Eds.), *Out of the garden: Women writers on the Bible* (pp. 13-26). New York: Fawcett.

Schudson, M. (1986). *Advertising, the uneasy persuasion: Its dubious impact on American society.* New York: Basic Books.

Tamez, E. (1994). Women's rereading of the Bible. In U. King (Ed.), *Feminist theology from the Third World* (pp. 190-203). London: SPCK/Orbis.

Theissen, G. (1991). *The Gospels in context: Social and political history in the synoptic tradition.* Minneapolis, MN: Fortress.

United Nations Commission on Women (1992). *The world's women: Trends and statistics 1970-1990.* New York: United Nations.

Van Maanen, J. (1988). *Tales from the field.* Chicago: University of Chicago Press.

Walters, S. (1995). Material girls: Making sense of feminist cultural theory. Berkeley: University of California Press.

Warner, M. (1994). In and out of the fold: Wisdom, danger, and glamour in the tale of the Queen of Sheba. In C. Buchmann & C. Speigel (Eds.), *Out of the garden: Women writers on the Bible* (pp. 150-165). New York: Fawcett.

Williams, D. (1994). Womanist theology: Women's black voices. In U. King (Ed.), *Feminist theology from the Third World* (pp. 77-87). London: SPCK/Orbis.

Winter, M., Lummis, A., & Stokes, A. (1994). *Defecting in place: Women claiming responsibility for their own spiritual lives.* New York: Crossroad.

Wolff, J. (1995). *Resident alien: Feminist cultural criticism.* New Haven, CT: Yale University Press.

Zaru, J. (1994). The Intifada, nonviolence, and the Bible. In U. King (Ed.), *Feminist theology from the Third World* (pp. 230-235). London: SPCK/Orbis.

Chapter 16

Making Sense of
Religion in Television

Alf Linderman

A "new paradigm" is evolving for studies of religion as well as for studies of the mass media (see Hoover in this volume).[1] The approach of culturalist scholarship with its focus on culture and meaning has become important to both religious and media studies. Thus, perspectives in which religious and media structures have been the primary focus are giving way to an increased interest in the construction of meaning. This increased concentration on meaning constitutes a nexus between media scholarship and religious studies.

First, as social and individual construction of meaning and thereby also the construction of basic value systems become the focus of media scholarship, the object of analysis acquires (functionally) religious dimensions. The study of how audiences understand and use the flow of messages in the mass media becomes, in part, a study of how people establish their general worldviews and ultimate values.

Second, recent developments of religious structures and currents are to a great degree related to the use of mass media for religious purposes.

A vivid example is American televangelism and the related development of religious/political networks and institutions. The religious media flow has an intertextual relationship to religious discourse in "traditional" religious institutions, but it also offers a context of meaning construction that in several ways transcends the scope of local religious communities (Hoover, 1988). The analysis of meaning construction is essential to the analysis of the difference this religious media flow makes in the minds of audiences, and for the structure of religious institutions. Thus, by enhancing our understanding of the process of meaning construction related to mass media texts, we gain a better foundation both for our studies of the (functionally) religious dimension in secular media and for our studies of recent media-related (substantially) religious currents and structures.

The aim for this chapter is to present a conceptual model for social and individual construction of meaning that is applicable to empirical studies of mass media reception. The particular focus is the reception of religious television, but in accordance with the above-indicated nexus between general media scholarship and religious media studies, the conceptual model relates to mass media reception in general.

Meaning is a complex concept to begin with (Wuthnow, 1987). Drawing on the pragmatist tradition, meaning is here used to point to that which constitutes (potential) guidelines for human action. Meaning has both a social and an individual side, and the two sides condition each other. I will return to this later.

The focus on meaning is rooted in a general shift of perspectives on media and their audiences. David Morley (1992) offers an interesting overview of the shift from "powerful media" perspectives to polysemy of texts and the interpretative agency of audiences (see also Jensen, 1991a, and White, 1994). However, this turn toward "semiotic democracy" is not unproblematic. As an example, it is argued that although John Fiske (1987) talks about "a process of negotiation between the text and its variously socially situated readers" (p. 64), he nonetheless overemphazises the polysemy of texts and audience autonomy. Together with many scholars in the field, Klaus Bruhn Jensen (1991b) notes that we need a theoretical framework that "may produce models for relating a social-institutional level of analysis with analyses of the interpretive strategies of individual communicants" (p. 26).

Jensen's own social semiotics of mass communication (1995), together with Keyan Tomaselli and Arnold Shepperson (1991), represent promising efforts in this new direction. They advocate the use of Peircean semiotics as the most promising theoretical source. Although siding with them in their turn to Peirce and to pragmatism in the search for a more nuanced and dynamic understanding of social and individual construction of meaning, and being much influenced by Jensen's presentation of Peircean semiotics, it is my ambition to see the dynamic model for the individual's relation to signs represented in Peircean semiotics as a complement to, and not as entirely incompatible with, Saussurean semiology with its focus on signification systems (cf. the "debate" among Jensen, 1991b; Fiske, 1991; and Newcomb, 1991). I will turn later to George Herbert Mead for a few concepts that prove useful for relating key ideas in semiotics to key ideas in semiology. To put myself outside already (somewhat) fixed categories, I choose the label "social semeiology" for this enterprise.

In my opinion, we need to retain the idea of conventional signification systems as a key factor facilitating human communication. Each act of communication is related to one or more socially established signification systems. These signification systems are the outcome of social interaction in a world ordered by structures and institutions in which power and influence are not distributed democratically. Any text resulting from an act of communication will signal its belonging to a signification system in that its elements will be organized according to rules and conventions within a particular system. This relation to a signification system constitutes constraints on the construction of individual meaning. However, this does not mean that the process of meaning construction is completely determined by this circumstance. Divergent "readings" are possible because each reader has a variety of possibilities for relating the text to different signification systems and for combining elements from different signification systems. We can use Figure 16.1 to illustrate the relationship between individually actualized meaning and social meaning.

According to Figure 16.1, social meaning is a function of individually actualized meaning, which in turn (in part) is a function of social meaning (cf. Giddens', 1984, structuration theory according to which human agency and social structure are enabling conditions for each other). First of all, the individual process of meaning construction is founded on the social meaning with which the individual is acquainted. Through the individual's previous experiences from social interaction in everyday life, he or she has acquired knowledge about how certain signs are used; that

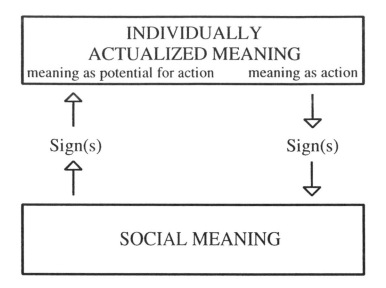

Figure 16.1. Social Meaning and Individually Actualized Meaning as Conditions for Each Other

is, what meaning certain signs are "supposed" to carry in a certain situation. The process by which the individual acquires this knowledge consists of the engagement in common activities with others (cf. George Herbert Mead's, 1934/1962, description of "social projects"). In this interaction, signs are used as individuals act and express themselves in many different ways. When the individual has made a certain meaning out of certain signs, there will be embedded in this meaning an inclination to act in a certain way. Thus, the individually actualized meaning can result in verbal or physical action by this individual that express how this individual processed the meaning in certain signs.

In this phase, when meaning is expressed, there is a potential for this meaning to become something more than just individually actualized meaning. Once expressed in the social arena, it can influence social conventions. It is through this continuous use of signs in social interaction that socially established signification systems can undergo continuous change and development.

In today's Western media culture, the mass media become important sites for the development of social meaning. In combination with other forms of direct social interaction in which the individual is involved, the continuous flow of messages in the media becomes an important point of reference as the individual develops a conception of signification systems and worldviews, and of values embedded in them.

Social meaning is the ever-changing result of ongoing processes of human communication and interaction. As various signs are used, social norms and conventions are formed about the use of these signs. Social norms and conventions are also formed about relationships between these signs and other signs within the system. Such social processes create systems of interrelated signs. However, this human interaction takes place in many different contexts, through various means of communication, involving various individuals and groups in different constellations at different times, and so on. When, and at what social and societal level, is it then justified to talk about signification systems and social meaning?

As a starting point, it seems justifiable to talk about realms of social meaning where there is an interacting and communicating community. That follows from the definition of social meaning as something related to social interaction. However, this initial answer is not sufficient. At what social level can we talk about relatively coherent signification systems and conventional social meaning? We can briefly look at a couple of examples.

In a study of cultural indicators, the general cultural environment of Sweden has been discussed (Block, 1982). In many respects, it seems justifiable to talk about the general cultural environment of one particular country or of one particular language as a system of signs where there exists common use and understanding of particular signifiers—where there exists social meaning. However, there are also signification systems in which such borders do not seem to be adequate. In particular, modern mass media creates new contexts of "interaction" and thus nurtures new contexts for meaning construction. One example is the so-called electronic church. A particular type of religious broadcasting serves as a point of reference for the development of religious identity in a variety of contexts and cultural settings. Although there will be many differences between how these messages are understood and used in different contexts, this flow of messages in itself constitutes a specific context of importance for the development of religious identity in many different cultural settings.

As a contrast to such large, conventional systems of meaning, there seem to be signification systems that are very limited in both time and space. A small, local religious sect could develop a realm of social meaning of its own. Within this community, particular signs could have their meanings very precisely defined; but these social meanings could at the same time be very different from the social meanings attributed to the same signs outside this community.

It is clear that it is not possible to make universal statements about at what level it is justified to talk about sign systems and social meaning. Levels have to be defined according to the character of that which is being discussed.

Although it is possible to talk about social meaning on many different levels, there are general mechanisms that determine how likely social meaning is to change. The larger the number of people who take part in using and maintaining a particular system of signs, the greater the stability of sign systems and the stability of social meaning become. The larger the community, the smaller becomes the relative importance of each instance of individually actualized and expressed meaning. This larger degree of resistance to change in socially established conventions within the larger community is not only related to the relative importance of each instance of individual meaning construction, but also, when formed within large communities, meaning systems become less firmly defined. There is more openness for concurrent variations in meaning within the larger community.

In the small religious group mentioned above, a single individual might relatively easily cause changes on the level of social meaning as the result of innovative use of signs. This, in turn, is not only the result of the relative importance of each instance of individually actualized and expressed meaning, but also the result of the character of the smaller group's own specific meaning system. Due to the size of the group, it is easier to uphold firm and strict conventions for the use of certain signs. In the smaller group, individually actualized meanings that differ from these conventions stand out more clearly as deviant meanings. These deviant meanings can lead to change or development of social meaning established within the group or to the group's "correction" of individually actualized meanings.

Such "correction" of deviant individual meaning could represent two different processes. Through direct social interaction, established social meaning could be reinforced. However, even without such direct social interaction, the significance of the established social meaning could make the individual "remember" the actualized meaning differently over time.

In recollection, the dissonance between the actualized meaning and previously internalized meaning is reduced (cf. Thorleif Pettersson's *The Retention of Religious Experiences*, 1975).

All signification systems are also conditioned by the societal structures within which they are established. Access to resources and technology are key elements in these structures. As mentioned above, the so-called electronic church could be seen as a vehicle for the construction and maintenance of a large-scale phenomenon that in a sense constitutes a religious "community" or network. For communities or networks in which communication via mass media is of great importance, there will be specific processes according to which social meaning can change. Individuals who occupy certain roles within the mass media—roles that are exposed to large audiences and perceived as important—can have a significant influence on the forming of social meaning for large groups of people. Pat Robertson could, for instance, have a stronger influence than their local pastor on many conservative Christians in different places. However, in accordance with the earlier discussion of social meaning, it seems clear that the social meaning maintained within the electronic church will be relatively "open" to concurrent variations on the local level. It derives its saliency from this openness at the same time as it conditions the social process of meaning construction (cf. Jensen's, 1995, notion of "surplus meaning," pp. 192-194).

Not only the size of the community and the social significance of particular institutions and particular roles or individuals play an important role in regulating the potential for change and development of social meaning. Gabriel Bar-Haim (this volume) describes postmodern society as a culture in which traditional local communities, where religious and agricultural rituals support social structures and relations, gradually disintegrate. The "profane" individual becomes sacred, while the "sacred" society becomes profane. Each individual becomes the center of his or her own network: a self-centered creation without sacred collective representations.

Bar-Haim describes a society that has "lost" something, but what it is that has filled this void might be further explored. According to Bar-Haim, individual networks of the postmodern society differ from traditional societies in that these individual networks do not include rituals in which the social "sacredness" is celebrated (Durkheim, 1965). In the place of such rituals, postmodern society offers so-called spectacles: events of civil, ethnic, regional, or cultural celebrations (national memorial days, ethnic events, etc.). There is no strong connection between the individual and the gathering in these postmodern spectacles; therefore, they do not offer any major sense of collective strength and togetherness.

Bar-Haim could be understood to say that postmodern societies are lacking social organisms engaged in common projects necessary to generate common signification systems. In my interpretation, however, what has taken place in a society in which the individual has a variety of social networks to relate to—not least through the use of media—is more a transformation of the character of social conventions than the disintegration of such conventions. In postmodern society, conventions have more functional than substantive properties. For example, terms like *happiness, fulfillment, religion, God*, and *value* have become defined more in relation to their function for the individual, than substantively with reference to a collective dimension as they were in Bar-Haim's "good old days." The sacredness of the social has indeed been replaced by the sacredness of the individual, but social signification systems are still formed in the process of social interaction and as a result of common uses of the media. However, the imprints on individual consciousness have different properties than those of "traditional" societies.

In a pluralistic society, each individual takes part in the reproduction of several different signification systems. Several different signification systems are available at each instance of individual construction of meaning. Through processes of socialization, the individual internalizes social conventions relating to many different spheres of life, modes of communication, and social structures. Through such processes, the individual internalizes a repertoire of signification systems (to which I will return later). Thus, it becomes particularly interesting to investigate how meaning is actualized on the individual level.

We now turn to Figure 16.2 illustrating the different components involved in the process of individual construction of meaning. It is the interaction among these components that constitutes the process of individual meaning construction, a process that includes elements of determination as well as interpretative agency.

The specific purpose of this model is to supply a framework for empirical reception analysis of religious television. Religious television is a particularly interesting type of broadcasting because some audience categories will be very familiar with religious discourse, whereas others will not. Religious broadcasters seem to assume that the word (of God) through the mass media can reach beyond the religious community and change people's lives everywhere. But if the perceived meaning of these programs is viewed as a function of certain situational and individual factors, we might perhaps expect people to change the message more than the message changes people! Furthermore, religious television is interesting because it serves as an example of how a traditional subculture is affected by the introduction of a mass medium. How religious television is perceived sheds light on the role ascribed to television in general.

Figure 16.2 illustrates how meaning is individually actualized as the result of the input given by various components. Arrows indicate how the components generate individually actualized meaning (causal relations), but these arrows do not, of course, cover all relations among the components. This model could be described as a formal theoretical model for causal relations—thus implying that I do not see a contradiction between a dynamic, processual, analytical perspective and formal logic (cf. Jensen, 1995, p. 144). However, the relative strength of these relations is an empirical issue and not something postulated by the model. As each component is briefly explained, the relationship between it and other parts of the model will be indicated, as well as how each component could be dealt with in empirical reception analyses.

The starting point in this model for individual construction of meaning is a particular discourse in which the individual is exposed to various signs. *Discourse* could be defined on many different meta-analytical levels (see Jensen, 1995, p. 63). In this model, discourse relates to the social use of signs in television, and specific genres are conventional guidelines for this use. In more general terms, discourse is the ongoing process of human interaction and communication within a certain community. Thus, discourse is another label for the ongoing process of communication that serves as the vehicle by which social meaning systems are created and maintained. This, in turn, means that discourse can be defined on many different social levels (cf. the discussion of social meaning above). It also means that a *discourse* can be defined as "an ongoing process of interaction and communication concurrently taking place in several different contexts, using several different modes of communication." For example, the discourse of religious television has an intertextual relationship to discourses in traditional religious institutions. To illustrate this openness

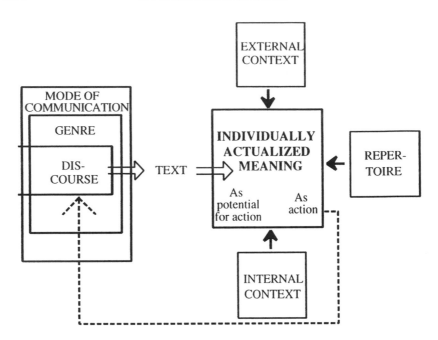

Figure 16.2. An Illustrative (Causal) Model for the Different Components Involved in the Situation in Which Meaning is Individually Actualized

toward more than one genre and mode of communication, the left side of the "discourse square" in Figure 16.2 is left open.

When we have defined *discourse* in Figure 16.2 as "social use of signs related to a certain genre of television," this naturally has significance for the external context and the individual repertoire of internalized signification systems. Television is commonly watched at certain times and in certain places, and genre is used to guide the selection of interpretative strategies.

The *external context* includes all aspects of the location in time and space of the individual act of meaning construction. Because *discourse* here is defined as television discourse, we have a number of natural limits to the range of external contexts in which construction of meaning could take place. For television reception, the external context includes where television is watched, what other people are present, whether there is any other specific "object" present that is perceived by the individual as relevant to the television discourse, and so forth. Moreover, to the external context can be added the larger context of society with its distribution of power and resources, and how this conditions the social use of signs.

Both the discourse in question and the external situation in which the construction of meaning takes place have significance for which parts of the individual's internalized *repertoire* of signification systems appear relevant to the individual. A specific media *text* will signal its intertextual relation to a certain conventional signification system through its composition. Such signals could either lead to a so-called preferred reading—a reading in which the text is decoded according to the signification system within which it was created—or it could result in an oppositional reading—a reading in which signals in the text trigger opposition and alternative processes of meaning construction. Within the present theoretical model, however, there is no given limit to the range of possible meanings in terms of how the individual relates the text to signification systems included in the individual's repertoire.

Although the individual can derive many different readings or meanings from a certain media text, this does not mean that individual construction of meaning is autonomous. Individual construction of meaning is always related to signification systems created within the community of sign users. Thus, Figure 16.2 refers to "individually *actualized* meaning." The point is that the individual is not bound to the use of the most "immediate" signification system (given the text, the external context, and the individual's previous socialization). There is a wide range of possible results of the individual process of meaning construction, but not all with the same probability. The meaning actualized when the individual uses the most immediately relevant social signification system could be called the "expected meaning." The model does not, however, quantitatively define the relative degree to which this particular meaning is expected. It is defined as "expected" due to its relationship to social conventions, but its frequency of appearance in real life remains an empirical issue. Thus, using the present theoretical model, it is possible to make some predictions concerning the outcome of media reception and simultaneously to recognize the individual element.

This brings us to the last component in the figure, designated the *internal context*. This is the psychological dimension. It includes emotions, motivations, and the individual's capacity to react. Needless to say, these

psychological aspects also relate to previous experiences that have generated the individual's repertoire of internalized signification systems.
The creation of this psychological component is thus related to, or a result
of, previous experiences of social interaction and life in general. Simultaneously, this aspect or dimension represents one particular function in
Figure 16.2. As this psychological dimension enters the model, the process
of meaning construction becomes open to individual creativity and dynamics. The internal context could be described as the responding and
active side of the individual (cf. George Herbert Mead's, 1934/1962,
elaboration on the role of "I" in the human self). This responding side ("I")
responds to that which is given in terms of the individual's social knowledge and competence—the latter being an essential part of Mead's "me"
(see Geyer, 1989). The interaction between this responding side, "I," and
the social knowledge and social competence of the self, "me," could be
described as follows:

> The responding part of the self ("I") responds to that which is given as
> the result of the immediate connection of the media text to certain codes
> for decoding, codes derived from the signification system(s) ("me")
> immediately (by "I") found relevant to the text in the specific external
> situation in which the construction of meaning takes place.

This process results in actualized meaning. Such meaning can, just as
it has been formed, be the "object" for the responding side of the self, and
can thereby be subjected to renewed reflection and subsequent response.
Thus, when signs are actually used, we arrive at a potentially infinite
chain of semiosis—as is the case in the continuous processual development taking place in the social sphere as meaning is acted out in social
context. There is no given limit to the ongoing process of meaning
construction. In this sense, this conceptual model for the construction of
meaning is very similar to the Peircean notion of infinite semiosis as it is
presented by Jensen (1991b, 1995). However, to me it seems like an
advantage not to have to struggle with Peirce's so-called "final interpretant" to get to the social level (Jensen, 1995, p. 24).

The relationship described above between the components interacting in the process of meaning construction could be illustrated with
another figure (Figure 16.3) that focus on the structure of interaction.

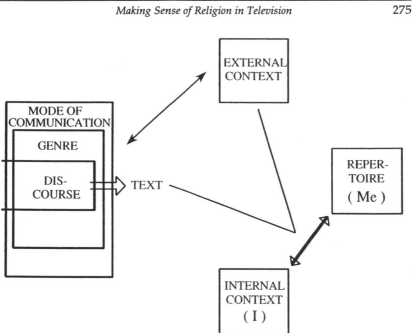

Figure 16.3. A Schematic Model for How Different Components Interact in the Situation in Which Meaning Is Individually Actualized

Our way of learning how the individual processes and perceives these signs is through the individual's verbal and physical action. The individual acts, and these actions become signs that can be the objects for new processes of meaning construction. When construction of meaning takes place within the individual—that is, without any explicit expression of this meaning (meaning as potential for action vis-à-vis meaning *as* action in Figure 16.2)—this meaning can be reflected on by the individual in its form as potential for action, but it is not accessible to anyone else. When the researcher asks questions concerning how a specific sign or text was perceived by the individual, the researcher initiates a process of externalization and reflection that would not have taken place if these questions were not asked (although similar processes might have been naturally initiated through the individual's normal everyday interaction). Such initiation of responses can lead to further development of the individual's meaning through the continuous process described above. As this process goes on, these expressed meanings, whether verbal or through other forms of action, make up a "text" in its own right. Through the structural analysis of such texts, we can establish an image of this process of meaning construction (cf. Wuthnow, 1987, p. 64). This image can then be described on the level of analytical discourse (Jensen, 1995, pp. 62-63).

Empirical reception analysis is thus the study of a process, a study that is simultaneously part of the process. The result of such an empirical reception analysis is not a description of how individuals perceived something per se, but rather, a description of how meaning is formed as meaning is expressed. This description by the researcher of how meaning is formed as meaning is expressed (i.e., the descriptive text by which the researcher expresses and communicates this description) is itself generated as a process of meaning construction, expression, and reflection on behalf of the researcher. However, this brings empirical reception analysis even closer to "reality," and to how signs are used in social interaction. Moreover, presuppositions concerning the generality of how various components interact in the human process of meaning construction can make it possible to draw certain conclusions based on empirical reception analyses that seem relevant beyond the specific situation in which the analysis took place.

We can now turn to the specific procedures of empirical reception studies. One initial step could be to define and analyze the (flow of) text(s) to be used as the point of reference for the individual process of meaning construction. Analysis of text(s), discourse, genre, and so forth, generates a first preconception of how this text (these texts) could be perceived by different individuals. For example, when studying religious (evangelical) television programs, we already know a great deal about those who usually watch these programs. We also know a great deal about how these programs generally are perceived by these viewers and what role these programs play in their lives. Hence, we can expect evangelical viewers to perceive an evangelical television program according to patterns found in previous research. Accordingly, we can expect different categories of nonevangelical viewers to perceive the evangelical program according to other patterns. Such knowledge could be used as guidelines for the empirical reception analysis: selection of respondents, important questions for questionnaires and interviews, and so on. However, the question of to what extent and in what direction the individual component involved in the process of meaning construction influences the actualized meaning remains to be answered by empirical data.

The external context, the physical location in time and space, could be used as a variable with more or less variation for different respondents. For most research on television reception, the data collection takes place in the homes of the viewers. This is a natural consequence of the circumstance that most television viewing takes place in the home—often accompanied by various other everyday activities. For reception studies that take this approach, it becomes important to describe specific features of different viewing contexts: the room where the television set is placed, who watches what with whom, what everyday activities go on concurrently, what human interaction takes place (e.g., Jensen, 1994). The significance of the external context can be explicitly addressed in the empirical reception analysis. If specific variations in external context constitute part of the methodological strategy—as, for example, if otherwise similar respondents watch a particular program in different settings—the study of actualized meanings could offer information about the significance of the external context as a factor influencing individual construction of meaning.

The individual's repertoire of internalized signification systems can, in the empirical reception analysis, be operationalized in a similar way to traditional background variables in sociological research. This also makes explicit in the reception study certain concerns of sociological research with structure and the distribution of power in society. Because the individual lives, and has lived, under certain conditions in certain social contexts, he or she acquires familiarity with certain social conventions. Through the process of socialization, the individual internalizes certain codes and conventional rules for decoding; and this acquired competence makes it possible for the individual to take part in social interaction in similar social contexts and under similar conditions. It is through previous experiences in social interaction that individuals develop the Meadean "me." If interpreted according to the present theoretical framework, traditional sociological background variables—for example gender, age, education, income level, various elements in childhood and adolescence, religious and political preferences and involvement—give a great deal of information about the individual's process of socialization. Because in the individual process of meaning construction this acquired repertoire of internalized signification systems is used as the point of departure, such traditional sociological background variables offer insights into how and why different individuals respond with different actualized meanings.

Although these background variables—that is, what such variables stand for in terms of the internalized repertoire of signification systems—can generate valid hypotheses about correlations between differences in backgrounds and differences in individually actualized meaning, such variables cannot conclusively predict how one particular individual at a given moment will use his or her repertoire of internalized signification systems. More subtle conclusions concerning how the individual used his or her acquired repertoire can be drawn as the individual reports on the references used in the process of meaning construction. Quantitative studies, in which relevant background variables are correlated with different "readings" of a media text, can therefore give only a crude image of the significance of certain background factors for the processing of this particular text. Qualitative approaches can explore further how and why different individuals have used their repertoire in different ways. The quantitative approach has advantages in that it gives information about the quantitative distribution of different "readings," information that can be generalized with a certain level of probability. The qualitative approach has its advantages in that it can include and make sense of readings beyond general patterns of meaning construction.

The last component in Figure 16.2, the internal context, is more difficult to operationalize in the present context, that of a sociological framework for empirical reception analysis. The way that the individual's emotions, motivations, and capacity to react in the situation in which the construction of meaning takes place can be measured (other than as that which makes individual deviations intelligible), falls outside the scope of this chapter. Nevertheless, the "internal context" is a vital part of Figure 16.2. This represents the responding and reflective side of the individual. If it were not for this "internal" dimension, the construction of meaning could be reduced to a formula consisting of the text, the external situation, and the individual's background and acquired signification competence. If it were not for the individual's responsive side, the individual's "I," individually actualized meaning would be equivalent to, or a mere reflection of, social meaning and nothing more. With the inclusion of the reactive and reflective "I," we include the so-called conversation (and struggle) between the socially given side and the active side of the self.

In the empirical reception analysis, we thus can measure the significance of the internal context in terms of different readings expressed by in-other-respects-similar individuals. We can also monitor the individual's reflections on that which the individual expresses, as we, in the interview situation, can follow how the individual converses with himself or herself and continually develops the meaning that is expressed.

One relevant issue related to the process of interaction between the individual repertoire and the internal context remains to be examined: Under what conditions will the individual *not* respond with readings of a media text that are a reflection of social, conventional meaning? Under what conditions will the conversation between "I" and "me" lead to responses and expressed meanings that are the result of creative and innovative strategies for meaning construction? The first and most obvious answer is that this will take place when there is something about the meaning that at least seems to be the most immediate meaning according to other respondents with similar backgrounds that does not satisfy the individual (see Geyer, 1989). This dissatisfaction need not be conscious; that is, it need not be the result of a completed process of interaction between "I" and "me." This dissatisfaction is an essential part of the *process* of interaction between "I" and "me." It is essential to the process leading to unexpected actualized meaning. Thus, if the immediate conventional meaning "proposed" by "me" in some respect appears to be problematic, the responding side ("I") seeks new interpretations. Even if, in principle, it is possible to discuss how various intrapsychological aspects could determine under what conditions the responding side of the individual will perceive conventional meaning as problematic, such discussions fall outside the scope of this chapter. Here, we will not go beyond the recognition of the process of individual construction of meaning as the meeting point for social conventions and subjective responses.

The framework just described has been applied to two reception analyses of religious television (Linderman, 1987, 1996). First, a Swedish program with religious music from a Swedish Pentecostal church was studied. This study primarily aimed to explore the significance of viewers' previous familiarity with religious messages (i.e., previous experiences leading to the internalization of religious signification systems). It was found that viewers with a history of engagement in religious life perceived the program as dealing with messages about salvation, eternal life, and so forth. Thus, these viewers found the program primarily aimed toward nonreligious viewers. On the other hand, nonreligious viewers without previous experiences from religious life perceived the program as dealing with a specific "hobby" of interest primarily to those who normally go to church—to those who think that religious music and church services are "fun" leisure activities. Thus, nonreligious viewers thought that the program was primarily aimed toward religious people. In short, both audience categories found the program as primarily aimed toward someone else. It seems like a fair guess that this outcome of the viewers' construction of meaning was unexpected by those engaged in the production of the program.

In the second study, attention was directed toward individually actualized meaning that falls outside the patterns of interpretation that could be expected. A conservative religious television program about the situation in South Africa and how religious revivals are sweeping the country was shown to students in both America and Sweden.[2] A few students came up with meanings that differed from general patterns of meaning construction. Although most American evangelical students found the program credible and informative, some dismissed the content as false and deceitful. These students applied to this religious program a general critical attitude toward commercial television. On the other hand, although most nonevangelical students did not find the program credible or trustworthy, some nonevangelical students reported that they found the program, at least in part, credible. One possible explanation for these "positive" perceptions among a few nonevangelical students is that they ascribe certain significance to television programs that to some degree relate to the format of documentaries.

In conclusion, it seems that the focus on how the audience constructs meaning out of religious television not only shows how this type of television works in the minds of different audience categories as they "make sense" of these programs, but also reveals how general qualities are ascribed to this medium by various viewers. Accordingly, such studies could be used for a discussion of what media-religion does in relation to traditional religious discourse and religious practices, but such studies could also be used for a general discussion of the role of television. Thus, the meaning-focused study of how people make sense of religion in television is a study located right at the nexus between religious studies and media scholarship.

Notes

1. This chapter is developed from my doctoral dissertation, *The Reception of Religious Television: Social Semeiology Applied to an Empirical Case Study* (1996). This development has been made possible by a research grant from the *Swedish Council for Research in the Humanities and Social Sciences* (ref. no.: F636/95).

2. For a content analysis, see Gustafsson (1994). For a reception study in South Africa, see Arntsen and Gustafsson (1996).

References

Arntsen, H., & Gustafsson, O. (1996, January). *Weathering the shifting currents: Positioning of self vis-à-vis the religio-politico rhetoric of the new religious political right: A case study from Durban, South Africa.* Paper presented at the Media, Religion, and Culture Conference, University of Colorado, Boulder.

Block, E. (1982). *Frihet, jämlikhet och andra värden.* Svensk inrikespolitisk debatt på dagstidningarnas ledarsidor 1945-1975. Lund: Studentlitteratur.

Durkheim, E. (1965). *The elementary forms of the religious life.* New York: Free Press.

Fiske, J. (1987). *Television culture.* London: Methuen.

Fiske, J. (1991). *Semiological struggles.* In J. Anderson (Ed.), *Communication yearbook* (Vol. 14, pp. 33-39). Newbury Park, CA: Sage.

Geyer, K. (1989). *Att dana människor.* Unpublished doctoral dissertation, Department of Theology, Uppsala University, Sweden.

Giddens, A. (1984). *The constitution of society.* Berkeley: University of California Press.

Gustafsson, O. (1994). A progress report on the analysis of the video: The Other South Africa. In A. Linderman (Ed.), *Conference papers: Media, religion and culture, May 24-26, 1993.* Department of Theology, Uppsala University, Sweden.

Hoover, S. M. (1988). *Mass media religion: The social sources of the electronic church.* London: Sage.

Jensen, K. B. (1991a). Reception analysis: Mass communication as the social production of meaning. In K. B. Jensen & N. W. Jankowski (Eds.), *A handbook of qualitative methodologies for mass communication research* (pp. 135-148). New York: Routledge.

Jensen, K. B. (1991b). When is meaning? Communication theory, pragmatism and mass media reception. In J. Anderson (Ed.), *Communication yearbook* (Vol. 14, pp. 3-32). Newbury Park, CA: Sage.

Jensen, K. B. (1994, July). *News of the world: Preliminary findings and theoretical implications.* Paper presented at the 19th Conference of the International Association for Mass Communication Research, Seoul, Korea.

Jensen, K. B. (1995). *The social semiotics of mass communication.* London: Sage.

Linderman, A. (1987, December). *Vadå kommunikation.* Paper presented to the Seminar for the Sociology of Religion, Department of Theology, Uppsala University, Sweden.

Linderman, A. (Ed.). (1994). *Conference papers: Media, religion and culture, May 24-26, 1993.* Department of Theology, Uppsala University.

Linderman, A. (1996). The reception of religious television: Social semeiology applied to an empirical case study. *Acta Universitatis Upsaliensis, Psychologia et Sociologia Religionum* 12. Stockholm: Almquist & Wiksell International.

Mead, G. H. (1962). *Mind, self, & society from the standpoint of a social behaviorist* (W. Morris, Ed.). Chicago: University of Chicago Press. (Originally published 1934)

Morley, D. (1992). *Television, audiences & cultural studies*. New York: Routledge & Kegan Paul.

Newcomb, H. M. (1991). The search for media meaning. In J. Anderson (Ed.), *Communication yearbook* (vol. 14, pp. 40-47). Newbury Park, CA: Sage.

Pettersson, T. (1975). *The retention of religious experiences*. Stockholm: Almqvist & Wiksell International.

Tomaselli, K. G., & Shepperson, A. (1991). Popularising semiotics. *Communication Research Trends, 11*(2), 2-20.

White, R. A. (1994). Audience "interpretation" of media: Emerging perspectives. *Communication Research Trends, 14*(3), 3-32.

Wuthnow, R. (1987). *Meaning and moral order: Explorations in cultural analysis*. Berkeley: University of California Press.

Media and the Construction
of the Religious Public Sphere

Stewart M. Hoover

The religious sphere has always been problematic for students of the media. This is evidenced by the relative paucity of works devoted to studies of relations between religion and the media. Aside from a few prominent studies of the phenomenon of televangelism (Hoover, 1988; Horsfield, 1984; Peck, 1993; Schultze, 1988), religion has been a "blind spot" of media studies (Hoover, 1995; Hoover & Venturelli, 1996).

There are both obvious and somewhat obscure reasons for this situation. For most of its history, media research has been dominated by positivist-empiricist modes and methods that have embedded in them a deeply held commitment to ideas of rationalism and secularism. To put it simply, the paradigms of early media studies were in important ways inoculated against nonrationalist phenomena and nonempiricist modes of explanation. It has been convenient to leave religion out of theoretical and empirical works, thereby avoiding some troublesome issues. Most prominent among these issues is the fact that religion is difficult for media scholars for the same reasons it has always been difficult for journalists:

On some levels it always defies the practices of verification so important to rational modes of inquiry in both guilds.

This situation has now begun to break open for two interrelated reasons. First, the easy and facile confinement of religion to the private sphere that has held sway in public discourse (and by extension in scholarly discourse) has been eroded by recent history. The rise of religious politics in the industrial North and the resurgence of ethnic and religious conflict elsewhere have put religion higher on the public agenda.

Second, and perhaps more important, scholarship has begun to evolve in ways that have moved questions of religion to the fore. In the field of media studies, this has resulted from the incursion of culturalist scholarship into the realm of meaning and ontology (Hoover, 1995). What has been called the "unpopular popular culture"—religion—is necessarily implied by studies that look at the ontologies and rituals of everyday life. That few such studies have so far directly addressed religion is probably a temporary condition.

In the fields of religious studies generally, the momentum toward understanding the media-and-religion connection is even more pronounced. What Warner (1993) calls "new paradigm" approaches to religious studies are increasingly problematizing the *private* sphere of life, the embedment of contemporary consciousness in commodity culture, and modes and practices of experience that privilege individual action over institutional prerogatives (Albanese, 1993; Marty, 1993; Roof, 1993b).

Religion scholars have, in a small way, begun to raise questions about the possible contribution of the media sphere to emerging contemporary religious consciousness.

> In the culture at large, questions of faith and spirit seem to have gone public: television programs, novels, magazine stories, and newspaper articles now give serious attention to the spiritual and religious questions of a generation that grew up suspicious of the faith and morality handed down to them by their elders. (Roof, 1993b, p. 166)

But these are still questions at this stage. Despite such ruminations, very little sustained attention has been given to the media. Commitment to such "new paradigm" or "reconstructionist" approaches (as Roof, 1993b, calls them) is far from universal. The whole notion that religious practice has moved increasingly to the individual level and away from the civic or public level where institutional structures and entities hold sway, is controversial. Among the most prominent critics of such an evolution are Bellah and his associates (1985), who have held the view that individualism and volunteerism in matters of faith are to be lamented rather than accorded legitimacy (Roof, 1993b, p. 169).

▒ Evolving Paradigms

Moving from a historical situation in which the relations between religion and the media have been problematic and have been treated within a dualistic framework (for a more complete discussion, see Clark & Hoover, this volume), the challenge of crafting a new scholarship of media and religion is a large and complex one. However, the momentum carries us forward.

We are clearly at a postmodern moment in these developments, in which new modes of cultural understanding and discourse are evolving. Among the most significant claims made for the postmodern are the ones that focus on its practices of symbolic construction and consumption. It is a moment that both celebrates the end of totalizing and determinate worldviews and recognizes the power of the individual to construct sets of cultural symbols into unique and personally salient patterns (Jameson, 1984). This process is fundamentally a process of appropriation, and as it is expressed in contemporary religious practice, it moves along two dimensions. First, it moves across *time*, symbolically binding perceived and factual histories to the purpose of the moment, as described in the case of contemporary fundamentalism by Marty and Appleby (1992). Second, it moves across *space*, bringing elements from other ethnicities, contexts, and traditions into a worldview made coherent in the experience of the individual. Work on the so-called new age religions of the industrialized West (cf. Albanese, 1993) illustrates this latter dimension.

Recognizing these temperaments obviously moves us away from reified notions of the nature of religious experience. Rather than its institutional attributes, this new paradigm in religion study looks at religion's embedment in personal and individual experience. Strangely reminiscent of similar valences in media scholarship, religion scholars now find themselves looking to the "audience" (religious practice) rather than at the "purveyors of texts" (religious institutions).

The "new paradigm" is partly rooted in the so-called supply-side or choice model developed by Iannaccone (1991; Finke & Iannaccone, 1993) and others. Adapted from the field of economic theory, this approach stresses the position of the individual and individual choice over the prerogatives of religious histories and religious institutions. The new paradigm also finds roots in new or alternative modes of religion measurement, such as narrative, interpretivist, and culturalist approaches (Ammerman, 1987, 1990; Roof, 1992; Stacey & Gerard, 1990; Wuthnow, 1992). Roof (1993b) describes the significance of this turn with respect to institutions:

> The term I use, "reconstruction," suggests that I prefer to move beyond the customary arguments on the decline of religion among sociologists, in favor of what I take to be a more nuanced interpretation of religion in America. My approach . . . privileges themes of volunteerism and innovation, the continuing vitality of American religious culture, and supply side, rather than exclusively demand-side explanations of change. (p. 157)

Many traditional ways of looking at religion are obviously challenged by such an approach. None more so, perhaps, than the notion of "belonging." That is, religions traditionally enforce a range of levels of conformity and loyalty on adherents, and our consensus understanding of religion typically entails such a dimension. What happens to the idea of belonging in a view of religion that privileges individual action over collective participation?

As Roof (1993b) and others are coming to recognize, institutional loyalty is not a necessary attribute of social and cultural participation. All cultural practices, including cultural rituals, are social constructions anyway. What this new perspective on religion allows for is the construction of religious culture out of a universe of symbols—an inventory if you will—that may or may not include the symbolic claims of the historic religions, and that nonetheless result in legitimate, substantive constructions. Warner (1993) responds to the widely held contrasting view as articulated in Bellah et al.'s germinal work of the mid-1980s:

> The authors of *Habits of the Heart* (Bellah et al., 1985) have most eloquently lamented these individualistic trends. Although they recognize

that Americans, no matter how individualistic, seek out like-minded others, they fear that the resulting associations are only "lifestyle enclaves," a term they intend to connote shallowness and mutual narcissism.... [They note that] "there is a givenness about the community and the tradition. They are not normally a matter of individual choice."

I do not wish to dismiss the concerns of Bellah and his colleagues, but there is considerable evidence that religious switchers are morally serious. (p. 1076)

So we are left with an evolving view of the nature of contemporary religious practice that should be challenging to our understandings of the relations between religion and the media. It is a view that implicitly challenges much of the research that has gone before in both religious studies and media studies. It challenges as inadequate an approach to religious media that focuses only on the intended meanings or "preferred readings" of religious producers. It challenges as well the notion that "religious media" is a category wholly coterminous with those texts constructed by religious groups or with religious intentions.

▓ Toward a Religious Anthropology of the Audience

What is needed is a religious anthropology of the audience to stand alongside the more rationalist anthropologies developed by postpositivist and culturalist empiricism (cf. Fiske, 1987; Hobson, 1980, 1982, 1990; Liebes & Katz, 1993; Lull, 1980, 1988; Morley, 1986, 1989, 1992). The outlines of such an anthropology are already visible in extant scholarship.

It might begin by centering on the notion of the audience as cultural and social practice. As Ettema and Whitney (1994) point out, "audiencing" (Silverstone, 1993) can be seen to be both symbolic and culturally constructive. We know who we are by our practices of textual consumption, and media texts now serve as important maps through which we see ourselves on local and global landscapes. We cannot ignore the extent to which audiences also *are constructed* (Ettema & Whitney, 1994; Seifert, 1994), and the not yet fully resolved questions of the power relations there (White, 1994, p. 5). Nonetheless, we can proceed from the assumption that, at the site of audience practice, culturally constructive activity takes place.

Thus, we have an active, sentient audience—one that, to an extent, can be said to act in ways that involve choice, appropriation, and re-integration of content (Hall, 1982), recognizing at the same time that the range of choices is not unlimited. Thus, texts are not overly determinative, and a negotiation of cultural power takes place at the site of consumption. This problematizes two elements of most received models of public communication: the role of institutions and their prerogatives, and the role of texts and their determinations.

Reflecting back on what has gone before in the way of scholarship on religion and media, we can immediately see a preoccupation with, and boundedness by, these very institutional and textual assumptions. The whole modus operandi for the typical study of televangelism has been the question of relations between these ministries and existing social and religious institutions (Hadden & Swann, 1981; Horsfield, 1984). Furthermore, the status of televangelists' texts and genres have by and large been seen with reference to the historic claims of churches and religious bodies (Fore, 1990; Schultze, 1988).

Most other work on religion and the media (cf. Soukup, 1989) has been more pragmatically and institutionally based, and almost by definition has focused its energies on institutions and their intended meanings of texts and genres. The audience, and audience practice, have hardly appeared.

To its credit, postpositivist media theory has stressed the audience, but it has been unsatisfying in its understandings of questions of meaning. Where the culturalist turn in media studies should have brought attention to the whole of meaning and meaning construction in media-cultural processes, it has instead cordoned off those sectors of human experience beyond the "rational" and "realistic," leaving us only partially enlightened as to the nature and scope of audience interaction with the media sphere (Hoover, 1995).

▒ Implications of the "New Paradigm" in Religious Studies

Warner's (1993) notion of the "new paradigm" in religion scholarship has opened up a wide-ranging debate over normative social theory and its understandings of processes of social and cultural change, religious evolution, and the status of the notion of secularization. We need not join these debates directly in order to draw important implications for our project here.

Warner's work provides an important clue to the problematic nature of the media sphere as a point of entry for religion scholarship. It might be assumed that sociology of religion shares with the field of sociology generally what Carey (1989) calls a "transportation" and Hoover (1995) calls an "instrumentalist" view of the media. That is, the implicit functionalism of the approach to media by much of sociology has assigned them a set of roles and responsibilities that serves a largely positivist view of social and cultural relations (Wright, 1986). This overdetermination of the media sphere has in fact turned up in the very few occasions on which it has been granted any purchase at all in recent religion scholarship (cf. Bellah et al., 1985, p. 294; Roof, 1993a, pp. 53-54).

However, Warner (1993) hints at a deeper problem for religion scholarship posed by the media sphere: its invocation of the boundary between public and private. Warner notes that "conventional social science wisdom" on the nature of religion has conceived of religion as "a property of the whole society" and that

> the institutionalized separation of state and church in modern society has offered religion only two alternatives: either religious values would become increasingly generalized so that they could remain the property of the whole, increasingly pluralistic, society, or, if they remained resolutely particularistic, they would devolve to an inconsequential private sphere. (pp. 1046-1047)

This "conventional wisdom" also severely truncates any potential significance of the media sphere to religion. If the media are seen in largely instrumentalist terms, and as institutions of the "whole culture," then their role in religion on the public level must necessarily be overdetermined. What is the point of subjecting media to cultural analysis when their only role is the more-or-less transparent representation of large, consensual symbols of a totalizing civil religion?

On the other hand, what is the interest in looking at the contribution of media symbols to private religious experience when the private sphere is—as Warner puts it—"inconsequential" anyway? The whole social science project vis-à-vis religion and the media, then, understandably becomes a rather mundane cataloging of the genres and tropes of "religious media" and their assumed and inferred costs and benefits to institutionalized religion.

What Warner sees as evolving theory in the field of religion sociology is a theme of "religious mobilization" in place of themes of secularization-enforced banishment to a truncated private sphere. In fact, the opening of the private sphere is the hallmark of most recent religion scholarship, Warner suggests, and should prove indicative as research moves ahead (p. 1048).

For our purposes here, it is enough to note that religion scholarship has thus begun to focus in a new way on the same levels of practice toward which media scholarship is now headed. What are the outlines of that new religious landscape?

▨ A Note on the Relevance of the American Case

It must be recognized that the argument presented here, particularly that rooted in developments in the field of religious studies, is rather consciously focused on the North American experience and the North American case. Although no broader relevance should be claimed without careful groundwork, several justifications for this representation come to mind. First, there is the fact of the media sphere and its global presence. Simply put, the media age has come to diminish the cultural significance of national and regional boundaries to an increasing extent (Beyer, 1994).

The experience of televangelism is a case in point. Although it was at first largely an American phenomenon, it soon became a global phenomenon on two levels. First, televangelists themselves took a global perspective, moving to distribute their programs well beyond the United States and the industrialized North (Shegog, 1991). Second, global media ensured that the phenomenon of televangelism was well known, even to nonadherents and the nonreligious, worldwide, particularly as scandals overtook the movement in the late 1980s (Horsfield, 1990).

This second valence of televangelism also predicts a second reason for the general significance of the American experience. That is, at this point in history, American culture becomes news across the world. For a variety of reasons, this is obviously not a situation to be celebrated; but it is nonetheless a fact. And we can assume that as the trends and practices in American religion gather force and momentum, they will become increasingly known elsewhere.

Third, the American experience is noteworthy because it is, to an extent, embedded in the larger experience of the industrial North. Although no other Northern countries share the level of religiosity, either private or public, of North America, trends do tend to pervade North America and Europe. There is evidence of a small but growing evangelical movement in Western Europe, for example. The "new age travelers" of the United Kingdom share much in common with some "new agers" (such as the Rainbow Family) in the United States and Canada. And most important, the global enterprises of commodity culture make available in most of the industrialized North the range of products and services that are coming to play a significant role in the religious "marketplace."

▓ The Significance of the Evolving Nature of Religious Experience to Understandings of Media Practice

Marty (1993) presents a catalog of the ways that what he calls "religious energies" are now expressed. The range of practices and expressions he describes serves as a valuable challenge to our project here. How we culturally account for such a set of phenomena becomes a critical challenge to a new, more systematic account of religious practice. We will review the most significant of these paths and then move to an appraisal of their implications for a religious anthropology of the audience.

First, Marty underscores the point that *personal* religious preoccupations are now more important than *communal* ones. Echoing Roof's and Warner's ideas about the extent to which the historically grounded and collective valences of religion now give way to individual and private processes of religious legitimacy, he suggests that the momentum in contemporary religion is now very much away from the collective. And echoing Albanese (1993), he stresses the extent to which these personal preoccupations must be accorded a degree of deference. There is authenticity here, a fundamental and substantive postmodern religious sensibility.

Also in keeping with recent work, Marty suggests that the *private sphere* is increasingly preeminent over the *public sphere* when we are talking about the energy of contemporary religious practice. Public religion, at least as it is expressed in rigid structures and institutions, is today less important than what goes on in private life. In a curious reversal of the "conventional" situation described earlier by Warner, we seem to be experiencing a "publication of the private." That is, privately legitimated religious practices and expressions still find their way into public. Movements and organizations still exist, but they are increasingly volunteeristic (Wuthnow, 1988) and rooted in a "marketplace" of religious choice.

This situation is supported, says Marty, by the rise of *individual autonomy* over *inherited authority*. Individuals now exercise more control over their religious lives, and the postmodern process whereby they appropriate and construct their own "structures of feeling" leaves the old authorities in a curious place:

> Assertion of authority has not disappeared, however, so much as it has found new outlets and modes. To use one grand sweep of a phrase, it has moved from the coercive to the persuasive realm. (Marty, 1993, p. 16)

This means that the former loci of religious authority, particular religious hierarchies and denominations (but also local bodies), are now embedded in a marketplace of religious choice. Their claims on adherents are no longer absolute.

Personal meaning becomes an essential element as well, says Marty. Other formerly regnant religious motivations, including the act of *belonging*, no longer exercise the pull they once did. As others have suggested, *meaning* has come to be a standard of nearly ultimate value in the calculus of personal experience. This is obviously a point of clear convergence between religion scholarship and media scholarship. As the focus on meaning has become determinative of culturalist media studies, it has suggested that the search for meaning must now be understood as an important point of salience for media audiences (Fiske, 1987). There is, as Linderman (1996) points out, more than one kind of "meaning," however. Much more can and will obviously be said in deconstructing this nexus, but a point of convergence exists.

The *local* and the *particular* are further favored over the *cosmopolitan* and the *ecumenical,* says Marty. In an era when individual and private legitimation are the order of the day, the need for larger, totalizing interpretations fades, again in a clearly postmodern turn.

Contemporary religion, says Marty, is more *practical* than it is *mystical.* Contemporary life excels in *praxis,* and effects and products become the important exchanges of personal life. Movements such as 12-step and self-help programs "resist" tendencies toward theological reflection, he notes. The spiritual has now become "commodified," he suggests, and is now articulated in personal and private life in a way that suggests practical action in a religious marketplace more than long-term devotion to any single mystical piety.

Related to this, contemporary piety is *affective* more than it is *intellectual.* Theological modernism and rational modes of religious expression are not the order of the day. Marty suggests that this is a longer-term trend in American culture, dating back to the "great awakenings," but has nonetheless found new purchase in today's religious sphere.

Finally, Marty posits that *particular expression* now finds precedence over *civil religion.* Contrary to some schools of thought on the subject, American culture seems not very interested in expressing its religion through the state. Despite religious activism that seems directed at bringing state power and state institutions to the fore in the promotion and protection of specific religions, there seems little public support for broadscale establishment, formal or informal. As Marty (1993) concludes, "Religion in America is easier to discern and define, than is American religion" (p. 26).

▓ Religion and the Media Sphere

What, then, are the implications of this emerging view of religion for our study of religion and media? First, we might suggest that the primary contribution of the media sphere to contemporary religious practice, thus described, is very much in the terms of a "marketplace." The process of religious commodification necessarily brings the institutions, practices, and texts of the media sphere to a central place.

According to Roof (1993a), the current postwar baby boom generation is settled rather comfortably in such an approach to religion.

Deeply influenced by a culture of consumption, boomers have grown up with religion made into a commodity and have looked on it in much the same way as other purchasable goods. Commercialization processes, packages, and prices almost everything in the religious market—from crosses to crystals.

The approach to religious truth changes—away from any objective grounds on which it must be judged, to a more subjective, more instrumental understanding of what it does for the believer, and how it can do what it does most efficiently. (p. 195)

Thus, this line of argument seems clearly to be suggesting that contemporary religious practice is embedded in the institutions of the media—the "consciousness industries"—and their cultural commodities. This situation is further enforced by the decline of other contexts of religious-institutional authority.

But some more finely nuanced speculations are possible as well. What does it mean that religion is today more *personal* and less *communal?* It means that religious experience is effectively integrated into the practices of the self that typify the media age. Communal involvement and loyalty are still possible, and still facts of contemporary life, but they are no longer *necessary* elements of religious experience or expression. This means that one of the major traditional challenges to "religious media"—the assumed illegitimacy of noncommunitarian, "vicarious" experience—is no longer as important a normative impediment.

The fact that these practices can take place in *private,* or find expression in *nonpublic* ways, further suggests new ways of understanding the role of the public media and their commodified symbols. Without the "inherited legitimacy" of community or group, private (though not necessarily isolated) choices become significant. The rise of the "12-step movement" in recent years is an example of this.

That the momentum has shifted from *belonging* to *meaning* is also significant to our project here. Articulated into the dominant modes of the broader culture, religious choice now emphasizes a new objective: meaning. Although the psychological motivations for belonging need not necessarily have changed, belonging can now be expressed in different ways. Translocal and transnational culture, made possible by cosmopolitan and global media, enables whole new senses of belonging.

But what about *localism* and *particularism* in the media age? Should not the very *translocal* and *transnational* character of the mass media contradict these impulses? Not necessarily. We know that the media are, in fact, both *local* and *translocal* and both *particular* and *universal*. Current trends toward the atomization and segmentation of audiences, and toward increasing localism in some media (such as radio), enforce new understandings of the structural nature of media and audiences.

The fact is that choices in the media sphere are, to use Marty's term, *"practical"* in a profound sense. Choice involves both rational action and practice that achieves that action. The rites and rituals of daily life now involve, among other things, interaction with the symbolic resources of the media sphere. That among those resources may be found texts, symbols, or ideas that may be seen to be religiously significant should no longer surprise us. And that the vast majority of what goes on in the realm of religious use of media is, in fact, embedded in what in another era we might have called the "secular media" should now have us thinking in entirely new ways.

But what of that residual category of textual practice that we might quaintly call "religious media"? A number of consequences present themselves. Not least among these is the sense that religious media texts must now be constructed with the assumption of a larger context of religious-media textual production and meaning construction, and cannot exist as a separate category altogether. The most recent research on televangelism should have made this obvious. In an experience similar to that described by Warner for the larger project of religious studies, recent televangelism scholarship has found itself looking for less deterministic, more cultural, explanations (Clark & Hoover, this volume; Peck, 1993). What seems obvious now is that this turn also points toward a turn that breaks "religious media" out of its genre classification and opens up the whole question of the extent to which all media, and the entire sphere of commodity culture, can be, and is, a religious sphere.

References

Albanese, C. (1993). Fisher kings and public places: The old new age in the 1990s. *Annals of the American Academy of Social and Political Science, 527,* 131-143.

Ammerman, N. (1987). *Bible believers: Fundamentalists in the modern world.* New Brunswick, NJ: Rutgers University Press.

Ammerman, N. (1990). *Baptist battles: Social change and religious conflict in the Southern Baptist Convention.* New Brunswick, NJ: Rutgers University Press.

Bellah, R., Madsen, R., Sullivan, W. M., Swidler, A., & Tipton, S. N. (1985). *Habits of the heart: Individualism and commitment in American life.* Berkeley: University of California Press.

Beyer, P. (1994). *Religion and globalization.* London: Sage.

Carey, J. (1989). *Communication as culture: Essays on media and society.* Boston: Unwin Hyman.

Ettema, J. & Whitney, C. (1994). The money arrow: An introduction to audiencemaking. In J. Ettema & C. Whitney (Eds.), *Audiencemaking: How the media create the audience* (pp. 1-18). Thousand Oaks, CA: Sage.

Finke, R., & Iannaccone, L. (1993). Supply-side explanations for religious change. *Annals of the American Academy of Political and Social Science, 527,* 27-39.

Fiske, J. (1987). *Television culture.* New York: Routledge.

Fore, W. (1990). "Living church" and "electronic church" compared. In R. Ableman & S. Hoover (Eds.), *Religious television: Controversies and conclusions* (pp. 135-146). Norwood, NJ: Ablex.

Hadden, J., & Swann, C. (1981). *Prime-time preachers: The rising power of televangelism.* Reading, MA: Addison-Wesley.

Hall, S. (1982). The rediscovery of "ideology": Return of the repressed in media studies. In M. Gurevitch, T. Bennett, J. Curran, & J. Woollacott (Eds.), *Culture, society, and the media* (pp. 46-90). London: Routledge & Kegan Paul.

Hobson, D. (1980). Housewives and the mass media. In S. Hall, D. Hobson, A. Lowe, & P. Willis (Eds.), *Culture, media, language* (pp. 105-114). London: Methuen.

Hobson, D. (1982). *Crossroads: The drama of a soap opera.* London: Methuen.

Hobson, D. (1990). Women audiences and the workplace. In M. E. Brown (Ed.), *Television and women's culture: The politics of the popular* (pp. 61-74). London: Sage.

Hoover, S. (1988). *Mass media religion: The social sources of the electronic church.* Newbury Park, CA: Sage.

Hoover, S. (1995, Winter). Media and moral order in post-positivist media studies. *Journal of Communication, 45*(1), 136-145.

Hoover, S., & Venturelli, S. (1996). Religion: The blindspot of contemporary media theory. *Critical Studies in Mass Communication, 13,* 251-265.

Horsfield, P. (1990). American religious programs in Australia. In R. Ableman & S. Hoover (Eds.), *Religious television: Controversies and conclusions* (pp. 313-329). Norwood, NJ: Ablex.

Horsfield, P. (1984). *Religious television: The American experience.* White Plains, NY: Longman.

Iannaccone, L. (1991). The consequences of religious market structure. *Rationality and Society, 3,* 156-177.

Jameson, F. (1984). Postmodernism, or the cultural logic of late capitalism. *New Left Review, 146,* 53-92.

Liebes, T., & Katz, E. (1993). *The export of meaning: Cross-cultural readings of "Dallas"* (2nd ed.). Cambridge, MA: Polity.

Linderman, A. (1996). The reception of religious television: Social semeiology applied to an empirical case study. *Acta Universitatis Upsaliensis, Psychologica et Sociologia Religionum 12.* Stockholm: Almquist & Wiksell International.

Lull, J. (1980). The social uses of television. *Human Communication Research, 6*(3), 198-209.

Lull, J. (1988). *World families watching television.* Newbury Park, CA: Sage.

Marty, M. E. (1993). Where the energies go. *Annals of the American Academy of Social and Political Science, 527,* 11-26.

Marty, M. E., & Appleby, S. (1992). *The glory and the power: The fundamentalist challenge to the modern world.* Boston: Beacon.

Morley, D. (1986). *Family television: Cultural power and domestic leisure.* London: Comedia.

Morley, D. (1989). Changing paradigms in audience studies. In E. Seiter, H. Borchers, G. Kreutzner, & E. M. Warth (Eds.) *Remote control: Television, audiences and cultural power.* London: Routledge & Kegan Paul.

Morley, D. (1992). *Television, audiences and cultural studies.* London: Routledge & Kegan Paul.

Peck, J. (1993). *The gods of televangelism: The crisis of meaning and the appeal of religious television.* Cresskill, NJ: Hampton.

Roof, W. C. (1992, October). *Presidential address.* Religious Research Association, Virginia Beach, VA.

Roof, W. C. (1993a). *A generation of seekers: The spiritual journeys of the baby boom generation.* San Francisco: Harper.

Roof, W. C. (1993b). Toward the year 2000: Reconstructions of religious space. *Annals of the American Academy of Social and Political Science 527,* 155-170.

Schultze, Q. (1988). *Evangelicals and the mass media.* Grand Rapids, MI: Academie.

Seifert, M. (1994). The audience at home: The early recording industry and the marketing of musical taste. In J. Ettema & C. Whitney (Eds.), *Audiencemaking: How the media create the audience* (pp. 186-214). Thousand Oaks, CA: Sage.

Shegog, E. (1991). Religion and media imperialism: A European perspective. In R. Ableman & S. Hoover (Eds.), *Religious television: Controversies and conclusions* (pp. 329-351). Norwood, NJ: Ablex.

Silverstone, R. (1993). *Television in everyday life.* London: Routledge & Kegan Paul.

Soukup, P. (1989). *Christian communication: A bibliographic survey.* Westport, CT: Greenwood.

Stacey, J., & Gerard, S. (1990). "We are not doormats": The influence of feminism on contemporary evangelicals in the United States. In F. Ginsburg & A. L. Tsing (Eds.), *Uncertain terms: Negotiating gender in American culture* (pp. 98-117). Boston: Beacon.

Warner, R. S. (1993). Work in progress toward a new paradigm for the sociological study of religion in the United States. *American Journal of Sociology, 98*(5), 1044-1093.

White, R. (1994). Audience "interpretation" of media: Emerging perspectives [Special issue]. *Communication Research Trends, 14*(3).

Wright, C. (1986). *Mass communication: A sociological perspective.* New York: Random House.

Wuthnow, R. (1988). *The restructuring of American religion.* Princeton, NJ: Princeton University Press.

Wuthnow, R. (1992). Introduction: New directions in the empirical study of cultural codes. In R. Wuthnow (Ed.) *Vocabularies of public life: Empirical essays in social structure.* London: Routledge & Kegan Paul.

Chapter 18

Summary Remarks
Mediated Religion

Knut Lundby and Stewart M. Hoover

All contributions to this volume center on mediated religion. They have taken the lead set in our introduction by understanding their project within the framework of media, religion, and culture. During the course of the book, there has emerged an integration of these elements into an understanding of *mediated religion in culture*.

In this spirit, the bibliographic chapter by **Clark and Hoover** broke new ground by unequivocally replacing an understanding of mediated religion as religious messages *transported by mass media to people*, with a cultural interpretation of religious or sacred symbolism *as shaped by the mediation itself*. Each of the succeeding chapters built on this by treating one or more aspects of mediated religion within a certain cultural context, on different analytical levels, and within varying institutional frameworks.

The foundation for analysis was further laid in the first section of the book. **White** investigated the processes of *signification* in which religion is mediated through texts in the reflexive struggle of actors in the construction and reconstruction of cultures. **Christians** went on to challenge mediated religion by questioning the technology of mediation itself through what he called a "cultural turn."

In the chapters dealing with *contemporary society*, **Murdock** addressed the changing contexts and practices in mediation of religion within the overall culture of modernity. **Martín-Barbero** followed, looking at mediated religion within changing configurations of community and youth culture. **Goethals** revisited mediated religion in the rituals of popular culture. **Bar-Haim** evaluated residual mediated religion in the megaspectacles of postmodern culture. **Lundby** looked further into mediated religion in collective representation in so-called media events.

The book's section on *changing institutions* opened by looking at the established churches. **Horsfield** discussed the consequences of media-cultural changes for their mediation of religion in contemporary culture. **Arthur** followed by pointing to the dependency of mediation in all religions, as a challenge for religious studies. The institution of televangelism was characterized by **Alexander** as a case of mediated religion resolving conflicting positions in contemporary culture. **Tomaselli and Shepperson** discussed the mediation of religion in televangelism based in a new adaptation of orality, to comfort believers experiencing a crisis of culture in their lives.

This led to the contributions on *individual practices*. **Peck** investigated the signification processes of psychologized religion in a mediated world. **Badaracco** looked at the active reading of public texts as mediation of religion in women's identity-formation. **Linderman** laid out an argument for how religion is mediated in meaning-construction, applied to religious television. **Hoover** closed by pointing out the direction for mediation of religion in the "marketplace" of mediated, individualistic culture.

▓ Mediation:
The Central Process

Throughout the volume, the authors have wrestled with the concepts of "religion" and "culture." Although it is clear that more definitional work needs to be done, our understanding of religion, as well as of culture, is implied when "media" become interpreted through processes of "mediations," as Jesús Martín-Barbero (1993) advocates. These concluding remarks will therefore be focused on this idea of *mediations* as reconfiguring links between religion and culture.

Martín-Barbero (1993) argues that because so many conflicting and integrating forces meet in communication, there has to be a shift from media to mediations. By *mediations* he means "the articulations between communication practices and social movements and the articulation of different tempos of development with the plurality of cultural matrices" (p. 187).

Terje Rasmussen, in his *Communication Technologies and the Mediation of Social Life* (1996), states that the term *mediation* is usually applied in a relatively unproblematic way in social theory. He considers this to be the case even as Martín-Barbero proposes the term to grasp the mixture and discontinuity, the *mestizaje* of modern cultures, to use the Latin American word for this plurality of cultural matrices (Rasmussen, 1996, p. 74n).

Because mediation is so important in contemporary studies of media, religion, and culture, it is a challenge to get a deeper understanding of these mediations in the case of religion as a part of today's mediated culture. These concluding remarks can only be suggestive, pointing the way to further research.

Nothing New, Yet Still Different

Mediations of religion are nothing new. To communicate within their cultures, religious institutions and religious studies have always had to rely on mediation through various media—from the oral, through writing and print, to electronic media—for the interpretation and sharing of religious symbols. This has always played back into the representations shaping religious meaning and the culture itself, as **Arthur** points out in this volume.

Modern media offer unlimited possibilities for symbolic manipulation through images or representations that were unknown until the past few centuries and that continuously develop as options for storytelling. However, all storytelling throughout history has been mediated. The *vetter* introduced in **Lundby's** chapter on the Opening Ceremony of the Winter Olympics in Lillehammer, Norway, are at hand to demonstrate. This case also reminds us of how easily old narratives may be reconstructed and remediated within today's media spectacles.

The *vetter* were living popular beliefs and figures among people of premodern times. The stories about them were collected as the modern industrial society emerged. The various *vetter* thus *became* folklore as part of the early modern project. The living *vetter* were mediated by use of print technology into collections of folklore, and the old beliefs and practices thus were transformed into "traditions." The first folklorists themselves became agents of the same mediating project, executing the transformation of the *vetter* and their like through the media at hand.

When the directors of the Opening Ceremony at the Lillehammer Games turned to the *vetter,* they performed a similar process of symbolic representation, this time based on the first transformations of the stories and the experiences of *vetter* by the early Norwegian folklorists. The Olympic project for which the stories about the *vetter* were adapted in the liminoid televised spectacle from Lillehammer in 1994 differ considerably from the mediations of the liminal storytelling about the *vetter* in the folklorist collections aimed at nation-building one and a half centuries ago. The fairy tales collected in last century's Norway were instrumental in the creation of a national identity (Hodne, 1994). The media spectacle of today's Olympic Games serves the purpose of supporting transnational relations and the ideal of a global Olympic identity. In that sense, the two generations of mediations of the *vetter* are parallel. Still, electronic mediations introduce new conditions and potential consequences, because the broadcast media are able to reshape narratives and redirect former mediations on a much larger scale than are print media.

▓ Electronic Mediations

Coronations in Britain during the dawn of modern electronic media offer illustrative cases of how emerging electronic mediations intervened into, and started to reconfigure, established symbolic universes. Here we draw on Kenneth Wolfe's (1984) work on the politics of broadcast religion.

The coronation of George VI in 1937 was the first to occur after the establishment of the British Broadcasting Corporation in 1922. The service in Westminster Abbey was covered by the new medium of radio. It fell to the newly employed director of BBC's religious service to give "the majestic rubrics of the historic service." He had to do this from a tiny box of a room above the triforium in the Abbey. The reporter was highly praised because he "brought the religious significance of the coronation clearly home to the vast numbers who listened" (Wolfe, 1984, p. 93). He did so without intruding into the service, for he was not really visible to those in attendance, positioned as he was under the ceiling of the cathedral. Still, the mediation of the coronation by radio changed the event by allowing people to take part by listening in. The most sacred sphere, however, was protected from such mediation. The BBC was not allowed to continue its coverage as the new king and his queen received the Eucharist. The broadcast switched to another church for sacred music.

The 1937 coronation could also have been transmitted to about 10,000 in the London area who had access to television. John Reith, BBC's director general, wanted to broadcast television from the cathedral, but those responsible for the coronation service would not allow cameras in the Abbey. BBC did, however, make the world's first television "outside broadcast" with mobile cameras placed on stands at Hyde Park Corner to catch a glimpse of the coronation procession as it passed by.

At the coronation of Elizabeth II in 1953, television was let in, but not without considerable discussion and restriction. Protection of the sacred was mixed with protection of class interests. In Westminster Abbey, as in many other cathedrals, a screen separates most of the congregation from the liturgical activities at the altar. Only a few of those sitting in the pews are able to see what is going on behind this screen. Television cameras had not been permitted there either.

The Archbishop of Canterbury thought television cameras at the altar would be too intrusive. Winston Churchill declared that certainly "modern mechanical arrangements" should be used to enable the public to see into the Abbey, but only what was seen by the general congregation and not what was seen by "high ecclastiastical dignitaries and state functionaries . . . whose duties require them to be close to the Sovereign." In the end, the Archbishop and the Dean gave in. Their fears of the invasion by television of the sacred environment were overshadowed by the advantage of presenting the event to the public in its "full religious significance" (Wolfe, 1984, pp. 497-498).

Today, it appears that their fears were justified. The new broadcast medium did not simply disseminate the service. Over time, the mediation introduced by television changed religion—and culture—as well.

▓ Mediation Theory

Changes in media technology provide one of the foundations for theorizing on mediation. Rasmussen (1996) points to "media theory" as one of the avenues to a social theory of mediation. Scholars such as Harold Innis, Marshall McLuhan, Walter Ong, Elizabeth Eisenstein, Daniel Boorstin, Jack Goody, Neil Postman, and Joshua Meyerowitz have argued that the technical structure of the medium is of primary importance. Whereas this understanding of mediation is based in a more or less deterministic view of media, Rasmussen argues that media theory should be balanced by "structuration theory." As proposed by Anthony Giddens, structuration theory overcomes the dualism of considering social processes in terms of actors versus structure by means of an understanding of structure as medium and outcome of action. Structuration theory provides insight into how societies of acting individuals and social institutions are produced and reproduced. However, as Rasmussen notes, structuration theory has itself no analytical focus on technology or media and their ontological pretentions, instead stressing materiality and the objective significance of social systems, which may prohibit it from developing critical insights. Rasmussen therefore argues that the "critical theory" of Jürgen Habermas brings in a perspective on modern paradoxical mediation, stressing the relationship between the uncoupling of social systems and the individual "lifeworld." This theoretical supplement also offers a normative foundation for critique and social change. A social theory of mediation then, following Rasmussen, has to take account of media theory, structuration theory, and critical theory without aligning with any of them in particular.

This applies to a structural analysis of changes in communication technologies and the consequences for mediation of social life. Adding perspectives that cater to the construction of cultural texts through signification practices (as in **White's** chapter here) within symbolic universes (as laid out by several contributors) and the symbolic interpretation of meaning (as in the section on *individual practices* here), the elements of a theory of mediated religion in culture begin to emerge.

These complex cultural processes themselves need to be mediated or re-presented by the researcher, reminding us that different perspectives and wordings will be applied, reflecting various positions. A philosophical approach is chosen by **Christians** when he calls for a critical theory of technology rooted in the thought of Martin Heidegger, whose most famous student, Jean-Paul Sartre, is the theoretical point of departure for **Peck** as she explores the mediation and signification processes of psychologized religion.

Furthermore, the levels of analysis are interrelated when mediations among *society, institutions,* and *individual practices* are involved. It might further clarify these issues to point out some problematics of mediated religion for research in each of these three analytic directions. All are set within the context of late modernity, which is "saturated by communication media, which increasingly put culture in focus, in a double process of mediatization of culture and culturalization of the media" (Fornäs, 1995, p. 1).

In this book, we have looked at religion and religiosity as implicated in this "doubly-articulated" process. **Peck** refers to the concept of the "mediazation" of culture described by Thompson (1990). Johan Fornäs (1995) calls Thompson's term "somewhat awkward," though he sees it covers much the same turf as his own concept of "mediatization," namely "the process whereby media increasingly come to saturate society, culture, identities and everyday life" (p. 1). In his book, *The Media and Modernity,* Thompson (1995) expands on the processes of mediated communication in society. What, then, happens to religion? This is the central concern of this volume, and it remains as a question for further research as we move ahead.

Individual Practices

Mediations create and re-create meaning. They do so within the context of individual experience. Against the backdrop of traditions of media research that grew out of *experimental* psychology, **Peck** here provides an assessment of media reception in terms of *existential* psychology, demonstrating how such an approach is entirely consistent with critical social analysis. Psychology plays a role in identity formation as well, but the process of mediation is located somewhere outside the bounds of the individual psyche. The status of the public texts **Badaracco** analyzes in her chapter places them squarely within the framework of mediation.

Linderman's approach to the specific texts of religious television introduces both a problematic of this process of mediation and a set of tools for analyzing it. Mediations are not determinative, even with reference to texts that presume to have an "impact"—as we have noted. To account for practices of reception with a framework of mediations requires a complex and nuanced project, as **Linderman** demonstrates.

Mediation assumes a complex web of practices and relationships. Understanding contemporary relations between religion and the media is thus not just about media texts and their reception, but also about the matrix of religious practice into which mediated messages and behaviors are introduced. **Hoover's** contribution here describes the nature of contempoary religious practice and the ways in which it accommodates itself to mediation.

These approaches at the individual level focus on *meaning*. On the other side of the coin of meaning, however, people always have some bonds of *belonging*. These belongings, as well as meanings, are shaped by mediations. Shared meanings offer belonging; at the same time, social belonging gives meaning. Both depend on mediations.

In the existential perspective, a similar distinction could be made between *being* and *meaning*, a position taken in this volume by the **Peck** and the **Clark and Hoover** chapters. Whereas the rather philosophical concepts "being and meaning" refer to ontology, "meaning and belonging" relate more to social relationships. The two pairs of concepts, however, are to certain extent related. Being a person in society implies belonging as well as meaning.

In late modernity, there is no longer a necessary link between meaning and belonging in religion, in the sense that knowledge of which religion or denomination a person belongs to would provide information about the religious meanings they hold. However, for particular cases—those who choose to keep their lives within strict frameworks—the link may be as strong as ever.

The "electronic churches" rally by means of the mediations of televangelism to recreate such a congruence in resistance to the conflicting mediations of the culture of late modernity (as discussed here by **Alexander** and **Tomaselli and Shepperson**). The price for its attempted retreat from pluralism is a condemnation to mediated rituals within communities of its own and an inability to create sacred meanings and religious belongings for a majority. There is a sense in which both the psychologized religion of daytime television and the fundamentalism of televangelism represent the same struggle. They are contrasting yet coherent solutions to the contradictions and conflicts of late modernity.

To put it in general terms, the challenge is to get to a further understanding of mediated religiosity as expressed by mediated meanings *and* mediated belongings in the individual practices of late modernity. This includes the extreme (but still fairly common) cases of belonging without believing and believing without belonging.

Because meanings are always part of symbolic universes and belongings always relate to communities, we are at the same time faced with the challenge of understanding the relationships between single sacred meanings and sacred universes of (post)modern culture, as well as the relationships between specific identifications and interactions within the changing and overlapping pattern of various communities in contemporary advanced societies. Both tasks obviously require a deeper understanding of mediations as both *cultural* and *social* processes.

There is an immediate need to specify and define the concept of "community" when it is applied. Communities may still be geographically defined, but there is a difference between the context of a city of several hundred thousand and a small town of some hundreds or thousands. In any case, geographic communities intermingle with various nongeographically defined communities, be they termed "interpretive," "fugitive," "communities of interest," or whatever. This matrix of communities sets the stage for the *mestizaje* of sacred and secular meanings, as well as for changes in religious and nonreligious belonging. According to **Martín-Barbero** in his chapter in the present volume, mediation through modern media is both the locus for the constitution of identities and a space for configuration of communities, which makes research into these processes important.

▨ Changing Institutions

The changing social and cultural matrix of communities in late modernity indeed also affects religious institutions, which are assumed to offer *de facto* religious community within their structural arrangements. For many people they do; but for as many, they do not. This is partly due to the fact that religious communities do not easily accommodate to the overall changes in patterns of community in society. They do not manage to reproduce the popular modes of community searched for by some, and they do not manage to create a meaningful contrast in the terms of community that is sought by others. Religious communities and religious institutions have thus become trapped in modernity.

This relates to the role of religious institutions in the mediation processes of society and culture. **Horsfield** notes in his chapter the absence of a recognition of the significant effects that changes in media have had on the churches. In the shift from largely nation-based cultures in which print was the main medium, to world-linked cultures in which electronic-based means of communication have become dominant, the major Christian institutions in Western culture have been closely identified with print-based culture and ethos, Horsfield reminds us. His argument centers on mediation when he holds that to "sustain the perspective that religious thought is also significantly influenced by shifts in media, it is necessary to establish a framework that lifts media out of the common religious frame of instrumentality and reestablishes it as a central and indispensable hermeneutic dimension of culture." The mainline religious institutions have lost influence. According to Horsfield, "in the power shift that has taken place, other social institutions tend not to use the media to communicate their reality, but rather are placed by the media on the web of culture in different positions and for different purposes."

These developments should not be seen as simply a matter of *secularization*. The relationship between changes in religious institutions and changes in other sectors of society could be treated through more detailed studies of changes in mediation practices. Such studies have to relate to the double process of mediatization of culture and culturalization of the media as well as to structural changes in society and in the relationship between individuals and society. **Goethals'** chapter on the reshaping of ritual by the "transport" of sacred time and space by the electronic media sets some parameters for discussion of the viability of religious institutions compared to mediated rituals in secular popular culture. **Bar-Haim** offers the contrasting view that religious institutions or "sacred centers" are weakened in today's society of loose networks, in which media play a central role in mediation of social relationships.

▓ Contemporary Society

The contemporary society of late modernity is a continuously changing society. In the ongoing transformation there is also a "re-enchantment
of the world"; religion does not disappear in late modernity, but changes
its face, as **Murdock** demonstrates. Religion is still part of both the
meanings and *belongings* mediated in society, though often in reconfigured
forms. This poses new challenges to those researchers, especially in
sociology and cultural studies, who have treated religion as a diminishing
residual category.

Idealist scholars in media studies and religious studies are challenged
as well. Both **Murdock** and **Martín-Barbero** in their reevaluations of
mediated religion in late modernity remind us of the prevailing class
divisions of society, though these conflicting lines are not constant either.
The political questions inherent in the ongoing reconfigurations of society
should be taken up. These reconfigurations relate to mediated religion in
society, as is obvious in the case of the New Religious Right based in
televangelism and electronic churches.

Changes in society are to a certain extent due to developments in
technology that influence mediations. Every society relies on mediations
of social interaction and other exchanges of meaning. Today, however, the
social is increasingly mediated by technical intermediaries, as noted by
Rasmussen (1996), who distinguishes between mediation in general and
communication-technological mediation in particular. Rasmussen's project aims to reconsider some fundamental elements of sociological theory
as it is applied to the new interactive media and communication technologies beyond print and broadcasting, as does ours. But to do so recognizes
the extent to which the new media are reshaping mediation opportunities
in society.

Ultimately, this will once again come around to the mediations of
religion. New phenomena, such as web-sites for worship on the Internet,
constantly emerge (Ess, 1996). However, the changes must be seen to go
deeper: into existing social structure. New communication technologies
affect the mediation of social life, as Rasmussen argues. Because religion
is embedded in social life, it cannot escape the changes. This relates both
to religion as institutions and belief systems per se, and to the ethical
challenge inherent in the fact that technology is intertwined with the
existential structure of human being, as here described by **Christians.**

And, as he adds, media technologies are "especially powerful mechanisms for reconstructing an inauthentic humanness." Will religious communities and sharp-eyed believers be able to perform the prophetic
and critical witness Christians seek? Will researchers of media, religion,
and culture be able to pose critical questions of mediated religion in
(post)modern culture? It is our intention that such a project has started
and been carried forward by this book and that it will continue to grow
and develop.

References

Ess, C. (1996, January). *Prophetic communities online? An examination of the revolutionary promise of cyberspace.* Paper presented at the Conference on Media, Religion, and Culture, University of Colorado, Boulder.

Fornäs, J. (1995). *Cultural theory and late modernity.* London: Sage.

Hodne, Ø. (1994). *Det nasjonale hos norske folklorister på 1800-tallet* (KULTs skriftserie nr. 24/Nasjonal identitet nr. 2). Oslo: Research Council of Norway.

Martín-Barbero, J. (1993). *Communication, culture and hegemony: From the media to the media-tions.* London: Sage

Rasmussen, T. (1996). *Communication technologies and the mediation of social life: Elements of a social theory of the new media* (IMK Report No. 16). Oslo: Department of Media and Communication, University of Oslo, Norway.

Thompson, J. B. (1990). *Ideology and modern culture: Critical social theory in the era of mass communication.* Cambridge, UK: Polity Press.

Thompson, J. B. (1995). *The media and modernity: A social theory of the media.* Cambridge, UK: Polity Press.

Wolfe, K. M. (1984). *The churches and the British Broadcasting Corporation 1922-1956: The politics of broadcast religion.* London: SCM Press.

Index

EDITOR'S NOTE: Page references followed by *n* or *f* indicate notes or figures, respectively.

About the Contributors

Bobby C. Alexander is Lecturer in the School of Social Sciences at the University of Texas at Dallas. He is the author of *Televangelism Reconsidered: Ritual in the Search for Human Community* and of *Victor Turner Revisited: Ritual as Social Change*.

Chris Arthur is currently Senior Lecturer in Religious Studies at the University of Wales, Lampeter. Among his publications are *In the Hall of Mirrors* and *Biting the Bullet*. He is editor of *Religion and the Media: An Introductory Reader*.

Claire Hoertz Badaracco is Associate Professor of Communication at Marquette University, Milwaukee, Wisconsin. Her research areas are politics and religion, public opinion, and leadership studies.

Gabriel Bar-Haim is Associate Professor of Sociology in the Department of Behavioral Sciences at the Tel-Aviv College of Management, Israel. His research areas are social theory, sociology of culture, and the anthropology of religion.

Clifford G. Christians is Research Professor of Communications and Director of the Institute for Communication Research at the University of Illinois. He has published widely in the areas of philosophy of communication and media ethics.

Lynn Schofield Clark is a doctoral candidate at the School of Journalism and Mass Communication, University of Colorado. Her current research focuses on identity-construction, media, and religion among adolescents and "generation X."

Gregor Goethals is Professor Emerita at the Rhode Island School of Design. Her academic interests are art history and the philosphy of religion. She is the author of *The TV Ritual: Worship at the Video Altar* and *The Electronic Golden Calf: Images and the Making of Meaning*. She now has a studio in Sonoma, California, and is Art Director for the Multimedia Translations Program of the American Bible Society.

Stewart M. Hoover is Professor of Media Studies and Professor Adjoint of Religious Studies at the University of Colorado at Boulder. He has researched and written widely on media, religion, and culture. He is the author of *Mass Media Religion: Social Sources of the Electronic Church* and coeditor of *Religious Television: Controversies and Conclusions*.

Peter G. Horsfield is Dean of the Uniting Church Theological Hall and Lecturer in Practical Theology at the United Faculty of Theology in Melbourne, Australia. Among his publications are *Religious Television: The American Experience* and *Taming the Television: A Parents' Guide to Children and Television*.

Alf Linderman is a research fellow at Uppsala University. He has conducted research on religious television in the United States and Sweden, and on meaning construction and media reception. He is currently involved in research projects focused on cultural indicators in newspapers, on religion in television, and on television audiences' construction of meaning.

Knut Lundby is Associate Professor in the Department of Media and Communication at the University of Oslo, Norway. Besides his recent work in the area of media, meaning, and social ritual, he has researched and published on issues of communication and community, particularly focused on studies in Southern Africa.

Jesús Martín-Barbero is former Professor in the Department of Communication Sciences, University del Valle, Cali, Colombia, and the past president of the Latin American Association of Communication Research. His previous books include *Communication, Culture and Hegemony,* and *Communication: Discourse and Power.*

Graham Murdock is reader in the Sociology of Culture at Loughborough University. He has written widely on the sociology and political economy of culture and communications and on cultural theory, and his work has been translated into over a dozen languages. He is currently completing books on broadcasting and on modernity.

Janice Peck is on the faculty of the University of Colorado at Boulder. She is the author of *The Gods of Televangelism: Religious Television and the Historical Crisis of Meaning.* Her writing on religious television and on television talk shows has also appeared in *Journal of Communication Inquiry, Communication Theory,* and *Cultural Critique.*

Arnold Shepperson is a researcher in the Centre for Cultural and Media Studies at the University of Natal, Durban, South Africa. He has published on semiotics, communication, and visual anthropology. He was formerly an electrician and draftsman in the South African mining industry, an experience on which his continuing interest in cross-cultural encounters in economic and civil affairs is based.

Keyan G. Tomaselli is Director and Professor in the Centre for Cultural and Media Studies, University of Natal, Durban, South Africa. He is editor of *Critical Arts: A Journal for Cultural Studies,* and author of *The Cinema of Apartheid.*

Robert A. White is Director of the Center for Interdisciplinary Studies in Communication at the Gregorian University in Rome and Professor of Communication Ethics and Communication Theory. He is former Research Director of the Centre for the Study of Communication and Culture in London and founding editor with Michael Traber of the "Communication and Human Values" series published by Sage. He is the editor of the "Communication, Culture, and Theology" series published by Sheed and Ward.